THE FOUR POWERS

OF

LEADERSHIP

W9-BBZ-036

PRESENCE
INTENTION
WISDOM
COMPASSION

David T. Kyle, Ph.D.

Health Communications, Inc.
Deerfield Beach, Florida

www.hci-online.com

Adaptation of Fig. 5.1, The Johari Window, from *Group Processes: An Introduction to Group Dynamics,* 3d ed., by Joseph Luft. Copyright ©1984, 1970, 1963 by Joseph Luft. Reprinted by permission of Mayfield Publishing Company.

Library of Congress Cataloging-in-Publication Data

Kyle, David T.
    The four powers of leadership: presence, intention, wisdom, compassion / David T. Kyle.
        p. cm.
    Includes bibliographical references and index.
    ISBN 1-55874-634-X
    1. Leadership. I. Title.
BF637.L4K85 1998
158'.4—dc21
                                                                    98-30733
                                                                         CIP

©1998 David T. Kyle
ISBN 1-55874-634-X

Publisher: Health Communications, Inc.
        3201 S.W. 15th Street
        Deerfield Beach, FL 33442-8190

Cover design by Larissa Hise

To Patt

CONTENTS

ACKNOWLEDGMENTS

I wish to thank many friends and colleagues who have encouraged me in the writing of this book. The strongest encouragement came from my agent, Joe Durepos, who saw fragments of this work and said, "Do it" when I had lost faith in it. Thanks, Joe. Significant encouragement also came from clients who wanted me to lay out the concept of the Four Powers in one volume. I owe a great debt to these men and women, who taught me, through their lives, what it is to be a leader.

To Peter Vegso, president of Health Communications, a great deal of appreciation for believing that this book had merit when he saw it in proposal form. To Matthew Diener, senior book editor; Lisa Drucker, associate editor; Mark Colucci, copy editor/proofreader; and Bob Land, proofreader—my deepest gratitude for the rigor that they demanded from me in the preparation of the book. Lisa, in particular, gave attention to every word and sentence in the manuscript. She taught me that writing is similar to polishing stone. There is a certain pleasure as the stone begins to shine, *and* it is very tedious. Without her assistance, the book would not be in its present form. Thank you, Lisa.

To my partner, Patt, my deepest appreciation for her support and love. The work we do with executives was born of her vision and insight, and the assessment process she conceived has assisted many leaders.

AUTHOR'S NOTE

As other authors have before me, I faced the problem of using gender pronouns—*he* or *she*, *him* or *her*—in writing *The Four Powers of Leadership*. Following the argument others have used, I have tried to use gender-neutral language and resort to *he* or *him* only for stylistic consistency.

THE FOUR POWERS OF LEADERSHIP

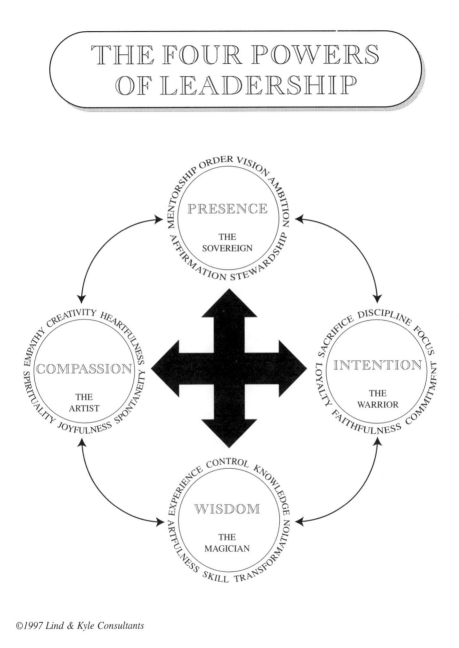

PRESENCE

THE SOVEREIGN

MENTORSHIP ORDER VISION AMBITION STEWARDSHIP AFFIRMATION

COMPASSION

THE ARTIST

EMPATHY CREATIVITY HEARTFULNESS SPONTANEITY JOYFULNESS SPIRITUALITY

INTENTION

THE WARRIOR

SACRIFICE DISCIPLINE FOCUS COMMITMENT FAITHFULNESS LOYALTY

WISDOM

THE MAGICIAN

EXPERIENCE CONTROL KNOWLEDGE TRANSFORMATION SKILL ARTFULNESS

INTRODUCTION

The Practice of Leadership
Some Simple Truths About Being a Leader

A part of all of us (even the leaders among us) desires, even longs for, some person to be a focus point, a divining rod or a guide who will help us find meaning and purpose in our life. We want someone to help us define our purpose, whether it is finding some ultimate "truth" or "revelation," accomplishing some great goal, or simply making a lot of money. We want leaders who know how to tap a larger, more exciting purpose to connect to our unique and individual purposes. One of the basic emotional "truths" about leadership is that *we want leaders who discover or create purpose in their own lives and then can articulate this purpose in such a way that we are motivated to follow them in order to find that same purpose for ourselves.* Although this "truth" is an emotional driver for most of us, a person's capability of inspiring and motivating people to follow his articulated purpose seems to be a unique characteristic of leadership.[1]

Leading, then, is not primarily about doing something, but rather about being something. The development of leadership is about becoming conscious of both the power within oneself and the power inherent within the position one holds. In a fundamental sense, the challenge of being a leader is about integrating personal power with one's positional power.[2] This does not mean that leaders are born with no skills to learn. Leaders aren't born, and there are a lot of leadership skills that need to be practiced every day. Developing leadership requires understanding and integrating into one's life, day after day, the fundamental "powers" that leaders must learn to access, cultivate, and balance in their personal and professional lives. *Being a leader is not about acting out a role, but rather about accessing the power to maximize one's unique and individual capacities and potentials.*

Individuals are not born with a leadership spoon in their mouth or programmed with leadership genes from birth.[3] Nor is leadership a set of skills one learns in a business school or by taking leadership seminars, although both may help.

Leadership is something one develops and grows into, not something one is born or trained to do. No particular personality trait—like being an extrovert or introvert—makes or breaks a leader.[4] No level of IQ or intuitive ability determines whether one can become a leader. It is also clear from countless studies that *good managers of people or things do not necessarily become good leaders.*[5]

Some individuals may exert their leadership through great personal charm and charisma; others through persuasion and inspiration; and others through keen intellect. In our current postindustrial information age, those with technical or financial genius or acute organizational and management ability tend to receive our acclaim as leaders.[6] The unique conditions of each period of time will call forth the different kinds of leaders we need, whether the conditions are prosperity or economic hardship, war or peace, technology explosion or spiritual development.

In their own way, each of these different types of leaders can galvanize a group of people, overcome or accomplish something that's never been done before, or propose a philosophy that changes people's lives. In essence, these leaders become magnets that attract people.[7] The ego gratification a leader derives from people flocking to him can be enormous. Hence the drive to use personality or technical talents to maintain one's following can sustain the appearance of good leadership for a long time. However, these unique talents and characteristics don't ultimately make a successful leader. All too often the label "leader" frightens and traumatizes an individual. Though they appear leader-like outwardly, many people labeled as "leaders" suffer crushing self-doubt and numbing fear. The result: *Many individuals in positions of leadership attempt to disguise their fear and shortcomings to make themselves appear more competent, talented, knowledgeable or capable than they really are.*[8]

Personality, talents or natural gifts can only take one to a certain level of leadership competency. A gap often exists between the inherent power to control and influence because of position and the ability to grow and develop deeper leadership characteristics. These deeper leadership characteristics provide the insight, understanding and wisdom a person must have in order to handle the complexity of followers' needs.[9] Given a new positional challenge, an individual must develop the strength to meet the overwhelming intensity of his leadership environment, improve his capacity to penetrate an ever-changing set of problems, and open the unconscious doorways to his own emotional and behavioral conditioning. Without this development process, a person will meet his own Peter Principle,[10] becoming a leader in name only.

Powerful and successful leaders—leaders who maintain their position for a long time—go through a developmental, learning and maturing process. They take their original magnetic quality or special expertise and develop it. They learn to reflect on themselves. They learn to see into and beyond what others see around them in the conditions and situations of their environment. They learn to focus less on themselves and more on the people who are attracted to working with them. They gain perspective on and develop humility regarding the depth of their innate capabilities. They also continually attempt to access other parts of themselves, which, in turn, engenders a fuller capacity for leadership. *These leaders discover that leading is a practice to be worked on every day.*[11]

Some basic principles about leadership practice have been around for a long time. We all know some of these practices instinctively. Knowing them is one thing, but committing to practice them daily is the critical challenge. Each of us has some unique quality that can serve as the cornerstone of increasing our capacity as a leader. *Our willingness to practice the principles and "truths" we already know is the critical choice that can develop our innate leadership capacities.* What follows are three principles, and some practices based on them, as a starting point for considering what makes a leader. No doubt you can add to this list from your own experience.

1. Successful leaders *make a conscious choice to continuously develop the positive personality traits and talents they have.* They also focus their intention to understand their positive and negative characteristics in order to measure their strengths and liabilities. These leaders actively work on both what enhances and what blocks their leadership abilities. In other words, they take themselves on as a continuous development project.[12]

2. Wise leaders *develop their capacity to observe and perceive* what others miss in any given situation. They learn to use their analytical skills and intuition not just as the basis of understanding the present events, opportunities or crises, but also to gain insight into the patterns that have led to those situations.[13]

3. Powerful leaders *discover how to work with the intangibles*— with group energy and tension, with creating vision, and with ways to motivate people to make extraordinary commitments.[14]

The following is a more specific listing of some of the pragmatic "truths" that flow from these three principles. These "truths" are woven through the various themes presented in *The Four Powers of Leadership.*

An individual's personal power must match one's positional power in order for one to become an authentic and influential leader.

Personal power is the conscious awareness and integration of the patterns of beliefs and perceptions that drive the leader's emotions, energies, choices and behaviors.

Leaders who have positional or legitimate power (CEO, president, chairman, owner, minister, etc.) may exercise the authority of their position ("I am the boss. Do what I say because I have control over your job, bonus, promotion, spiritual view, etc.") but find that people fail to give them willing enthusiasm, followership or loyalty if they don't have matching personal power.

Understanding how to exercise and integrate positional and personal power is the active and ongoing learning goal of the leader. It is this integration that forms the basis for creating strong personal and organizational commitment, goal focus, and behavioral results in followers.

The shadowy, negative sides of a leader's personality must be consciously explored and understood if the leader is to avoid becoming manipulative and abusive.[15]

Abuse of power is the projection of inner needs and emotional wounds onto a leader's followers or adversaries.

This book examines many aspects of the shadow side of leadership power and how to bring them into the light of day.

The daily task of a leader is to perceive the larger patterns that influence a situation in order to make wise and balanced decisions.

The ability to perceive patterns is like throwing a rock into a pond and watching how the ripples extend and eventually reach the shore. If one focuses only on where the rock entered the water, one misses the power and influence of the shock wave it sends through the entire system of water, rocks and shore.

By understanding and reflecting on the differences between one's own thinking and decision-making process and those of one's followers, one can minimize frustration and increase patience in working with people under one's leadership.

Corollary: Leaders who learn to expand their natural personality style, mode of thinking and behavior by knowing when to match the different styles of their followers will increase the alignment and synergy between themselves and those who want to be led.

The work of leadership is to create results, build teams, and expand the competency and capacity of followers to increase their own leadership potential.

Not working from one's technical competency is the big challenge for a leader. When stressed, we like to do what we do best rather than what is best as a leader.

Strong leaders are good participants in teams and good developers of team members. They enter into the give-and-take of participation, and are good coaches and mentors of others. As a coach and mentor, a mature leader always has his eyes open for his future replacement.

Developing people to be more competent and capable than oneself is a critical ego challenge for a leader.

Encouraging people to challenge his thinking, leadership style and decision making is a mark of a leader's maturity.

The role of a leader is to create a context for people to focus their intent and energies. The leader creates a container to hold people's will and power. The container is built by articulating and maintaining the following:

- A critical set of values that gives followers boundaries of safety and security and an environment of vulnerability in which trust and risk can occur.

- A transpersonal purpose that connects the individual follower's personal purpose to the purpose of the leader and/or organization.

- An evolving, dynamic vision of results in which followers can see that what they do today creates new possibilities for the future.

The leader's vision creates motivational energy and sustained excitement for both the leader and his followers. The vision should create enough ongoing tension in followers that it pulls and challenges them to move from the dilemmas of the current situation toward accomplishing the pragmatic details of the vision.

The vision should be simple enough that followers can describe it in their own words; it become *their* vision, not just the leader's.

If the leader must constantly promote the vision, then the vision itself is not motivating people and challenging them to realize it.

The work of the leader is to *manage the tension* between the current reality of the situation and a vision of future results for the organization. Too much tension will discourage people because the vision will seem impossible. Too limited a vision will create very little tension and will result in a lack of motivation.

Leading followers toward a vision means constantly reminding people that what they are doing has never been done before.

The operational challenge of the leader is to keep people moving toward the vision by asking the question "What do we need to do creatively and differently?"

The joy of following a leader with a challenging vision is that leaders and followers "make up the world" each day and learn how to accomplish the work of the vision together.

"Making the world up as we proceed" is the basis for a *learning leadership pattern* that challenges the leader to be at the edge of his own growth and development.

Leaders and followers who are learning together are in a continual state of challenge. In this state they are discovering new forms of creativity, and they permit each other to experiment and make mistakes.

Leaders who commit to a learning leadership pattern make time for individuals and groups within the organization to solve problems, and build structures that support all individuals concerned so that they can experiment with new ideas, methods and modes of operating.

The daily task of the leader is to identify, confirm and keep followers focused on the critical strategic issues that must be solved in order to fulfill the vision.

Focusing on strategy is a way of teaching followers to think about solving critical issues that could make or break the organization or the vision.

Insightful leaders encourage followers to focus on doing the right things. They show the pathway from strategy to tactics, from concept to concretization, and from mission to goals and objectives.

A leader continually finds concrete and measurable means to demonstrate accomplishment and success to his followers.

Human beings are problem-solving animals. Fulfillment, satisfaction and joy all lie in doing something never done before.

Goals, results and solutions achieved are only markers of what's been learned. Recognition of the achievement—whether praise, prize or money—is not the long-term motivator.

Celebration of accomplishment becomes the building block for the next level of learning.

As we shall discover in our exploration of the Four Powers of Leadership, the ability to live out these "truths" of leadership does not come from following techniques or formulas. These truths are observations, behavioral markers of people learning to become more consciously human.

Leadership is the result of uncovering critical perceptual and emotional blocks in one's life, uncovering old limiting patterns of behavior, and finding access to one's essential creativity. The leadership need of our time is for a regaining of the true "elder leader."

The "elder leader" is not necessarily one advanced in age as much as one who has gained maturity in the qualities of Presence, Intention, Wisdom and Compassion. These qualities emerge through self-reflection, daily practice and self-motivation, which allow one to stretch oneself beyond the common norms of day-to-day work activity.

Many of our best leaders are not particularly good managers in a technocratic sense, but they clearly know how to manage themselves and teach others how to challenge themselves to greater achievements by focusing on the most critical issues at hand. For this kind of leader, managing an organization becomes more than attempting useful time management techniques, meeting a budget or giving a good performance review. In fact, many of the leaders we will examine would not use the language of management at all. Rather, they would speak of challenge, testing, learning or discovery. The emphasis in their speaking is for their followers to deepen their understanding, create more inner capacity, and become colleagues, comrades, and partners with them in the venture they envision. Often, however, when people assume the leader role, they venture into new and unexplored inner territory. The drive and challenge of the leadership role can create a gap between the demands of the new position of leadership and the lack of personal power they've developed to fulfill that role.

THE GAP BETWEEN PERSONAL AND POSITIONAL POWER

When people are promoted or seek a higher position because their skills and competencies have made them successful at one level, their leadership behavior often changes dramatically once they assume their new position. When shifting from one level of positional power to a higher level of positional power and responsibility, a gap emerges. This gap occurs between the inherent and defined power of the new position and the personal power and influence the person has developed that created access to the new position.

This gap is a chasm for many people. What they each achieved as leaders in their previous respective positions seems impossible to achieve in their new ones. The difference between what these individuals imagined the new positions to be and what the positions actually demand from them may be frightening. Many people come to feel they are "faking" the job. Others put in longer hours, thinking that more time will help. Still others hide behind the new authority of the position, believing they only need time to learn the new job. Many managers promoted to director positions, or directors moving into VP roles, or VPs becoming CEOs have shamefully admitted their fear and anxiety at not knowing how to use their new power. Consultants are often asked to work with recently promoted executives who "suddenly and out of character" become abusive to employees or who, rather than motivating people, were ordering them around because they were the boss.

These fearful and angry individuals are caught in the learning gap between personal and positional power. They don't understand that to avoid the Peter Principle of "arriving at their highest level of incompetence," the talents and capabilities that put them into the new position have to be stretched in new and different ways. Laurence J. Peter, who described this incompetence phenomenon in his book *The Peter Principle*,[16] noted that the fear of being found out as incapable of the new position begins to shut people down from the fundamental learning and growth that is needed to bridge the personal-positional power gap. Not only does this gap reveal how and where people need to grow, it also can activate the shadow, or negative, characteristics of their personality. These seemingly new negative behaviors and attitudes were probably part of the individuals' personalities but didn't show themselves in previous positions. Given new pressures, stresses, demands and responsibilities, these shadowy parts of their characters may appear, adding to the uncertainties of a new job and revealing new aspects of themselves that they don't know how to control.

THE FOUR POWERS AS A MAP
FOR LEADERSHIP DEVELOPMENT

The gap of power is the fertile ground in which a person can cultivate the powers of Presence, Intention, Wisdom and Compassion.
These four "powers" are the fundamental archetypes that become the
container for leadership development. The discussion of archetypes
presented in this book will provide the framework within which the
"tools," models and insights relevant to leadership can be used. Each
chapter centers on one of the four archetypes, and describes the
shadow, or negative, characteristics of each archetype and how they
are activated when a person assumes positional power. Understanding how the shadow parts of leadership work in human beings
can provide insight into how to heal and integrate the power challenges within one's personal and professional life as a leader. Gaining
insight into how these four powers work in one's life can also provide
a basis for mapping out one's leadership development. The more conscious one is of these four powers, the more successful one will be in
accessing their latent potential. The following brief description represents the positive characteristics of each of the Four Powers.

Intention is the power of the Warrior archetype. Most leaders
begin to build their career upon this archetype. The Warrior has
learned to be self-disciplined, intensely task focused, and committed
to the time and energy required to fulfill whatever the leader or organization needs of him. A person with Intention is willing to sacrifice
for some larger, transpersonal purpose. This individual demonstrates
strong loyalty to people and principles, and is faithful in fulfilling
whatever is required to serve the "kingdom," the organization or the
leader. As a person advances in leadership positions, the Intention of
the Warrior archetype needs to merge more with its opposite—the
Compassion of the Artist, which provides flexibility to the Warrior's
rigid qualities. As the Warrior archetype matures, it will also
add firmness to the power of Presence and intensity to the magical
qualities of Wisdom.

Wisdom is the action of the Magician archetype. When someone says, "That's like magic. How did you do that?" we are experiencing Wisdom in action. Wisdom appears magical because it is a combination of skill and knowledge about something that, through much experience, has moved from practice to art. To master the art of something means a person has gained a certain level of control and has the ability to use art to transform situations. It is Wisdom and Intention that most leaders rely on to advance within organizations. One gets a promotion through hard work and experience. Insofar as this was the pathway to success for aspiring leaders, leadership often becomes identified with spending longer hours at work than anyone else and acquiring the breadth and depth of experience necessary to solve problems. Because these qualities of hard work and mastery of knowledge and skills are in most leaders' comfort zone, leaders come to rely on their Intention and Wisdom powers when difficulties arise.

Compassion is the power of the Artist archetype. Understanding this power in leadership requires understanding the meaning of the word *compassion*. The Latin *com-* means "with," while *passion* comes from *passur* or *pati*—"to suffer."[17] Compassion is literally having the passion to *suffer with* people. Empathy and creativity are the means by which the Artist confronts difficult and challenging situations. The core of the Artist's passion is the tendency toward strong feelings and emotions—excitement, ardor, intensity, zeal, devotion and affection—as well as love for people and things. The Artist's Compassion warms the leader. The Warrior's Intention can leave the leader cold and calculating. When Compassion bursts into flame it brings forth in the leader the qualities of spontaneity, humor, creative innovation, and heartful and joyful activity. Compassion is a leader's spiritual center. Compassion is the compass point that directs the other powers. The Artist, then, ignites the Warrior with devotion, generates affection in the Sovereign's relationship with his followers and provides the Magician with clearer understanding and insight in order to serve the "kingdom."

Presence is the archetype of the Sovereign, or the king and queen

characteristics in leadership. The power of Presence in a leader provides context—an energetic, compelling force—from which a person
can create an emotional bonding or personal relationship to a project,
company or country. For a leader, the power of Presence within him
embodies qualities of personal and organizational ambition, and
provides vision that gives meaning to an immediate activity. Presence
nurtures others through mentorship. It encourages diversity, risk taking and vulnerability in others. Presence expresses stewardship of the
enterprise and provides order for the organization, as well as affirming, recognizing and "blessing" people. Most of all, Presence is that
intangible quality of identification that people make with a leader
who motivates, inspires and excites them.

The process of cultivating the Four Powers works through the
dynamics of opposite polarities. Presence is balanced by Wisdom,
while Intention and Compassion balance each other. At any given
point in a leader's development, one power may pull on its opposite
in order to express itself. Or the conditions of the "realm"—the organization, community, etc.—may demand that the leader emphasize
and use one or two powers more than the others for the good of the
people or projects at hand. A classic example of balancing opposites
in leadership development is the Warrior/Artist tension. In the Middle
Ages, Irish warriors weren't allowed to defend their borders until
they not only mastered the sword (warrior skills), but could also sing
and dance (artist skills). Similarly, Japanese samurai warriors had to
master calligraphy, meditation and the tea ceremony, in addition to
mastering fighting skills. Both cultures recognized that without the
balance between Warrior and Artist, one would lack an emotional
framework (Compassion) to direct the focus of one's activity
(Intention). Without this developmental balance, one would not have
enlightened, skillful protectors, but rather, dull, mechanical soldiers.[18]

Using the four power archetypes as a psychic map for understanding
one's own leadership terrain will help one explore a well-marked pathway for leadership development. This map has been around for thousands of years. Truly successful leaders stumbled onto the map through

trial and error, or were taught it by an insightful guide. As will be seen, many people throughout history have pointed to these powers.

Woven throughout the book are countless stories and examples of clients and public leaders who exemplify the positive and negative characteristics of leadership. These stories and examples will help clarify the principles, models and tools presented throughout the book. Within the chapters on the Four Powers, you will find practical suggestions, methods and techniques for developing your positive leadership potential as well as ways to work with your negative, or shadow, leadership characteristics. The examples, concepts and practices of leadership presented in the book will provide access to what one may need to learn about one's own leadership capacity and potential.

Assuredly, we are all leaders if we are willing to awaken to something deeper and more profound in our lives. The activities of leadership become the learning ground, the environment to unravel who we truly are. So often, the person given the positional power of leadership remains lost in the activity of making "things" happen. He fails to take the time to uncover the place of Wisdom and Compassion in himself that can create the remarkable quality of leadership our organizations and culture need. Understanding how to uncover and practice these two fundamental threads of human awakening guides the quest for the kind of leaders that are needed in this difficult age. *The Four Powers of Leadership* attempts to illuminate this age-old endeavor of finding the appropriate leadership development for the time in which we live.

Challenge
The Need for a New Leadership

In *Fortune* magazine's January 13, 1997, issue, one lead article was titled "Get with the *New* Power Game." "If you want to get ahead of the curve and stay there, you need to understand that power today isn't what it was twenty years ago," read the teaser for the article. "Want to amass power? Give it away. Want to look powerful? Forget the pinstripes and the big corner office. Try chinos and a cubicle." The article went on to describe the old and new ways to exercise power as a leader. The emphasis of the article was on the outer accoutrements of dress, offices, power tools (cell phones, laptops, etc.) and what one drinks.[19]

An interview in the same issue showcased Larry Bossidy, the CEO of Allied Signal, a $14.3-billion industrial company. This interview focused on how he leads an organization as large as Allied. The questions were typical leadership fare: How do you get employees to feel urgency and commitment? How do you establish total quality in a company? How do you develop strategy and visions and make it work?[20]

Both articles point to a continual interest in successful leaders and how they exercise power. Both articles also represent the usual superficial approach to the subjects of power and leadership.

A steady interest exists in information on leadership and the use of power. Witness the number of popular bestsellers like Stephen Covey's *Seven Habits of Highly Effective People*[21] and the Peter Drucker Foundation book *The Leader of the Future*.[22] At any given time at least one or two of the books on the *New York Times* bestsellers list will be a leadership or power-oriented book.

Leadership remains an increasingly important topic primarily because we see so little positive demonstration of it in the world today. During the past ten years, dozens of books on leadership have been written to help us understand this most critical topic. Four books by leading authorities have contributed greatly to our understanding. Studies by Warren Bennis in *On Becoming a Leader*,[23] John Kotter in *The Leadership Factor*,[24] John Gardner in *On Leadership*[25] and Jay Conger in *The Charismatic Leader*[26] all describe the lack of leadership and the need to exercise it more creatively and positively in the world today.

These four studies, and many others done over the last several years, attempt to research the characteristics and behavior that make up the "what's" and "how's" of leadership.[27] Each study attempts to address the general lack of leadership demonstrated in the world today, and our dire need for creative and effective leadership. Each study also urges various means of training and development of leadership within schools and organizations. These works provide both inspirational and practical insights into the need to and means of encouraging individuals and organizations to develop leadership capability.

This book, however, is more in line with the "new" organizational and leadership thinking found in Peter Senge's *Fifth Discipline*,[28] Robert Fritz's *The Path of Least Resistance*[29] and Margaret Wheatley's *Leadership and the New Science*.[30]

The Four Powers of Leadership also follows the psychological, spiritual and social-historical traditions of Robert Moore's *King, Warrior, Magician, Lover* series,[31] James Hillman's *The Soul's Code*,[32] and William Strauss and Neil Howe's *The Fourth Turning: An American Prophecy*.[33]

The growing demand for these "new thinking" books is demonstrated by the increasing interest of the baby-boomer generation. Many of these "boomer" individuals who "woke up" in the 1960s and 1970s are now in positions of leadership throughout our culture. These are people who are hungering for more depth, insight and understanding in their personal struggle with leadership and power challenges. They want to learn how to integrate leadership into a balanced way of living personally, and how to fit a personal value structure together with business and organizational demands that are often at odds with their personal value system.

You are reading this book because, like so many of your friends and associates, your job and the opportunity to grow and take leadership in your personal and professional life are what you are focused on today. To advance in your job, you want to know how to manage and lead.

Corporations spend millions of dollars every year on management and leadership training. The hunger for knowledge is great. Personally, we all are willing to buy everything from *Chicken Soup for the Soul* for inspiration to *Seven Habits of Highly Effective People* for practical advice. But cultivating leadership takes more than reading a book or attending a seminar.

The promise of this book is to provide some insight and an opportunity for self-reflection, and to increase your motivation so that you continue the cultivation process that each of us must undertake in order to fulfill the *next natural step* in our development. It is hoped that one or two ideas, a story here and there, or some of the models or techniques will help you further your next step and give you more enthusiasm to trust your own powers. As will be described in the next section, the need to develop more capable leaders at every level of society presents a challenge that will determine the direction society takes over the next five to ten years. Although the tone of this next section may sound a little strident, its purpose is to reframe what most of us know but increasingly don't pay attention to because it is so confusing and is, in many ways, beyond what we can influence. Understanding the leadership crisis requires turning our attention to the positive and negative nature of the powers that leaders activate in themselves and others. To be reminded of the conditions that require leadership also challenges us to learn how to cultivate our own leadership capacity in order to meet the overwhelming issues confronting our society and world culture.

The Leadership Crisis

Today, the leadership crisis is most clearly revealed in its dark, or shadow, side. The manipulation of people by means of the media and consumerism, as well as through control of political and economic systems, is a prominent example of the shadow side of leadership. The contrast between positive and negative leadership power, and the struggle to develop leaders who can integrate both aspects into their lives, represents a serious need that must be satisfied in order to understand how to meet the enormous challenges of the twenty-first century.

THE ABUSE OF LEADERSHIP POWER

To understand leadership one must first explore the question of how leaders use power, manipulation and control. Both the world situation and the problem of leadership are tied to the use and abuse of power. Using and abusing power starts inside a man or woman. All individuals carry within them the tension between the conscious ego structures of values, morality and ethics, which guide their behavior, and the unconscious shadow part of themselves, which is projected onto others. The dark, negative things one perceives in others represent the tangled web of complex forces, innate urges and destructive tendencies that one suppresses in order to take on the values, morality and ethics that guide a society. These two forces—the conscious and unconscious, positive and negative—are at work in one's mind and heart, in one's relationships, and in the stances of power one takes in the world through work and other activities. The conflict between these two forces will be explored more fully, later in the book.

Robert Moore, professor of psychology and religion at Chicago

Theological Seminary and a Jungian analyst in private practice, believes that the heart of this crisis lies in how individuals express or repress the inherent power within their minds and souls. Moore argues, from the position of cross-cultural anthropology, religion and psychology, that present-day society has failed to initiate people into the rites of using positive, healthy power in their leadership roles.[34] Furthermore, he asserts that a psychological crisis of the masculine exists.[35] While this is particularly true of the male personality, it is also true of the masculine part of the female personality. His view is that during the past several generations in Western culture, the positive characteristic of masculinity within men and women has continually suffered emotional wounding from very early childhood. This wounding is apparent in the lack of fathers and husbands in the home, and the increased physical and sexual abuse men perpetrate against children, among other things. Because of this wounding, individuals who are in leadership roles tend to be caught and held in childlike patterns of fear about the exercise of power. The result of this wounding has been the inability of most leaders with positional authority to successfully access healthy personal power, but not become abusive of followers. Moore, as well as a number of other thinkers, further suggests that the exercise of patriarchy—male influence, dominance and power—over the last five thousand years has led to the breakdown of our values, spirituality and ecosystem (the last stemming from the deterioration of respectful relationships between us and other life forms).[36] *How to become healed of these deep psychic wounds in order to exercise positive masculine power, and particularly leadership power, in more creative and balanced ways is the key leadership issue for global survival in the twenty-first century.*

The late Joseph Campbell, in his work *Myths to Live By,*[37] proposed that the world monoculture of materialism has focused leadership into a dead end of economic narrowness. He argued that *business and financial power dominate the drive for purpose and meaning in our individual and collective lives.* This economic narrowness substitutes for a deeper, richer, and more mature creativity and spiritual expression in our personal relationships and within our communities.

An intriguing suggestion Campbell makes about this economic dominance in our world today is that one can determine the values and primary focus of a culture by the height of the buildings that dominate a town or city. For thousands of years, religious values dominated the psychic and geographical center of a town or city, represented by the presence of a temple or church, which generally was the largest and tallest building. Personal and societal life were directed by this religious focus. Politics, law, economics and artistic endeavors all were determined by religious leadership and power.

As new political philosophies grew, particularly in the West during the Renaissance, the skyline began to change. By the time of the French and American Revolutions, the city hall and the capitol structures grew both larger and increasingly bureaucratic—a reflection of their cultural dominance. Later, industrialism usurped government's seat of power in the Western world, and skyscrapers increasingly came to dominate the city skylines. Now, the tallest structures are not the buildings of religion or government, but of commerce and economics. It is the Sears Tower, the Transamerica Building and the Empire State Building that command the view in their respective cities. In turn, the power of leadership moves from the religious and political values of concern and community to those of competition, earnings per share and the bottom line. What now dominates the worldwide skyline is the financial institution.[38]

THE LEADERSHIP OF THE MONEY PEOPLE

It is no longer political leaders of governments who determine the course of world events, but the leaders of finance and banking, who control transnational corporations and influence international economic policy. They meet at world summits, set the values of currencies, manipulate world industries and markets, and provide for the financial bailouts of entire countries. For the countries they represent, their financial decisions bring political, military and ecological consequences. For example, it is economic survival and opportunity that is creating a new political entity in the "United States of Europe," or to use its real name, the European Economic Union. From a united "Common Market," political and cultural borders are giving way to a common currency and an economic force that has challenged the dominance of the United States over the last forty years and the Japanese over the past fifteen years. The European Union is determining both political alignment and the restructuring of Eastern and Western Europe. This realigning has changed the balance of economic and political power worldwide.

In terms of political restructuring, the dogmatism of communism and its economic failure turned the Soviet Union and Eastern Europe away from their production-oriented economies and toward the market-driven economies of the West. In turn, the movement to a market economy created a fundamental change in Eastern Europe's political and social structures.

The former Soviet Union's Mikhail Gorbachev turned back seventy years of Marxism when he said, "We are a superpower militarily and a third-world power economically." All his actions (including a serious change in military focus) demonstrated that the Soviets were going to change as quickly as possible to survive economically. In a domino effect that spread with breathtaking speed from the Berlin Wall to country after country, Eastern European Bloc nations opened up their political and social systems and quickly became independent. The risk to his leadership that Gorbachev took to bring a peaceful end to a paranoid era is unparalleled in modern times. In the end, it was economics that demanded that he change not only an economic structure, but a way of life.[39]

In great amazement, the world realized that the mighty Soviet Union had been an empty economic shell that ultimately became bankrupt and was swept away. The staff who reported to Gorbachev indicated to numerous delegations from the West during the late 1980s that the conversion from a command economy to a market economy would take a generation.[40] But the sudden reversal of

Gorbachev's fortunes and the coup in the Soviet Union in 1990 extinguished the chances of the slow evolutionary change Gorbachev had envisioned.

SERVANTS OF THE GLOBAL LEADERSHIP

When Boris Yeltsin and the genuine democratic leaders in the former Soviet Union came to power in 1991, Russian citizens were hopeful that positive economic change would occur. Since the 1996 election of Yeltsin, the country has remained divided and in deep despair that real change can happen for working people. Yeltsin and his opposition leaders have brought a corruption and devastation to the Russian economy and social system that parallels the robber barons of the 1800s in the United States. However, what will ultimately determine future conditions in Russia is not the politicians or the Russian Mafia; it is, rather, the agents of the World Bank and the International Monetary Fund (IMF), who are forcing a financial and social restructuring that will enable Russia to fit into the world consumer system.

If Russian leaders have become pawns to the Western consumer engine, our own religious and political leadership have become subservient to the global economic and financial leadership. Again, the emphasis of what is being described is the shadow or dark side of the leadership dilemma. Financial leaders influence political leaders to keep military spending at very high levels to fuel the economy even though the "Evil Empire" is gone. Also, the United States is the number-one seller of military arms to second- and third-world nations.[41] Because of its military-economic intentions, the United States has a vested interest in keeping political conflict going by funneling arms into these unstable nations so that the economic war machine can run alongside consumerism in order to make sure the world economy is always being fueled.

It is the shortsighted economic leadership of first-world timber companies, chip manufacturers, oil companies and the like that rationalizes the deterioration of basic human, moral and spiritual values; this unenlightened leadership turns away from tough political, economic and democratic challenges in such places as China, Colombia or Indonesia. This shortsightedness and rationalization protect transnational investments. Both human and natural resources in undeveloped nations are raped. The people of these countries are stripped of their self-determination and cultural, religious and political identities as dominant Western economies offer jobs and loans to third-world countries in order to get cheap resources and labor. The first world rationalizes that, in exchange for the jobs and IMF loans granted to third-world nations, first-world countries can deplete rain forests and set up sports shoe factories or car plants so that people in these countries can have the "opportunity" to eventually become consumer participants in the "modern" world. Many of these third-world peoples don't want modern consumer "opportunity," but enough money is given to the top leaders in these countries that it is easy for developed nations to buy their way in and set up shop.

With transnational corporate machines grinding out a constant supply of goods to buy and consume, the greed and drive for more and more things wound the collective heart and reduce the collective will, culminating in our abusing the young, neglecting the aged and overfeeding the population—all as a result of the constant demand to *consume* as an end in itself.[42] Personal consumption drives 80 percent of the gross domestic product. The latest fashions, the newest computer, the bigger-screened TV, the new-model car all pressure the public to buy constantly those things one doesn't really need. The $100-billion advertising industry is the mechanism that continuously maintains the pressure to constantly buy. In television, movies and our daily life, buying things is presented as the primary value and the purpose of work, as well as what one does for recreation and what drives one's perception of personal worth and meaning. Each person takes in this constant propaganda assault and tries to work out some form of accommodation to it. The failure of most leaders is that they are not helping to address the fundamental issues and, more important, not exercising creative and compassionate vision to find a way out of this cultural dead end.

THE OUTLAW MONEY LEADERS

The leadership of the financial power structures dominating our planet doesn't have to fit into any accepted social, political or religious system. Throughout the world there is conflict between legitimate judicial systems and illegal syndicates. The illegal economic power of drug lords in South America, Southeast Asia or the former Soviet Union have their own armies, communication and transportation systems, and influence or control—by means of the sheer force of billions of dollars—over national economies and governments. It is this drug-controlled economy that adds another variable to world financial leadership competition. The promotion of drugs (and worldwide financial manipulation of millions of people) is probably the single largest symptom of leadership dishonesty.

The pharmaceutical, tobacco and alcohol industries are the most profitable and powerful in this country. These "legal drugs," particularly tobacco and alcohol, kill more people than all the "illegal drugs" combined. Even the ravages of heroin addiction do not compare to the wide and devastating impact of these legal drugs on the health and well-being of the majority of the world population. Alcohol, for example, is the number-two killer of people in the United States.[43] Tobacco is far more addictive than any hard drug and has been proven to cause a variety of fatal cancers. Despite all the pressure to obtain financial settlements from tobacco companies in the United States, our government, rather than stopping tobacco companies, is helping them to export this lethal product into third-world countries, where the markets are wide open to buy American cigarettes.[44] A 1996 World Health Organization and World Bank study on world disease predicted that tobacco-related diseases will cause one in ten deaths throughout the world by 2020. In 1990, tobacco claimed 3 million lives worldwide; in 2020 it will claim 8.4 million. When government agencies are challenged as to why death is being exported, the explanation given is that it helps in the balance of trade.

A so-called war on drugs is meaningless until the fundamental reason for "drugging ourselves" is addressed. It is the failure of political and religious leaders to meet the real problem of drugs: a world consumer culture led by financial leaders who have defined the superficial world of material consumption as comprising the basic purpose and meaning of life. Everything in one's life is focused through the lens of economics. Job position, work, debts and having things—not family, friends or an inner life—become what is primarily important to people. Mood-altering drugs, whether legal or illegal, have simply become the sacrament in the religion of consuming things.

Illegal drugs are called an escape and a cover-up. But they are not effectively prohibited because they satisfy some unexplainable need in people, and they help to fuel the world economy and line the pockets of many of the most important people in the world. Political leaders wage war on drugs in the same way as they wage war on poverty, arms control or any of the other causes du jour that fool people into believing that the real problem is one thing when it is really something else. These same political leaders, however, support the legal drugs of pharmaceutical, tobacco, alcohol and coffee companies because these industries support their campaigns and fuel local economies.

When seen on television or read in news reports, the blatant lies of tobacco corporation executives and political leaders who argue that nicotine is not addictive or a cause of lung cancer, make it clear that economic power is abusive. What has happened with the selling of tobacco happens with other unhealthy products that corporations and governments worldwide push on the public for short-term economic gain.

Whether it is marijuana, cocaine, alcohol, sugar, coffee, chocolate, TV or something else, people seem very susceptible to using some substitute that they believe will help them touch some larger-than-life feeling within themselves—some inner world that has meaning and beauty. But the substitutes are just that: dark mirrors that merely reflect one's emotional, physical and spiritual death. The feelings of euphoria, sudden insight or bursting of energy that they bring offer a moment of hope and relief. Then they become mere habits and cover-ups of a deeper pain. *The real addiction is the drive to want to feel some goodness in the midst of the craziness and pain most people seem to experience.* Something about the way in which we now live no longer permits people to feel. Instinctively, one knows there is a different way to live, but most don't know what it is or how to find it. There is a longing some express for a new set of leaders to show a way out of the inner pain and toward a different home inside oneself. People want guidance in the midst of the chaos and a way to feel safe and happy in their communities. This longing and suffering open individuals to the influence of both positive and negative leaders.

THE CRY FOR NEW LEADERS

Most of our political and religious leaders stand mute or join in with approval, urging that financial progress based on consuming must go on for the good of all. But in many countries throughout the world, and in small and unassuming ways, dissent grows. Among some there is the restless questioning of whether the god of economic consumption is enough for the human spirit to worship.

The unarticulated cry of millions across the planet is for someone who can teach people to live again not by economic bread alone! There is a an undertow of resistance from concerned citizens that political and corporate leaders cannot continue to rape the earth for short-term profit. Movements, groups and coalitions are raising up leaders and voices around the world in an attempt to respond to the plethora of personal, social and environmental needs of the people of this planet. These are thoughtful, strong voices that urge sustainability and a simplicity of living within the frantic media-driven world culture. These are the voices of the democracy movements in China, Burma and Mexico; of the Simple Living movement in Europe, India and the United States. It is the nonmoney resource systems growing in Australia, Canada and, notably, in the United States in Ithaca, New York. These nonmoney systems acknowledge that the skills and capabilities of people in a community, not paper money, form the true resource basis for healthy living. The rising tide of consumer rejection can be seen in the simple act of the average citizen throughout the world who turns off the TV and puts it in the closet. Again and again, people individually and collectively all over the world are saying no to a leadership that would turn them into robots serving a consumer machine and saying yes to leaders who affirm community, individual creativity, strong family, and ecological and spiritual modes of living.[45]

But just as positive, caring voices responsive to human concern and activity are growing, another kind of dissent is also growing through religious fanaticism, ethnic conflicts and political absolutism. Whether in Northern Ireland, Israel and the West Bank, west Africa, southern Mexico or Sri Lanka, ethnic, political, economic and religious conflicts blur together. People fight for their "rights." But *whose* rights becomes the question. One group's rights seem to take away the rights of another group. Dogmatism grows in the "holy war" fundamentalism of Islam, the "take over" Christian fundamentalism of the United States, the right-wing Orthodox "absolute" fundamentalism in Israel, the separatist "destroyer" fundamentalism of the Tamal Tigers of Sri Lanka, the "terrorist" fundamentalism of both sides in Northern Ireland and the "uncompromising" Sikh extremists in India.

The leaders of each of these groups claim that their one moral or religious position is the only way. These groups claim the authority to kill, hurt or control those who don't believe their way. Many leaders of such groups urge a puritanical purging of materialism and consumerism, while at the same time urging followers to provide them with financial support. These leaders cry out to their followers to "give money so that we can succeed and triumph!" Success is defined by how much money will influence politicians, purchase media or buy guns. In their own way, these leaders give meaning, purpose and hope to their followers. Although little positive change actually results from these efforts, the presence of some kind of organized action that is purported to help followers gain control of their lives or environment keeps their hope alive, however cynical or destructive such hope may ultimately be to the followers themselves, or to the world at large.

Positive and negative leaders both operate effectively in times of deep confusion, transition and uncertainty. Individuals want predictability and control in their lives. Negative leaders tend to pull people more deeply into their fears so that they act protectively and exclude any others who are not like them. Positive leaders in times of deep cultural transition urge individuals toward community, shared values, and a discovery of living and working from one's own inner strength. Each of these forms of leadership works from the position of being a victim of circumstances or of learning to access new and creative resources to solve the difficult problems at hand. Followers receive their power to participate based on whether they are directed inward to their own creativity and resourcefulness or are guided to be dependent on outside codes of conduct and prohibitions.

To live and learn from our inner resources is difficult at best in good times, let alone chaotic times like these. To live from the inside out takes moral strength, inner courage and a community of support. It takes the wisdom of elders, the patience of teachers, the inspiration of leaders. It requires an individual to take a step beyond the economic dominance of a monolithic world culture. To live from the inside out calls for a strong vision, intuitive insight and the courage to begin living differently day to day.

Many people throughout the world are beginning to experiment. Through their spiritual and religious beliefs, through their myths and stories, through their arts and community rituals, they are attempting to create new alternatives that are separate from the dominant worldwide economic culture. But there is a race for survival, and the question is, How fast can we change from solely depending on the external world of economics and finances—of *things*—to creating a balance between our inner and outer lives? Most people have become cynical and numb to the question of whether there are leaders of sufficient strength and presence who can stand against this dark power of economic, political, and religious control and abuse. The deep collective despair is whether hope can return, whether a new form of leadership can emerge in these dire times to help answer this desperate need.

John Gardner, in his book *No Easy Victories*, says: "Leaders have a significant role in creating the state of mind that is the society. They can serve as symbols of the moral unity of the society. They can express the values that hold the society together. Most important, they can conceive and articulate goals that lift people out of their petty preoccupations, carry them above the conflicts that tear a society apart, and unite them in pursuit of objectives worthy of their best efforts."[46]

Without a new leadership to help raise up a new image, a new possibility of something different from what one has, most people will continue to live in a narrow economic definition of reality that excludes an inner spiritual world. Without a new form of leadership, there will be little opportunity to create and teach new rituals and affirm the old traditions that give value and meaning to life. Without a new, determined leadership, there will be little urgency to bring people into contact and balance with the natural world, and no one to provide a path back to the creativity and community with other people that is possible. There is a deep need for a different kind of leadership than what dominates the world stage today. This is a leadership that must help meet the challenge of redefining how to live in the world spiritually, socially, politically and economically, lest humanity become increasingly lost in a sea of chaos.

THE CRISIS OF THE CROSSROADS

The *crisis of the crossroads* has existed as long as people have been on the planet. Crisis is part of the evolutionary journey. Crisis can help one wake up a little more to oneself and to others. The crisis at this moment demands not only a leadership that is open to solving world problems, but one that has the vision to help cross the threshold to a different way of living life on this planet. The leadership that will surmount this threshold crisis will need to synthesize both old and new forms. This coming threshold crisis may be what social historians Strauss and Howe describe in their book *The Fourth Turning* as the twenty-year Crisis Cycle that has recurred every hundred years in Anglo-American culture for the past five hundred years. Our last crisis period, they argue, began at the stock market crash of 1929 and ended in 1946 after World War II. The next crisis period, they contend, will be triggered sometime between 2005 and 2007.[47] Or, in a larger sense, this crisis may be what the Jesuit philosopher Teilhard de Chardin called an evolutionary *change of state* that comes when a species is getting ready to either make an evolutionary jump or go into extinction.[48] Whatever the analysis of the situation may be and what part of the cycle this threshold time represents, the focus and response that can become galvanized by thoughtful leadership is what can make the difference both now and in the future.

There is an old African ritual about meeting such a critical crisis that the storyteller Michael Mead recounts.[49] It is a ritual in which a group of men and women line up opposite each other and chant back and forth. This particular chant is used when the problems in the village are very great and the people have no answers. In this chant they call to the gods to come to the crossroads to help them go in a different direction. In the chanting, the physical movement and emotional intensity between the men and women permit a powerful energy to emerge. The power that is generated and called forth is an intangible, psychological, spiritual energy that feeds both the individual and the community so as to provide a new level of strength and resolve to meet the crisis. It is through this generation of physical, emotional and spiritual power that insight, clarity, direction, and a new way to live and act in the world are restored to the community.

In the spirit of the crossroads ritual, our challenge today is to "chant," to call together with all our strength that a new direction and a new leadership be given to us. Let us begin the call/response at the crossroads of our crisis by exploring the heart of the leadership issue: the structure of power.

1

The Structure
of Power

A Map for
Understanding Power

The Four Powers of Leadership is a description of leadership characteristics based on fundamental structures of the psyche (the conscious and unconscious parts of a person's body/brain/mind/soul matrix) that is within all human beings. These "powers of leadership" are four among many different kinds of psychic structures potentially within us. These "powers," or structures, are patterns and images (gestalts) that are somehow held within a person and that cause one to respond, react and behave in specific ways. In psychology these structures are called *archetypes*. The word *archetype* comes from ancient Greek, meaning "original pattern."

The Swiss psychiatrist Carl Jung established the modern psychological usage of the idea of archetypes.[1] He understood them to be the "primordial images" of the unconscious. From Jung's point of view these primordial images remain hidden within us but manifest themselves in our consciousness through stories, myths and fairy tales. These poetic frameworks reenact the primal situations of birth, death,

1

motherhood, love, change, coming of age, conquest, etc., in specific themes, patterns and motifs. For example, such poetic stories as the *Epic of Gilgamesh* (the ancient Sumerian epic), Homer's *Odyssey*, the Arthurian legends, the Krishna stories of India and Dante's *Divine Comedy* play out within them a vast array of archetypal images. The archetype (the ancient, a priori energy) stands unseen behind these poetic images, but through the structure of the image itself, the archetype becomes available to conscious awareness, and therefore accessible to daily experience.

James Hillman, a student and expander of Jung's work, in his book *Re-Visioning Psychology*[2] broadens the definition of archetypes in the following six ways:

"Archetypes are the *deepest patterns of psychic functioning* [bold and italics mine]; they are the roots of the soul governing the perspectives we have of ourselves and the world."[3]

Archetypes in this sense are mental and emotional frameworks that we don't see. They are *structures that we look through*, much like looking through a window. The archetypal window outlines or creates a pattern for what one sees in the world. For example, it is "seeing" that there is a common pattern to all human beings no matter their race, culture or history. These commonalities are first seen in the same body structure, mental capacity, emotional responses, etc.

In particular, the archetypal patterns are revealed in how people raise children and develop a family unit; they are also seen in the ways communities are organized, no matter where they are in the world. In another vein, through the windows or archetypes out of which one continually looks and from which one repeatedly sees, regardless of time period or geography, one can observe such things as recurring themes of history, similar human thought and belief systems, the rituals that provide meaning, and the myths, stories, and fairy tales that capture collective experience and that are retold in each generation.

"Archetypes are *fundamental metaphors* [bold and italics mine] that describe root ideas, first principles, patterns of instinctual behavior, worldwide rituals and experiences."[4]

Such basic notions as God, art, society, life, community, nature, etc., that one holds as given are formed by and developed through these basic patterns held deep within. The metaphor that "we are created in the image of God" is an example of this aspect of archetypes. The drive to understand oneself through God is fundamental to how individuals create spiritual meaning and religion. At the broadest level, the struggle with economics today—capitalism or socialism or something else—is a fundamental metaphor for the search for personal and collective choices in values and meaning for work and societal structure.

"Archetypes form the *mental and emotional structures*, and generate the *basic energy and power* that motivate the attitudes and behavior of individuals and groups of people."[5] [Bold and italics mine.]

The power of an archetype possesses one in the sense that one can become unconscious as to how its energy has formed one's actions and responses to people and situations. Individuals act through a given archetype by living out unconsciously the image(s) of the mental and emotional attitudes provided by one's environment, family, culture and historical period. Although one will live out these unconscious archetypal patterns automatically, one can be conscious of them through dreams, myths and broader cultural "stories." These personal and cultural images create the conditions of how one's physical, mental and emotional energy will be directed. The basic life energy in each person—the psychic force or libido—is neither positive nor negative, moral nor immoral. If one is unconscious of the pattern or structure, or of how to access this primal energy, it will be difficult to control this force in one's daily life.

If one's life condition and psychological makeup were such that one needed control over every aspect of life, what might be accessed by that individual is the archetype of the tyrant. In an extreme case, this individual might try to exert control over the world as Hitler attempted. (The real Hitler not only took on the tyrant/

savior archetype, but also was able to tap a deep-seated archetype in the German people that channeled both the energy of their frustration from the effects of World War I and their pride in the cultural dominance of German history.) On the other hand, if one consciously accessed the archetype of the Christ and identified with Jesus, one could easily give oneself in service to the world. The power and energy of this image let one reach beyond one's own needs and open to what Christians call the power (or archetype) of the Holy Spirit to serve humanity. Mother Teresa, Albert Schweitzer and thousands of missionaries who give themselves in service take on this healing servant archetype.

These archetypal structures within all people are both unconscious and conscious. They are channels and generators of power that one's ego can either inhibit and block (and therefore stop the natural flow of psychic energy) or to which one's ego can surrender. In whatever manner one chooses, these archetypal powers release and express themselves in ways that can have great impact on oneself and others.

The decisions one makes throughout life develop the particular cluster of archetypes that makes up the pattern of one's life. Being more conscious of one's own particular pattern of archetypes permits one to enter into dialogue with them in order to reinforce, unblock or change the pattern that influences how the psychic energy moves through one's life experience.

"Archetypes *organize* into clusters or constellations, or hosts of events from different areas of life. [Bold and italics mine.] This clustering appears first in behavior, second in images and third in a style of consciousness."[6]

The hero or heroine archetype offers an example of this organizing. This archetype appears in all cultures throughout both Eastern and Western history. To follow Hillman's sequence, the *behavior* is the first identifying quality of the hero archetype. It is the drive to explore, to respond to challenge, to risk one's life and prove one's capabilities. The second characteristic in his organizing schema is a set of *images*. For any of us these hero images can range from

Hercules and Superwoman to Jesse James, Percival, Rambo, Luke Skywalker and Joan of Arc. What gives power to these images is that the hero is on a quest to discover inner qualities through encountering outer difficulties, challenges and adventures. What these hero images give us is guidance in how to seek independence and achievement, develop overpowering capabilities, conquer forces larger than ourselves, sacrifice ourselves for others, or be single-minded, disciplined and virtuous. This extension of the warrior-hero archetype is particularly influential in the modern organizational setting. Leaders in organizations look for "champions," "heroes" and "superpeople" to get the project completed or the job done.

The third defining trait of the hero is a distinct *style of consciousness.* These archetypes can easily be called forth in us by leaders and others around us. Something exists deep within individuals that wants to be the hero, to respond to the challenge, to overcome, to exceed one's own capabilities and to test oneself against forces larger than oneself.

The value of understanding how archetypes become organized through behavior, image and style lies in its giving one immediate clues as to the kind of energy that is driving the individual, the group one is participating in or leading, or the outside forces of these archetypes that seem to be in control. Learning to self-reflect on how different patterns of behaviors, images and consciousness operate in oneself enables each individual to see the character of the archetypes that are at work, the sources of people's motivation and action, and the way to make conscious choices and decisions in responding to these forces.

"Archetypes *are collective.* Archetypes are rooted in, but go beyond, individual habits and personal differences. Second, archetypes provide the connection between what goes on in the individual soul, and what goes on in all people in all places and in all times. *Archetypes allow psychological understanding at a common humanity level."* [7] [Bold and italics mine.]

All the various aspects of human experience—what one calls good and evil, all the various viewpoints, beliefs and attitudes that one calls crazy or sane—are within human beings. What we each choose and manifest in our individual personality provides a common link to know and understand others similar to us elsewhere in the world. Suffering and grief, joy and hope touch every human being in a manner that goes beyond language and culture. The archetypal patterns link people in collective unity as humans. No matter what differences exist among people, a deeper collective unconscious exists, and it continually sorts out the common connectors that permit one to recognize others as part of one human family.

"**Archetypes transcend culture, history and differences in racial and genetic characteristics.** *Archetypes appear similarly in all peoples through all time.*"[8] [Bold and italics mine.]

The particular images of the archetypes may be different in different cultures and in different times, but they hold the same power and potential for every human being. In this sense an archetype uses the structures of dream, myth, story, poetry, song and ritual so that we can come to feel our common patterns with all peoples.

Whether it is an African story that teaches the principles of a child learning responsibility in the bush by not keeping the rats his father killed for food; Hans Christian Andersen's Ugly Duckling teaching self-esteem; a Chinese tale of a man who turns into a fish to experience the creature's feelings; Jesus teaching the parable of planting seeds; or the nightly dreams that show one part of one's personality that is being denied, one is part of myth-making human culture, which keeps reexploring the same fundamental issues of learning, growth and change. People make up stories, create rituals of play and drama, sing songs to lament and praise, and paint, sculpt, write, make movies and recite poetry to discover and pass on to others who and what one is.

SUMMARY OF ARCHETYPAL "POWERS"

The foregoing definitions clearly show that archetypes operate in people in complex and often unconscious ways. The important element of these definitions for purposes of leadership is that the person who is expressing the archetypal powers of a leader holds the potential to significantly impact people in either positive or negative ways. It is the creative and destructive impacts of the Julius Caesars and the Napoleons, the Indira Gandhis and the Mother Teresas, the Hitlers and the George Washingtons, the Joan of Arcs and the Marie Curies, the Christopher Columbuses and the Robert Pearys, and the many, many other men and women who have attained the power of leadership over the people who followed them. But it is also the impact of one's boss at work, the pastor at church, the doctor at the clinic, the therapist in the consulting room. They also influence one positively or negatively by their conscious or unconscious use of these leadership "powers." *For one's own protection, as well as the potential development of oneself as a leader, one needs to understand these leadership structures and the use and abuse of their powers.*

In addition to the four leadership archetypes that will be described, any archetype can overpower the ego-self of an individual and take possession of the personality, to the detriment of the person and of the people that person leads. President John F. Kennedy was so possessed by his own Camelot myth that he believed no one could kill him and rejected the suggestions of his aides to ride in a closed-roof car in Dallas. Archetypal possession allows Christian leaders like Jimmy Swaggart or Jim Bakker to consider themselves to be morally above reproach for doing the very things they preach against. Archetypal possession is also seen in the captain of a military unit who wantonly leads his men into a senseless battle because he wants to be a hero and, as a result of his action, jeopardizes the safety of his command and kills himself. It is also present in the doctor who holds the power of life and death over his patients, insisting that he operate on them when they really do not need the operation, simply to make money. It is displayed in the seemingly sensitive, caring teacher who through understanding, listening and appreciation of students creates an atmosphere in which he is able to sexually seduce students for "their learning and growth." The power the individual holds over people in each of these examples seems to access the blind spot, the underside, the gray or shadow part of an energy that all leaders can potentially exploit if they are not wise or careful with the patterns of power—the archetypes—they invoke.

Episcopalian minister and Jungian psychologist John Sanford, in his study *What Men Are Like* (coauthored by George Lough),[9] shows that archetypes are strong at a very early age. He states that "we are especially close to these archetypal influences in childhood. They fill the imagination, and shape and direct [our] healthy development."[10] He goes on to say that "the images they produce in the mind of the child are creative; they appear spontaneously in the child's imagination and play. This living contact with the archetypal world is experienced in a unique and pristine way in childhood and it needs to be nurtured by the parents. For from this early contact with the archetypal world emerges the later creativity of the adult."[11]

Many know from experience this child's world of archetypes in imaginary playmates or vivid daydreams with kings and queens and fairy beings. This child's world of archetypes comes alive through pretend events and fantasy worlds that extend from pirates to soldiers, to animals, to playing teacher, nurse, mommy, daddy or whatever else arises in one's imagination. If, somehow, this life of imagination is suppressed or lacking in one's childhood, one can become cut off from one's own soul, from the source of inner power. Sanford comments: "the preparation that we need for adult life is a long and healthy immersion in the creative world of fantasy, for which our souls have a natural and in-built propensity and need. For lack of the proper early nourishment of the soul a man (or woman) may in later life become dried up and uncreative."[12]

In discussing the tension between the positive and negative aspects of these archetypal powers, it is clear that the roots of their development begin very early in one's life. If family experience repressed one's imagination, then one may suffer today from a lack of creativity and, as a result, may demand great control over one's world. This control may cause one to access the shadow side of the powers that press in on one and want to be expressed through one's behavior. For many, the world of fantasy and daydream may keep one buried in the unconscious and may cause difficulty in coping with the daily routine of life. Here the powers lack focus and direction, and their energy is quickly dissipated.

No matter whether one has had a positive or negative childhood experience or even a damaged childhood, these archetypal powers are accessible in ways that can open and heal and enable one to tap some deeper and richer part of oneself. Sanford suggests that within each person there are the structures or archetypes that let the healing force of God work in one's life. It is from the archetypes that a very ancient idea comes "that everyone has both human and divine parents. In Christian language, we are the child of certain parents but also a child of God. For this reason . . . early contact with the archetypes cannot be stressed too much."[13] Sanford concludes that through contact with the archetypes in childhood, the way "is made for the possibility in adult life that [a person] will have the archetypes as his inner companions just as he did when he was a child."[14] These powers will be companions and work positively or negatively on one's psyche throughout life, no matter what the conscious childhood experience of them was.

POWER AS THE CORE ISSUE OF LEADERSHIP

Power is the primary definer of leadership. The dictionary defines power in four interrelated ways. First, it is "the ability or capacity to perform or act effectively." Second, "a specific capacity, faculty, or aptitude." Third, "strength or force exerted or capable of being exerted." And fourth, "the ability or official capacity to exercise control; authority." The first two definitions represent the personal power inherent in an individual. The second two definitions represent the use of power through position. Power is a condition of both being and doing.

By these definitions the recognized position of a leader gives a person certain responsibilities that are exercised by exerting decision, control and judgment over conditions, people and events. This *positional power* of a leader may or may not coincide with the *personal power* that the leader demonstrates. In positional leadership, the power the person exercises is given through the role. The role of president of the company, master of the scout troop or prime minister of the country defines the scope of powers and rights the person has over the situation. In personal power, one does not have to hold a title or be given the power through some authoritative agency. Rather, power comes from some inner source within the person through "a specific capacity, faculty, or aptitude." Many people one knows have this "sense of power" about them. Some people describe this power as *presence*. When the person walks into the room, for example, all eyes seem to turn to this individual. People with presence have a quality that attracts individuals to them. People like being around them, talking with them, doing things with and for them. Or some people say the person "has charisma and lights up the room with her energy." Someone with *charisma* seems to pull one toward him. One feels more energized and motivated to do things when around him. This characteristic of presence, or charisma, that some people exhibit has a compelling or motivating power.

If a very strong archetype has been constellated in the charismatic individual, it can often trigger a complementary archetype in others as well. If, for example, the charismatic archetype of an individual is expressed in strong interpersonal qualities by extending appreciation, love and caring to people, then being around that individual may open up in one repressed feelings and emotions with which one hasn't consciously been in touch. Such an awakening may activate devotion and service to the person or to the person's philosophy, and a willingness to give oneself to others because the person asks us to, compelling one to act very differently from how one had been before encountering that individual.

In an organizational setting, personal and positional power activate archetypes in both the leader and in the follower. An employee can be uncomfortable around the president of the company simply because that person holds the power that could influence the employee's career, position in the organization or economic status. The president asking an employee to do something, and the employee responding with strong motivation and commitment, may not be the result of the personal presence of the individual who is the president. The role the individual plays, separate from our like or dislike of the person, may activate a variety of mutual archetypal responses. For example, the father or mother archetype in the president can in turn activate the employee's "good little child" archetype, and the employee may become compliant in pleasing the president as "mommy" or "daddy." Or it may be the "bad boy (or girl)" archetype, and the employee may become resistant and do everything possible to fight the "mommy" or "daddy" represented by the president.

If both personal and positional power come together in the same individual, then the classic figure of the *charismatic leader* emerges. Both the *role as leader* and the *personality presence* merge, and a strong personal response of attraction or repulsion compels one to respond to the leader in some way. Being in the aura of the leader will affect people. No matter what such a leader's personal interaction with an individual, he will influence the individual in some manner. The various combinations of archetypes, or powers, that an individual leader accesses in his psyche and expresses through his personality determine the nature and character of that person's particular leadership.

Many leaders who have positional power wonder why things seem not to go right when they exercise their "power rights." A manager who says that he or she is the "boss" to an employee and that the employee should "do better work or else" will find only short-term influence over the individual and probably a continuing resistance over the long run. But a fellow worker who has personal power may inspire the same individual to do a good job because it is "so creative and so much fun" to work with that person. Other employees may say, "[So-and-so] is the person I'd love to work for because [he or she] brings out the best in me." But, often, when some of these charismatic types are put into the positional leader role, they find that their "equality leading" through example ceases to work; it does not influence others to meet predetermined standards or conform to set policies and regulations. The charismatic leader will often resist these kinds of imposed standards and structures, and try to exercise power in a manner that meets his or her own personality style or archetypal needs.

How aware a leader is of his positional and/or leadership power isn't as important as how conscious or unconscious that person is in acting out the various leader archetypes. For it is in the presence or absence of the power of the archetypes that one will demonstrate effectiveness, or lack thereof, in influencing and motivating other people.

In *The Leadership Factor,* John Kotter describes effective leadership as "good leadership." That is, leadership that "moves people in a direction that is genuinely in their real long-term best interests. It does not march people off a cliff. It does not waste their scarce resources. It does not build up the dark side of their human nature. In this sense, one could say Adolf Hitler displayed strong leadership at times, but obviously not effective leadership." [15]

From this preliminary discussion of archetypes, we turn now to the discussion of the Four Powers of Leadership, outlining both their positive and negative aspects. Each of the Four Powers—Presence, Intention, Wisdom and Compassion—resides in everyone. The opportunities one has and the choices one makes determine to what degree those powers are activated and expressed.

2

CHARACTERISTICS OF
THE FOUR POWERS

CONTEXT FOR THE FOUR POWERS

The four leadership powers, or archetypes, presented in this book are based on the work of many people, particularly Carl Jung and several of his students. The development of the leadership archetypes has been influenced by John Weir Perry[1] and his work on the king archetype; Robert Bly and his discussion of the power of images and what he calls the *shadow bag* that we all carry within us; Michael Mead and his use of ritual and storytelling, and his understanding of the Warrior; James Hillman and his understanding of what it is to "go down" into the darkness of our soul; and Robert Moore and his configuration of the four archetypes that make up the focus of this book. Robert Moore's discussion of four archetypes stimulated this book's consideration of how leadership power operates in men and women. Finally, the drive to explore these leadership issues comes from practical experience in various kinds of organizations with managers and executives who are attempting to remove the blocks and release the potentials of their own powers of leadership.

What Moore sees as a crisis in modern Western culture has

compelled him, as a theologian and therapist, to present the four archetypes in his books and to groups all over the country. He sees this crisis in his clinical practice with individuals and his work preparing men and women to be ministers and leaders in the church: It is a lack of initiation into *mature masculinity*,[2] as opposed to the prevailing initiation into a male dominance system. *He defines being initiated into a mature masculinity as discovering how to access the four masculine archetypes that are present in both women and men in such a way that one can draw power from them but not be possessed by them.*[3]

Furthermore, Moore contends that archetypes are possessive and can dominate us because they are, by definition, imperialistic. They create compulsive behavior (such as workaholism) if a person does not learn through some form of "ritual elder initiation" how to balance and work with these very powerful energies. He presents four archetypes that can possess us or be repressed by us: the *King,* the *Warrior*, the *Magician* and the *Lover*.[4] Each archetype has male and female aspects, so a more accurate configuration would be the male/female Sovereign, the male/female Warrior, the male/female Magician and the male/female Lover (which this book terms the Artist).

To provide a more modern leadership language, this book terms the Sovereign as the power of Presence, the Warrior the power of Intention, the Magician the power of Wisdom and the Artist the power of Compassion.[5]

These dual descriptions are mythic images that are both transcultural and transhistorical. The image of king or magician, for example, appears in many diverse cultures. Though having different historical contexts and meanings, these recurring archetypes demonstrate that the same characteristics described in modern Japan, ancient India, medieval Europe or Silicon Valley are always within all of us.[6]

The various aspects of the powers of these four archetypes will illuminate our exploration of leadership characteristics, the positive and negative aspects of each of the archetypes operating in leaders. Before examining these characteristics, a brief summary of the earlier discussion of archetypes will create a context for the description of how these four powers are cultivated within us:

- *Archetypes are structures deeply imprinted in our psyche, or soul, collectively and individually.* They are a part of us, but independent of us at the same time. They exist almost as if they were separate personalities in us.
- *These powers are amoral.* That is, they are centers of energy that can be used in positive or negative ways. In some sense they "just are." They exist as autonomous energies within us.
- *Archetypes are transformative in their power.* When the energy of the archetypes is working, it changes us and often influences people and events around us.
- *A person can access an archetype in constructive or destructive ways, or in a combination of the two.* The more we know about an archetype, the more we can learn to *work with* the power it makes available to us.
- *We can be possessed or oppressed by archetypes.* When we are oppressed, we become extremely self-critical—we are under attack by the archetype. When we are possessed by the power, we are the archetype; we act out its role and are under its control.

Moore points out that a single image in which to see all four archetypes present is the historical figure of Jesus.[7] Whether one is Christian or not, the image of Jesus has dominated our Western cultural focus for two thousand years. Because of this dominance, the Jesus image has deep roots in our collective unconscious, psychologically, emotionally and spiritually.

The four leadership powers emerge from Jesus' life and provide the characteristics that illustrate the four archetypes as "powers." One of the strongest archetypal images we have of Jesus is his death by crucifixion. The title that has been given for his sacrifice is "King of Kings." In Christian theology he is not only proclaimed as "King of the Jews," but is placed as *"King (Sovereign) of the Universe."* In this universal proclamation as king, his *Presence* fills everything.

What he is, rather than what he does, illustrates the key element of Presence. Second, Jesus is seen as a *Warrior* in his faithfulness (loyalty) to his Father, God, and in his refusal to be intimidated before Pontius Pilate at his trial. Or, in a similar way, in his chasing the money changers out of the Temple in Jerusalem. His capacity to focus his *Intention* produces results and demonstrates his intense commitment to the transcendent—the larger sphere beyond his own actions and understanding. In the role of *Magician,* Jesus is seen as healer and miracle worker. Whether feeding five thousand, raising Lazarus from the dead or making a blind man see, he shows the deep knowledge and skill necessary to access some miraculous power. One can do tricks or one can be wise in the use of power. Jesus demonstrates the *Wisdom* of using skill and knowledge appropriately. Finally, we see his creativity and empathy as *Artist* in his saving the prostitute from being stoned, gathering around him poor fishermen and affirming their potential as leaders, and forgiving the thieves who were crucified with him. Each of these are supreme examples of Jesus' "passion to suffer with" others that is the basis of his *Compassion.*

Using Jesus as an integrating image of the Four Powers of Presence, Intention, Wisdom and Compassion gives us a helpful framework for exploring the leadership characteristics of each of the archetypes. As Carl Jung has pointed out, the figure of Jesus in Western culture over the past two thousand years has shaped the depth of the leadership image that is buried deep within our collective unconscious.[8]

Let us examine now the negative or shadow side of the four leadership archetypes, demonstrating how this shadow energy is at work in all of us. If Jesus has represented the positive archetype of the Four Powers in Western culture, then Satan—the devil—has been his negative counterpart.

THE SHADOW SIDE OF POWER

Within all our personalities are negative attitudes and behaviors that either unconsciously and unexpectedly, or sometimes consciously and with devilish delight, attack, judge, hurt, and in inscrutable ways try to gain control over and dominate others. Carl Jung suggested that this fact of psychological projection came from what he called the shadow part of our unconscious.[9] Conscious awareness could be described as light and the unconscious part of our lives, the shadow, as its mirror image, which follows behind us. We are unaware of this unconscious shadow part of ourselves until we see it projected like a spotlight onto someone in the form of our fear, guilt or anger. This shadow concept is not a recent psychological invention. We can go back to the well of spiritual literature and see yin/yang, dark/light, conscious/unconscious, life/death portrayed in the battle between the gods and the demons of Hindu Vedic scriptures or the contest between the powers of good and evil in the Zoroastrian religion of Persia (present-day Iran), in which Ahura Mazda—the Wise Lord—was equal to and constantly counterbalancing his opposite, Ahriman—the Evil One.[10] Of course the three monotheistic religions of Western tradition all start with the creation story (borrowed from Sumerian myth), in which a shadow—the Serpent—emerges from the Tree of the Knowledge of Good and Evil. This serpent in Christian tradition is the fallen angel, Satan, who has aligned the demons and forces of darkness to do battle with the God of Light for control of our souls.

Flowing through ancient Greek culture are the various shadow gods, such as Hermes, the trickster-thief; Hades, lord of the dark underworld (which became our conception of hell); Dionysus, the ecstatic drunk; and Pan, the god of nightmare (who became the horned image of the devil in medieval Christianity).[11]

These images reemerge in Western literature through Plato's shadow cave in the *Republic*, Dante's descent into hell in the *Inferno*, Shakespeare's darkly drawn *Hamlet*, Goethe's *Faust* and Nietzsche's

Beyond Good and Evil. In a more popular sense, we have the fairy tales of the Brothers Grimm with ever-present dark sides; the vampire stories of Bram Stoker; Poe's tales of horror; and the apocalyptic shadows of Huxley's *Brave New World* and Orwell's *1984*. Throughout our accumulated history, literature and art bear the traces of our modern concept of the shadow.

For all our intellectual understanding, our daily experience of the shadow is hidden from our conscious awareness. The Jungian analyst Edward Whitmont described the shadow as "everything that has been rejected during the development of the personality because it did not fit into the ego ideal."[12] Another analyst, Adolf Guggenbuhl-Craig, amplifies this notion of rejection: "We define the shadow as those elements, feelings, emotions, ideas, and beliefs with which we cannot identify, which are repressed due to education, culture, or value system."[13] The teacher William Eichman describes the dark side of our personality not as a "side, or a shadow, or a persona—it is a tangled web of complex forces, programs, and effects which we repress from ordinary consciousness so that we rarely see its true nature."[14] Marsha Sinetar says that this dark side unfolds in its own time to reveal to us "our uncontrollable impulses, the habits we simply can't break; the unacceptable, contradictory tendencies moving us in opposition to the way we intended to go."[15] And finally, Jungian psychologist Karen Signell describes how we experience the shadow in our daily life thus: "In daily life, you may catch only a fleeting notion of your own shadow's existence in your avoidance of certain topics or your vague feelings of guilt, self-doubt, discontent, or discord. You may suddenly notice vague worries and feelings in a flush of embarrassment, in an awkward moment of nervous laughter, in a burst of tears, in a flare of anger."[16]

Robert Bly, in his *A Little Book on the Human Shadow*, describes the shadow as a long bag we drag behind us throughout life. When we were two or three years old, he says, "energy radiated out from all parts of our body and all parts of our psyche. A child running is a living globe of energy. We had a ball of energy, all right; but one day we noticed that our parents didn't like certain parts of that ball. They said things like: 'can't you be still?' Or 'It isn't nice to try to kill your brother.' Behind us we have an invisible bag, and the part of us our parents don't like, we, to keep our parents' love, put in the bag. By the time we go to school the bag is quite large."[17]

Bly goes on to describe all the bag stuffing we do, so that, out of conformity to parents and culture, we are dragging behind us a huge bag of repressed feeling, behaviors, and perceptions of ourselves and the world. That original energy ball of the child tends to become very limited, and the potential power of expression and creativity is curtailed by social conformity.

Bly continues by describing what happens if, at some point, we try to open the bag to experience directly the power of the shadow contents of ourselves: "when we put part of ourselves in the bag it regresses. It de-evolves toward barbarism. Suppose a young man seals a bag at twenty and then waits fifteen or twenty years before he opens it again. What will he find? Sadly, the sexuality, the wildness, the impulsiveness, the anger, the freedom he put in have all regressed; they are not only primitive in mood, they are hostile to the person who opens the bag." The man or woman who opens that bag without understanding what it contains rightly feels fear. As Bly says, anyone looking up and seeing "the shadow of an ape passing along the alley wall . . . would be frightened."[18]

Robert Louis Stevenson, in *Dr. Jekyll and Mr. Hyde*,[19] displays this double, light/shadow personality. Many writers who have thought about the shadow find the complexity of issues raised by Stevenson's story to be informative. Bly observes this about the story that "Morally and ethically he [the doctor] is wonderful. But the substance in the bag takes on a personality of its own; it can't be ignored. The story says that the substance locked in the bag appears one day *somewhere else* in the city. The substance in the bag feels angry, and when you see it, it is shaped like an ape, and moves like an ape."[20]

One manager, Roger, who worked at a large computer-chip manufacturing company, had a reputation for fairness and effective relationships with subordinates. His positions were primarily in staff roles, managing one or two people. Because of his successes, he was given line responsibility of a manufacturing section with forty people in it. Within weeks of his new assignment, complaints poured into the employee relations department. Verbal abuse, sexual harassment, job intimidation, unreasonable assignments and schedules were among the charges against this person. Senior staff couldn't believe it was the same man. His angry ape had come out of the bag *somewhere else* in the company.

The Jungian analyst John Sanford notes that Jekyll states early in the story that there was a duality in his nature. Jekyll observes that "man is not truly one, but truly two." Like so many of us, Jekyll intellectually had a psychological insight about himself but found it difficult to translate it into his emotional and behavioral life. We all carry the devil, the dark force of evil, within our shadow bag. However, Sanford observes that what Jekyll did when he created a drug that permitted his shadow, Mr. Hyde, to emerge from him was to *decide* to be Hyde. Jekyll wanted to explore and play with the power of his shadow. Believing we can control our shadow side can be dangerous because, as in Jekyll's case, we can become our shadow. As Sanford says, "The deliberate decision to do evil leads to our becoming evil." Jekyll, like most of us, believes he can control his shadow once it is out of the bag. By becoming Hyde (his shadow) Jekyll began turning into Hyde without the drug (the power stimulus). Jekyll's decision in the face of his lack of control was to assert his ego will and determine not to let Hyde emerge. Part of his attempt to stuff Hyde back into the shadow bag was to become religious in order to protect himself from the evil. But this strategy doesn't work. Hyde is out of the bag, and he is too strong for Jekyll's fear and pretense of being a good person. Jekyll's persona, his mask to the world, is now crumbling beyond his control. As we will explore in the various shadow aspects of the Four Powers, the means to meet the power of our shadow is neither in expression nor repression, but in learning to hold both the dark and the light in us consciously.[21]

We can avoid getting caught in Dr. Jekyll's situation and being overcome, and ultimately destroyed, by our shadow. The first step, as we shall see throughout our inquiry into the Four Powers, is to begin to understand and observe shadow characteristics as they emerge in our life.

When parts of us have been repressed and held back from expression, as is the case with the shadow side of our personalities, these parts of us somehow change and become twisted into a personality that our "nice" daylight personalities would never accept as being us. Most of us keep our bags closed, control our actions, and apologize for inappropriate behavior. But if we don't make friends with whatever is in that shadow bag we drag behind us, the chances of the unexpected happening will increase. The Hyde part of our personality will show up *somewhere else*, possibly overpowering the values, beliefs, attitudes and behaviors that we think comprise our true selves.

The struggle between the light and dark sides of personality was clearly portrayed in the *Star Wars* movie series with young Luke Skywalker facing the shadow side of his personality in the form of his own father, Darth Vader.[22] The continuing question that Luke had to struggle with was whether he would choose the light or the dark side of the Force. In his training session with Yoda, the Magician, he was challenged to go down into a dark passageway and confront the shadow within himself. He confronts and fights Darth Vader in the dark cave. When he finally cut off the head of Darth Vader and opened the helmet, he was shocked to find his own face. Anyone aspiring to be a leader must confront his own unknown face—the shadow within himself—if he is not to be destructive to the people he leads. All the great leader tyrants of history opened the shadow bag and let out the power of fear, hate and violence. Unable to accept these shadows as their own, they each projected these shadows onto the world around them and, as a result, destroyed many, many people as well as themselves.

The fear that many executives experience when they are promoted to greater positions of power and authority catalyzes this dark side of personality. The ego of the executive at a lower level of positional power was strong enough to contain improper behavior and attitudes toward those who reported to him. As the positional/personal power gap widens, the ego structure of the person may not be large enough to hold within it the new positional power. New decisions must be made that are more ambiguous, complex, and do not fit the normal values, standards, and morals upon which the executive's ego has been built. Within this growing tension and personal uncertainty, the executive often feels "possessed" by fear, anger, and uncertainty on the one hand; and grandiosity, inflation, and superiority on the other. This opposing tension within the person begins to project the negative characteristics of rejection, scapegoating and what Edward Whitmont describes as "the archetypal experience of the other fellow who in his strangeness is always suspect."[23] A statement that the executive may have made in the past such as, "I would never be like John, who rages at people," is the behavior that he now expresses to those around him. Others will notice these dark characteristics, but the executive, caught in the shadow, will be blind to them. His denial will be the loudest when someone confronts him about his own rage. This split between a leader's conscious ideals and image about himself as a good person can put him on the strange road of becoming Mr. Hyde even when he never intended it.

Many executives, when confronted with their behavior of intolerance and attack on subordinates, reject out of hand that they were too aggressive, demeaning, embarrassing or cruelly hurtful to their employees. Their response to feedback on their behavior is, typically, shock. They will say, "I was just being honest, direct and firm. No, I didn't do what you said. You [referring to the person providing the feedback] are exaggerating." Their own view of how they ideally should treat people at times doesn't match the ways they actually treat them or the feedback given to them.

Most leaders do not see their own shadow at work. What we might call "shadow" they may simply call "being tough." In these shadow leaders' drive to "get results," they excuse the often devastating effects of their shadow behaviors on people.

Fortune magazine periodically runs an article titled "America's Toughest Bosses." The February 1989 edition includes a list of individuals who at that time were some of America's toughest bosses.[24] Here is a sample of what subordinates said about these bosses and how the bosses each described themselves:

Richard J. Mahoney, Chairman, Monsanto

How others see him: "He has a big ego. . . . subordinates have to stroke him a lot. . . . listens to others but doesn't understand . . . little empathy with subordinates . . . can't believe he is wrong."

How he sees himself: "I am demanding, not mean. Forgiveness is out of style, shoulder shrugs are out of fashion. Hit the targets on time without excuses."

Hugh L. McColl Jr., Chairman, NCNB Corp.

How others see him: "We sit on the edge of our chairs. . . . he manages with aggressiveness and perfectionism, and he expects us to cope with the tension."

How he sees himself: "I expect the Herculean. There's no golf in the middle of the day, no coasting to retirement. If you're not leading, you're out of here."

Harry E. Figgie Jr., Chairman, Figgie International

How others see him: "From horrendous to delightful, from idiotic to brilliant . . . working with him was a nightmare. . . . really abusive . . . the Steinbrenner of industry."

How he sees himself: "You don't build a company like this with lace on your underwear. We bought small companies with no management depth. There is no room for error."

Robert L. Crandall, Chairman, AMR Corp. (parent of American Airlines)

How others see him: "His toughness is very visible. . . . has a towering temper and swears a lot . . . focuses all his energy on the issue and sees everything in black and white. Those who have been with him for years learn to counter his faults with logic and reasoning."

How he sees himself: Declined to be interviewed.

Frank A. Lorenzo, Chairman, Texas Air
How others see him: "He thinks he's a great manager, but he's not. . . . incredibly impulsive . . . not trusted inside or outside the organization . . . good dealmaker though."

How he sees himself: "I have to be tough but fair. We built this company from businesses that were failing. We didn't just take over a big company and blow out the cobwebs."

The author of the article, Peter Nulty, concludes the piece after describing in more depth these and other highly placed business leaders. Four observations stand out from the article about tough (shadow-dominated) bosses:

- Tough bosses have difficulty telling constructive toughness from the destructive kind.
- The tough boss believes that his power to fire someone is the hardest thing for a subordinate to handle. Some subordinates say being fired can be a relief.
- While toughness may consist of abuse, it is usually unrelenting pressure that causes the problem for subordinates.
- Tough bosses eventually find people who can handle their boss's terror.

Nulty concludes: "As global competition heats up and turmoil rocks more industries, tough management should spread. So look for more bosses who are steely, super demanding, unrelenting, sometimes abusive, sometimes unreasonable, impatient, driven, stubborn and combative. And have a nice day."[25]

All of the bosses quoted on the preceding pages display the problem of recognizing the difference between their shadow qualities and other parts of their personality. What their *subordinates saw* as very negative *they saw* as the elements that contributed to their success. These men may be very kind and loving to their children, and be generous and giving of time and money to their community; but in their leadership roles, they have built their success around strong powers of shadow leadership that they may be unable to recognize as different from the "nicer" parts of themselves.

Most Jungian analysts conclude that the shadow, particularly as it occurs in our dreams and in our scapegoating of others, is the same sex as ourselves.[26] The person whom leaders generally project their shadow upon and scapegoat is typically of the same sex, as well as their mirror opposite in personality style and temperament. An example of a classic shadow mirroring occurred with a corporation's CEO and COO.

The entrepreneurial CEO was leading a multibillion-dollar corporation that hired a COO who had a professional, big-company style. In all ways, the COO was the opposite to the CEO. The COO was a strong extrovert as opposed to the CEO's being an introvert; an intuitive thinker as opposed to the CEO's being an analytical thinker. The COO had very strong interpersonal skills as opposed to the CEO's difficulty in relating to people. The CEO's unrelenting and focused work ethic was the complete opposite of the COO's laissez-faire attitude that things would be done when they needed to be. Most everyone in the organization appreciated the warmth, charisma and interest in people that the COO exhibited. The constant feedback to the CEO about the COO was mixed. The COO was popular with the employees because of his interpersonal skills, but he was unpopular with many senior executives (and the CEO) because of his lack of urgency in completing projects. The COO's failure to meet work deadlines infuriated the CEO.

Within a few months of the COO's starting the job, the CEO began a constant barrage of criticism toward him. He did so privately to other executives, as well as publicly, verbally "reaming out" the COO in staff meetings. Close observation and knowledge of the CEO's background showed that much of the COO's interpersonal style,

positive attitudes and behaviors in difficult situations were what the
CEO had split off from in childhood and put into his shadow bag.
Other executives could see clearly the value and contribution of the
COO, but in most ways the CEO was unable to acknowledge the
COO's "good points" and the value of his contribution to the organization. The CEO was a classic Magician who had consummate skill
in making deals and manipulating the whole of his business through
control of a great deal of detail. But he wasn't a Magician when it
came to the interpersonal skills of managing people, coaching subordinates and being a "spiritual" leader of the organization. His shadow
verbal abuse in scapegoating the COO for not being the deal maker
and consummate business leader, as well as demeaning him and iso-
lating him from critical information and decisions in the organization,
revealed the CEO's shadow at work.

When discussing his projections onto the COO, the CEO began to
concede that his reaction to the COO could be about unresolved
issues in the CEO's own life. Of particular focus was the CEO's controlling manipulation of people and situations, his lack of interpersonal skills, and his intense, all-consuming workaholic pattern. For
this CEO, confronting his shadow projections was one of the first
steps toward understanding the areas in which he needed to grow and
develop. Even more important for the CEO was to make some
choices about changing his behavior toward the COO so that he could
begin to integrate his shadow projections and become a more effective leader. Edward Whitmont observed that in order to understand
ourselves, it is critical to examine those onto whom we project our
shadow. "It is not until we have truly been shocked into seeing ourselves as we really are, instead of as we wish or hopefully assume we
are, that we can take the first step toward individual reality."[27]

It is this inability to recognize when our shadow is active and having an effect on people around us that is one of the most crucial areas
for development and growth in our lives. With positional power available to us as leaders, the abuse of that power through the shadow
can cause a Mr. Hyde to emerge from within us. However, there is a

positive aspect to having the shadow emerge in our lives. When shadow behavior emerges, it reveals where individuals need to take the next natural step of growth in their lives. The shadow is a measure of the gap between the positional power one holds and the personal power one has to fulfill in that positional role. Each of us has a shadow bag. The circumstances, relationships and work of our lives give us the opportunity to bring this negative material to awareness and to learn to heal ourselves from the suffering we carry in that bag. Each description of the Four Powers will address their shadow aspects. Being able to name and face our shadow characteristics is the first step in working to integrate the power of the shadow in our lives.

THE WARRIOR
THE POWER OF INTENTION

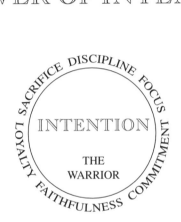

THE WARRIOR AS STANDARD-BEARER

Darlene was the president and sole owner of a graphics company with annual sales of $25 million. She had forty employees and ran the company "by example." The primary example she provided was working twelve hours a day, seven days a week. She came from a family of Romanian immigrants, put herself through college and earned an M.B.A., started a one-person graphics business, and grew it by hard work and a strong motivation to succeed. She was energetic, driven, tough on quality issues and loyal to her employees.

As the company grew, she moved further away from the day-to-day operations, and the business began to experience difficulties. She brought in new partners who supposedly would bring more experience and stature to the organization, enabling growth of annual sales to $50 million. Soon she realized what so many other entrepreneurs have discovered: the loyalty, dedication and self-sacrifice she willingly gave to the business were not what her new partners had intended to give.

Darlene found that she had not only the vision of what the business could be driving her efforts, but also the faithfulness and determination to do whatever it would take to make the organization grow. *Ultimately she had Intention: the strong ability to focus her total attention and give of herself in whatever way needed, to accomplish the task of making the business successful.* But she discovered that she was not effectively communicating and transferring her faithfulness and determination to the new people who were joining the organization. When this inability to transfer was pointed out to her, she realized that she needed to learn how to shift from relying on her own Warrior capability of completing the job successfully to developing those same Warrior qualities in her employees.

Whether one is an independent entrepreneur or a team player working in a large corporation, the Warrior archetype, embodied in the characteristic of Intention, places one into positions of leadership. Most of the positive aspects evident in leadership today derives from this particular power. Hard work and determination supported by honor and duty become the hallmarks of Intention. *Sacrifice, discipline, focus, commitment, faithfulness and loyalty are the key attributes of the Intentional leader.* Promotions most often derive from these characteristics. They result in praise and rewards, whether in the form of high grades in school or increased salaries and promotions. "If one is willing to pay the price, one will receive the reward" is the Warrior message of our culture.

Yet, it is true that not everyone succeeds when they work hard. Indeed, such qualifiers as gender, race and creed limit success. More often than not in our culture, it has been the white male who "makes it." Further qualifiers for gaining access to positional power are who you know, being in the right place at the right time and having the right set of credentials—all of which play a part in whether we receive rewards for our Warrior efforts. These considerations notwithstanding, the public message remains strong and consistent: "Work hard (and long), and you'll receive your reward." The rags-to-riches story plays out in many different ways: It is the corporate success story of a Donald Peterson starting out as an engineer at Ford Motor Company forty years earlier and then retiring as chairman and CEO of the company; it is the Silicon Valley miracle of Hewlett and Packard starting out in their garage and creating a multibillion-dollar electronics company.

COMMITMENT, LOYALTY AND SERVICE

The Warrior power involves more than just hard work. *At the core of the Warrior is the capacity for radical commitment to transpersonal loyalty and service.*[1] The Warrior has the strong Intention to dedicate himself to some higher cause. Leaders with strong Intention motivate themselves, and the people who join with them, to work hard not just to make money or beat the competition (although this may also be part of the motivation), but also to fulfill some idealism that is fundamental to their purpose in life. Their commitment and loyalty to the job, project, team or cause is radical because the Warrior never wavers in choosing between commitment to the service of his ideal or purpose, or attending to something in his personal life.

Consider the accounting team in a large organization that gives up weekend after weekend to install a new accounting system because the manager had been able to create a powerful commitment to the idea that it was the right time to install it. In the history of the company, they were the ones who would make the difference and change how the organization operated from that point forward. They were willing to give up skiing, time with their families and so on because they were dedicated to something greater than their individual needs. They were dedicated to ensuring the future success of the company and to improving the system for all those who would succeed them in the accounting department.

For all of Steven Jobs's shortcomings as a leader, the genius of the Apple computer company lay in the transpersonal dedication he communicated to employees, the promise that together they would revolutionize the world through the personal computer. People who walked into the Apple offices during its early days felt as if they had entered a roomful of zealous missionaries. These Apple employees wore T-shirts emblazoned with "Working Ninety Hours a Week and Loving It!" And anyone who witnessed them at work believed this proclamation because from the reception desk to the boardroom, everyone seemed to embody it. Over and over one heard employees say they "lived at Apple" because it was so much fun and that Apple was "their life." These people displayed a radical commitment to transpersonal loyalty and service that went beyond making money, as one employee's admission testified: "I can't believe they pay me for this!" Much of this transpersonal Warrior feeling left Apple during the era of John Scully. But even under the new management struggling to keep Apple alive, an underdog spirit that Apple can change the world is still alive. This feeling exists strongly among "ol' timers," who remain dedicated to Apple products leading the personal computer "revolution."

FAITHFULNESS AND DISCIPLINE

With the strong commitment to a transpersonal purpose comes the moral characteristic of *faithfulness*. The U.S. Marines inculcate this characteristic into the new recruits as the basis of their discipline. *Semper Fidelis* ("Always Faithful") is the Marines' motto: faithful to their corps, to their country, to their officers, to their buddies. Out of this faithfulness comes courage, persistence, stamina and determination to "get the job done" no matter what it takes. To be faithful requires discipline. *Disciplined faithfulness* means practice; it means doing something consistently, over and over again, until it's done right. Discipline keeps the practice going when things are difficult. Faithfulness is the persistence that permits the growth and development of something that moves an activity from skill to mastery.

It is as a result of faithfulness and discipline that quality naturally arises. A Warrior achieves quality because he has such a radical commitment to some purpose that he would not accept making the effort to achieve something unless it was near perfect. In this respect the Warrior may not be efficient. There may be a lot of trial and error as to what "quality" and "near perfect" mean for the Warrior leader and his followers. But part of the discipline of the Warrior leader is the commitment to "do it right" no matter what the cost or price. In this respect, Warrior leaders are often labeled fanatics.

Strong intentional Warrior leaders have a highly developed sense of standards. They have yardsticks to gauge quality, and the inner drive to "do it better next time." With this strong intentional focus on doing the task at hand, and stretching one's capability by doing it, the Warrior develops a great tolerance for enduring pain and discomfort, whether it be physical or psychological, in the service of his goal.

For example, Warrior sales leaders typically travel in and out of three or four different cities and airports in a single day; stay in a different hotel every night; have breakfast and lunch meetings, and business dinners that last until ten o'clock; and work at a laptop computer until one in the morning, day in and day out. When asked why they give up family life, weekends and normal day-to-day living, they say that their constant drive is to do better this month in sales than they did last month. The goal isn't primarily money, but rather, "crafting the deal better next time," "making the extra effort to meet with two more customers each day," "getting each of my sales guys to produce better results." No matter what the sacrifice, discomfort or cost to these sales Warriors, they want to be the best salesperson possible.

This dedication to work and to the success of both the company and the individual causes the Warrior to choose work-based loyalties over personal relationships. When conversing, Warrior leaders who have this dedication and loyalty will talk with great fervor about their families, children, wives and the future activities they will have with them. But when questioned about the lack of time they have with their families, Warriors typically reveal some sadness; but overriding that sadness is an abstract and transpersonal commitment to such things as "helping the company survive," "taking the organization to the next level," "serving the needs of people" and "meeting the challenge and opportunity." Often these men and women, by virtue of their lifestyles on the road, become solitary knights doing battle with customers, airlines, sleepless nights, delayed flights on Friday nights and the loneliness of mere telephone contact with family. Yet, they move on, always faithful.

This dedication to task over relationship is not limited to traveling businesspeople. Most executives continually face the Warrior dilemma of choosing work over family. In one Christian service organization, many of the top executives tell their wives and families "it's the Lord's work" that keeps them on the road, traveling the world, when in fact they simply love the work; and though they struggle with the guilt of being absent so often from their families, they wouldn't have it any other way. For most of these executives, both "the Lord's work" *and* "the road work" motivate them. A genuine transpersonal cause drives their dedication and actions; when they have the chance to be at home, they are always eager to be going away again. One executive director's wife even refused to unpack his bag, telling him not to pretend that he was staying at home when, in his mind, he was preparing for the next trip.

Focus

Another strong characteristic of the Warrior is his mastery of his particular field of endeavor. *This means having experience, skill and knowledge about what one is doing, and the ability to sustain intense focus and concentration.* When an intentional Warrior leader faces an issue, he knows what to do, or at least knows the way to approach the situation. The Warrior leader's skill must be credible, and he must "practice" in his field—not just for others who follow him, but for the personal discipline and integrity that such practice gives him. But most important of all, the Warrior leader seeks balance among his various skills.

In the Roman tradition, the god Mars had two characteristics. He had great skill with weapons and was equally skilled at dancing. In the samurai tradition, the Warrior was not only a great swordsman, but also was equally skilled at poetry or calligraphy.[2] In the old Irish tradition a Warrior couldn't guard the border until he had mastered swordsmanship, dancing and singing ballads. The true power of the Warrior combines science and art. The Warrior energy brings together the right brain and the left brain. Each skill or side of the Warrior's capabilities not only balances the individual, but also cultivates focus and discipline. Einstein played the violin and rowed a boat to provide a balance to his abstract mathematical thinking. He believed that the kinesthetic, or physical, quality of playing the violin and rowing a boat helped him think better. Perhaps this physical activity was an anchoring force that provided grounding yet allowed his mind to soar. Without this balance you don't have disciplined Warriors, you have "soldiers." That is, you have men and women who can be mindless and who follow orders without considering moral or ethical implications. As modern history makes clear, "following orders" provides an easy step to being cruel and savage.

Being a Warrior doesn't mean that we need to look through the military lens to understand the power of Intention. The multitalented Warrior gives dimension and intentional power to his leadership. Part of the power of Ted Turner as a leader is his multitalented capability to meet difficult challenges and to achieve success. In true Warrior fashion, he often achieves this at the expense of relationships around him. But the diversity of his right/left brain, creative ideas and approaches to things, and his hard-nosed business sense form a combined force that stimulates the people around him to follow his

Warrior power. He is a businessman, the owner of a professional baseball team, as well as a serious sailor and fly fisherman. Having a passion for a different kind of television, he challenged the established networks and started a new one that sets the standard for international news coverage and that viewers can access twenty-four hours a day, from anywhere on the planet. Committed to world peace, he launched the Goodwill Games, an alternative to the Olympics that brings together not only world-class athletics, but also the world arts and business communities, for a huge festival of cooperation every four years. Finally, his Warrior intensity was evident when he challenged the wealthy of the world by giving a billion dollars to the United Nations. Ted Turner's transpersonal commitment to global and societal renewal continually motivates him and those who have worked with him. Renewal, as John Gardner conceives it, is made up of pluralism, alternatives, diversity and dissent. Not permitting these to exist in the environment, according to Gardner, signals that the leader is unlikely to meet the challenge of change and unlikely to allow his organization to evolve in creative ways.

A final focus characteristic of the Intentional Warrior is the capacity to be proactive in difficult situations. From the standpoint of Warrior power, two main issues exist. First, a Warrior needs good instincts and "radar" to discern from clues in the business and organizational environment when an "enemy" is threatening the organization. Continual alertness to the possible competitive, strategic or organizational threats needs to be a prime focus of a Warrior leader. Second, the Warrior leader needs to determine the appropriate amount of power to use in a particular situation. A leader can react out of fear and use all his resources to fend off an "enemy," or he can weigh the conditions and circumstances, and use only the amount of power that the situation demands. Part of Warrior focus is maintaining the appropriate power response to each situation that arises. A good Warrior is always a minimalist with respect to the use of power.

POWER AS A FORCE

In the martial arts a student is taught from the very beginning to avoid the use of his skill until he has no other alternative. But when the student uses the force of his skill, he is to use it in the way that is the least destructive to the person or the situation at hand. The old gunslinger who is constantly challenged by the younger shooter in the western is a good example. The young shooter can't understand why the old fighter is so reluctant to fight him. Typically the old gunslinger will say, "You never fight unless you're gonna kill the man. And I've killed too many men I never wanted to fight!"

The Warrior leader in organizations has to have the "sense" of what will threaten or be an "enemy" to the organization, and then know how to appropriately respond to the situation with both wisdom and decisiveness. CEOs or presidents of companies may panic when a merger threat arises, and spread that fear throughout the organization by means of "fire drills" for the staff, designed to help the organization figure out how to prevent the takeover. But Warriors exhibit strength, caution and decisiveness before the threat becomes reality, thereby creating calm, assurance and direction for their staff and followers.

Phil was sole owner of a medium-sized television/media products company. The manufacturing site was in Los Angeles, and the sales office was in New York. He had developed a particular product niche that was gaining competition. With manufacturing costs increasing in Los Angeles, profits were shrinking. The "enemy" of costs and competition was getting close. Phil had been conservative in his financial management and had good cash reserves. He believed his product base could grow in some new directions and had developed plans to accomplish this growth. However, his professional staff was growing older, and he was experiencing difficulty energizing and motivating them to come up with new and creative marketing ideas. Also, he personally was dissatisfied with the Los Angeles traffic, congestion and general lifestyle. Given the various professional and personal "threats," Phil took action in a very Warrior-like fashion.

The combination of threats led Phil to a bold use of his power. Carefully taking into account his own needs and those of his business, he moved his company from Los Angeles to a small college town in the Pacific Northwest. He figured out that his costs for manufacturing would be cheaper, the professional staff who wanted to move would find it energizing, and he would meet his own personal lifestyle needs in a manner that would give him the energy and enthusiasm he needed to take the company through its next step of growth. The influx of new personnel, ideas and motivation resulting from the move, combined with the stability of his sales force continuing to work out of New York, accelerated the growth of the company, made it more competitive and enabled it to bring out new products more quickly than it had been able to in Los Angeles.

This type of forceful, determined, bold action of Intentional Warrior leaders creates new alternatives to problems and enables organizations to move to their next natural stage of growth. In summary, then, Warrior power needs to be present in the leader in order for the leader to:

- Focus on the most critical tasks at hand
- Do the unpleasant things that must be done to guarantee success
- Take stock of a situation and find the critical path to success
- Muster the right resources and work hard, steadily and courageously, on difficult issues
- Continually create a team effort by recruiting other "Warriors/ Knights" to work with the leader
- Demonstrate absolute faithfulness and loyalty to a purpose that is greater than merely the satisfaction of his personal ambitions and goals
- Know how to meet threats with appropriate power

However, if these characteristics become twisted, the power of the Warrior can open an organization to the most destructive aspects of the Warrior's god, Mars. Mars, it is well known, can revel in battle, death and destruction as ends in themselves in order to satisfy some twisted compulsion. It is this twisted shadow of the Warrior's Intention that we now examine.

THE SHADOW WARRIOR

Anne Schaef and Diane Fassel in their groundbreaking book *The Addictive Organization* demonstrate very clearly the basis of the shadow side of the Warrior:

> An addiction is any substance or process that has taken over our lives and over which we are powerless. It may or may not be a physiological addiction. An addiction is any process or substance that begins to have control over us in such a way that we feel we must be dishonest with ourselves or others about it. *Addictions lead us into increasing compulsiveness in our behavior.* . . . Process addiction refers to a series of activities or interactions that hook a person, or on which a person becomes dependent. *The common process addictions are work, sex, money, gambling, religion, relationships and certain types of thinking.* [Italics mine.][3]

The intense concentration and single focus of Intention enable the Warrior to accomplish things successfully. Yet, he can all too easily cross the line of dedication to his purpose and become addictive and compulsive. In other words, the long, daily "to do" list of activities can become an addiction. Shadow Warriors can become physically addicted to the "high" from the adrenaline rush of constant activity. Completing activities compulsively to check them off the "to do" list can substitute for meaningful and strategic work. Leaders that are addicted to work for the sake of work will compulsively drive subordinates to put in long hours and engage in "fire drills" just to keep them busy. Like any addiction, workaholism thrives on denial, confusion, self-centeredness, dishonesty and perfectionism.

Work Compulsion

The destructiveness of work addiction in the shadow Warrior manifests itself clearly in the midst of deadlines and time pressures. Joan, a director of finance, appeared to have a positive relationship with her department. She took time to explain projects and seemed to set deadlines in conjunction with her subordinates. But as deadlines approached, her behavior would change radically. Joan's personal interaction with her subordinates seemed to disappear, replaced by a highly critical and judgmental attitude. At such times she demanded absolute perfection, didn't care how many hours it would take to complete a task, and totally disregarded the feelings, needs and personal issues of her staff. *This lack of valuing personal relationships and instead focusing totally on the task is one of the key characteristics of the shadow Warrior.* When Joan's own boss confronted her about the treatment of her subordinates, she denied her behavior and had her direct reports sign statements that she worked with them in positive and supportive ways.

Personal coaching with this individual revealed her own belief that she *should* be able to do everything herself. *It was hard for her to admit that she needed people to work for her.* Furthermore, Joan felt that her subordinates were not as capable or dependable as she: No one could complete projects in as timely a manner or as perfectly as she could. These two beliefs drove her to micromanage and control everything her staff did, and she believed that she was really helping them when she drove them unmercifully. Joan's own inflated belief that she was better than everyone else drove her to work sixteen to eighteen hours a day, reviewing each subordinate's work in order to make sure every detail of a report was perfect. If the report wasn't perfect, Joan would have her subordinates rewrite the reports as many as four and five times. Each returned report to a subordinate would be accompanied with meticulous notes and directions from her. Her absolute rule with her subordinates was that no verbal or written communication went to a senior manager except with her written approval. Joan's distrust of her subordinates' competency and her fear of being seen by senior management as anything less than perfect drove her to a level of compulsive work that began to negatively affect her health.

Most addicts both deny the addiction and surround themselves with people who support their behavior. When subordinates were interviewed, they acknowledged the pressure Joan brought to bear on them but also excused the negative effects of her behavior as part of the challenges of the job. Her superiors acknowledged the high turnover in her department but couldn't fault her because she always "got the job done." She had not taken a vacation in five years, and the senior management saw this as great dedication and evidence of her being a true "comer" in the company. In the end they rewarded Joan's workaholism with a layoff due to a company reorganization. The true tragedy of this story is that four months after the layoff, Joan committed suicide. The note said simply, "If I can't work, I don't want to live." This is obviously a dramatic case, but the same pattern repeats itself over and over again in the workplace. The compulsive work of the shadow Warrior is the one addiction we socially approve and support. It results in our earning more money and receiving promotions.

Being competitive, doing a better job and getting ahead comprise the bottom line for many companies. But—and that "but" represents a high cost for many people in the workplace—companies that support the addiction of workaholism[4] in their employees are supporting what Bryan Robinson calls "work abuse." This abuse causes increased physical stress, high blood pressure, heart attacks, emotional trauma and a whole host of destructive relationships in the workplace due to work compulsion. Robinson, in his book *Work Addiction*, puts it bluntly:

> Work addiction, although it is the most accepted and encouraged of all the addictions, is a serious disease that destroys relationships and kills people. Held hostage by their illness, work addicts live in misery and despair amid accolades, slaps on the back, fat paychecks and gold plaques. It is the only disease that draws cheers from onlookers as the work addict dies a slow, painful death, both psychologically and physically. Our society needs an overhauling on its views of work, at the personal, human and corporate levels. We must learn to make distinctions between healthy work habits and work abuse.[5]

From this pattern of compulsive task performance radiate several other characteristics of the shadow Warrior. When the power of the Warrior becomes twisted, several things begin to occur: poor personal relationships, confusion about emotional and sexual behavior, playing the hero at the expense of others, ends justifying means, the sadistic exercise of power over others, and sacrificing others to achieve one's objectives.

Relationships

A common shadow Warrior pattern is to feel guilty about not spending time with spouse and family, while rationalizing why one stays late at the office, misses social engagements, and fails to attend a son's or daughter's activity. The loyalty aspect of the Warrior becomes twisted in voicing high values for spouse and family but behaviorally demonstrating no genuine involvement with them. Typically working twelve- to sixteen-hour days, and most weekends, leaves shadow Warriors little time for meaningful relationships with those close to them. Too often, shadow Warriors rationalize the work addiction by saying that they are working the long hours for "them." The "them" may be the shadow Warrior's family, team or company— or even the country or the Lord.

Consider a consultant, Tom, who was coaching shadow Warrior executives. He knew all the symptoms and rationalizations. But when the negative archetype becomes activated in oneself, one goes blind to what one rationally knows. Like any addiction, it overpowers and dominates to the exclusion of everything else.

Tom and his two partners started a new company with all the promise and enthusiasm of a new marriage. They had a good market opportunity, and the company began to grow very quickly. Staff grew to nine full-time and three part-time people within a few months. Receivables began to stretch out over sixty to ninety days, and cash flow to pay salaries and bills became critical. Tom could see that he and his partners were going to lose the business unless they generated more revenue. In true Warrior fashion, Tom was determined that the company would not fail.

The quickest way Tom thought he could solve the problem was to move from managing the company full-time to filling up his schedule with consulting work. By sheer force of will he filled his schedule. The average number of billable days for a consultant per month is twelve. The other days are used for marketing, proposals, preparation, etc. In order to meet the financial challenge, Tom filled up eighteen to twenty days of billable time. Tom began to travel, keep his share of management responsibilities in the company and be available to his wife, who had become ill with a chronic disease. When Tom was home, he wasn't home: He was on the phone, in front of the computer or just worrying about what he had to do next.

Tom believed he was concerned about and supportive of his wife but could not hear her strong plea for him to be emotionally present. The commute from his company's offices in the Bay Area to his home in the foothills of the Sierras was three and one-half hours each way. After several months, Tom no longer slept well at night and gave up his exercise program of over twenty-five years. These changes, combined with airplane travel, excessive driving and unhealthy food, contributed to his looking and feeling awful. In one of the long rides back from the Bay Area to his home, Tom realized, to his horror, that he couldn't feel anything inside him. Tom had lost contact with his soul.

Work addiction had consumed Tom, and he was in the same place where he had observed so many of his clients. When Tom returned home, his wife confronted him, saying she no longer could tolerate the kind of life he had created by shutting her out emotionally and not being with her physically. Tom's wife's confrontation was painful to accept, but the recognition of his own loss of any sense of contact with an inner life helped him begin to break the denial that he had rationalized and justified for the sake of the business. The recovery from the addiction was not easy and took some time. Like any addiction, it is something Tom seems always to face in himself. Tom learned that what made him a success can also kill him if practiced to excess. Fundamentally, this aspect of the shadow Warrior focuses energy on building a product, organization or some other external part of one's life rather than building close relationships, deepening family bonds or spending time with oneself.

Emotional and Sexual Behavior

Another aspect of the shadow Warrior in relationships is his attitude about emotionality and sexuality. Some shadow Warriors idealistically position their spouse as the "sacred one" for sex, but extramarital affairs provide the place for fun, emotional release and the expression of sensuality. Neglecting the development of intimate relationships, the shadow Warrior does not focus emotional or psychic energy on spouse and family. The shadow Warrior's energy is devoted to his own success, with his family all too often a showcase that fits into his career strategy.

The shadow Warrior often believes it is his right to have sex with whomever he desires. Sex is one of the expected rewards, along with money, status and recognition. Sexuality in this respect is tantamount to a reward that one earns for being in the position of power and, as such, loses any greater meaning. The shadow Warrior approaches sexuality as he would any other task or activity—without intimacy or personal relationship. Sexual partners become objects from which to derive pleasure. As they say of this kind of behavior in the military: "This is my rifle, this is my gun; this is for fighting, and this is for fun." This, however, is not just a male issue. Many woman Warriors who are determined to climb the career ladder may use sexuality to accomplish their shadow Warrior aims.

For both men and women, the sexual shadow behavior becomes more easily constellated in the Warrior archetype because of the impersonal, objective driving character of this power. The Warrior archetype is in contrast to the Artist, who fosters a breadth of feeling, emotional richness and sensitivity toward others. The shadow Artist can indulge himself sexually, but the indulgence will have a different kind of impact on his leadership behavior. The point to be made is that impersonal and abusive sexuality, as well as sexual harassment in general, usually occur when one is strongly activating the shadow Warrior.

This separation of intimate emotional relationships from the expression of sexuality, endemic to shadow Warriors, receives attention in media exposés of Warrior leaders who seem to have little concern for the results of their sexual exploits until they are publicly "caught." Religious and political leaders seem particularly susceptible to this shadow side of their power. A notable example would be former Senator Gary Hart, who, during the 1988 presidential campaign, was caught engaged in an affair with Donna Rice on Bimini while his wife and family were campaigning for him. He was caught by the very journalists he challenged to follow him around so as to disprove the rumors about him. Another example is the televangelist Jimmy Swaggart, caught photographed in his exploits with a prostitute while he preached against pornography and pleaded for donations to his multimillion-dollar ministry.

With little public remorse, Dick Morris, the Republican consultant to President Bill Clinton, used his affair with a prostitute while he was working in the White House, as a chance to write an exposé about the Clinton White House.[6] In the book, he describes his affair as an unfortunate bump in his career. But the most powerful recent example of shadow Warrior sexuality is the acknowledgment by President Bill Clinton himself. The president denied in his first run for the presidency his twelve-year affair with Gennifer Flowers and then under oath confirmed it. His personal credibility suffered further from the strong circumstantial evidence of his sexual misconduct with Paula Jones and from his admission of "an inappropriate relationship" White House intern Monica Lewinsky.

All these men, after the exposure of their affairs, had their wives stand with them while they denied or confessed their "sins." Each wife publicly pledged faith in her spouse, although behind-the-scenes interviews indicated all these wives had struggled with their husbands' exploits for long periods of time. Hillary Rodham Clinton became not only her husband's defender, but also his attack dog, claiming that Independent Counsel Kenneth Starr's investigation was a right-wing conspiracy to destroy Clinton's presidency.

The shadow Warrior's blindness to his sexual exploits extends to his conviction that others won't see what he is doing. If others do see it, the shadow Warrior expects their absolute loyalty in keeping silent. The shadow Warrior considers it his "divine right" to express his sexual potency as part of maintaining his leadership potency and sees this as "natural" for someone in power. This rationalization of the Warrior energy receives support from women who seek to be close to power and are willing to play the leader's game. But this is not just a male leader problem. Women executives describe how their own sexual energies become charged up in the high-octane world of power, politics and business. These women's own arrogance and shadow power can blind them just as these forces blind their male counterparts. Whether by demand or by seduction, these women can manipulate their subordinates into pleasuring them.

Long hours at work, constant travel, conferences and board meetings all become convenient venues for the expression of sexual energy. The shadow Warrior channels his deep emotionality into his work, rather than directing it toward his spouse or family. The physical and emotional "safety value" of sensual/sexual activity makes it both appropriate for tension relief and "reasonable" in the leader's view. The spouse at home is for stability, support and propriety. Executives dismiss the impact of affairs on their personal and family life as unimportant. Their only concern is that they don't want their sexual liaisons to jeopardize their images as "family men" or infringe upon the comforts their spouses provide. But they also will admit that the Warrior commitment to work gives them little time to have meaningful emotional and sexual relationships with their spouses. One executive was in such denial about the effect of his extramarital activity that he could not accept the consequences, even when his wife sued for divorce after confronting him.

Sexual energy often increases as a leader experiences more and more the power of position and his growing ability to exercise that power. When the increased sexual energy is not integrated into a healthy emotional relationship that is bound by a personal, ethical or spiritual commitment, it can move into the darker impulses of the personality and have devastating consequences on the "kingdom."

Heroics

The shadow Warrior will seek his or her own glory rather than accepting recognition for contributing to the efforts of other individuals or the team. In some cases, the shadow Warrior will totally suppress the acknowledgment or recognition of any other person. The shadow Warrior characteristic manifests itself in the leader who demands that all attention be on himself. The shadow Warrior will sacrifice other people's careers, accomplishments and opportunities, and will focus everything on himself as the sole recipient of "glory." A classic example is the arrogant platoon leader who forces his men into dangerous situations that can result in their being killed, in order to prove his ability to the commander. He takes daring risks to show the courage necessary for decorations and promotions, but he does so at the expense of his platoon. This shadow hero exists in contemporary boardrooms as much as in wartime battlefields, and his Warrior energy can be just as destructive in either place.

In many corporations, the vice president of sales exhibits shadow Warrior heroics. When this darkness emerges from the shadow bag, such an individual will do almost anything to his sales staff to "make the numbers." Gary, the senior vice president of international sales of one company, had the reputation of being the "hero of the numbers." Near the end of a given quarter, sales figures could be off by 30 to 40 percent, and he would publicly declare to the company, "No matter what, we'll meet the numbers." To the amazement of everyone and the great pleasure of senior management, the "numbers" would be made. But, after five or six quarters of this kind of heroics, the toll it was taking on his group demonstrated itself in chronic sickness, turnover within his organization, nervous breakdowns and a whole host of other human carnage. Gary had been a hero (for a while), but the long-term effect on his organization was devastating. His negative heroics exemplify these characteristics of the shadow Warrior:

- Ends justifying the means by the excessive exercise of one's positional power
- Sadistically exerting power over others through put-downs, demotions and intimidation
- Pushing people too hard without seeing the toll it takes on them— often expressed as, "All people should work as hard as I do."

In the case of this sales VP, making the numbers meant manipulating the finance department into doing some creative accounting so that products booked in the previous quarter but not shipped until the current one could be considered part of the "new" numbers. Gary also made deals with customers to buy products with the understanding that they wouldn't have to pay for a couple of quarters, and took other steps that were not part of the company strategy.

Gary's almost daily verbal abuse of his sales force for poor performance, his constant claim that others could not produce as he could, and his repetitive public humiliation of other employees in the company created fear, intimidation and low morale. His biting sarcasm and taunts about employee incapability and incompetence broke people's sense of self-worth and self-esteem. When employees quit and joined competitors, Gary would call their new bosses and deride the employees as incapable and worthless.

Gary made it known how little he slept. It was typical to receive calls from him at three or four in the morning, when he would demand information or give an employee a new assignment on top of the regular workload. Fourteen- to sixteen-hour workdays were typical for the people working for this man. Because of Gary's own capacity and drive, he wouldn't recognize a person's illness or acknowledge the need for rest, family time, relaxation or vacations.

The problem with this situation was that senior management became this man's codependent. They admitted that in his zeal he pushed the limits of some things, but then they would rationalize that "he got the job done for us." They were not willing to confront him about his destructive behaviors and treatment of people. Instead, they excused him, saying that perhaps he had the "wrong team," and continued to praise him for his "heroism" in meeting sales goals.

In the end, this codependency cost the senior leaders of the company dearly. Gary was finally caught in an illegal deal, bringing about an SEC investigation that ruined the company's credibility with its customers, drove down the stock from twenty-eight dollars to five dollars a share within a few weeks and forced the CEO to resign. It took a new CEO and a new management team several years to rebuild the company and pull it out of the hole in which this shadow Warrior VP had buried it.

The Warrior archetype as the pattern for success is so ingrained in our business culture that we will support it even when its dark side predominates. Today, a strong and prevalent ends-justifying-means attitude is eating away the core of our business and societal value systems. Those holding power over us are often not held accountable for their actions. The ethical breakdown in society permits the shadow Warrior to convince followers that it is okay to cheat, lie and manipulate people and situations. This ability of a shadow Warrior leader to manipulate followers into betraying personal and societal values makes it easier for followers to become cynical in all types of behavior. As followers, our own shadows can play into a leader's shadow Warrior's negative compulsions and desires. Coming to terms with our shadow Warrior in our role as follower or leader is a prime necessity for our personal and collective renewal.

CULTIVATING THE WARRIOR WITHIN[7]

The Intentional Warrior archetype places a strong demand on people in our culture. It is the backbone of our work ethic. "Work hard, and you'll get ahead" is what all of us have heard preached from parent, teacher, minister and boss. Our own experience has generally borne out this admonition. A little more effort, a few extra hours, a little better service, a new idea, a firm loyalty—these are what resulted in the raises, promotions and opportunities for advancement. Leaders preach it, and we become it—men and women who will rise to our highest capabilities. The other side of that is the Peter Principle. This idea originally was published in 1971 as *The Peter Principle: Why Things Always Go Wrong* by Laurence J. Peter.[8] Peter coined the term *Peter Principle* from a simple observation: In a hierarchy every employee tends to rise to his level of incompetence. *This principle states that most people will tend to keep receiving promotions and advancing until they are in over their heads and incapable of doing the job.*[9] This principle further states that as we move upward, at some point, we each arrive at a new position (how we arrived there is irrelevant) where the scales tip toward the lack of capability and competence in doing the job. In this new position, we haven't the foggiest idea of what to do, but instead of admitting our inabilities, we begin to "fake it." We pretend to know what we are doing. In Peter's view, this is the point where everything starts going wrong. In essence the "faker" doesn't know what he doesn't know.

Being the Faker: The Shadow of Incompetence in the Warrior

The faker[10] generally believes that he is getting away with not knowing what to do. The faker rationalizes and argues with himself that he will learn as time goes by and nobody will know the difference. In reality, what people reporting to this person recognize very quickly is that the faker *is* faking it. The faker may have good intentions, and even when faking, he may work long, hard hours to cover up his lack of ability. The problem lies in the faker's positional power; whether he fakes it or not, he can influence decisions, actions and an array of conditions that may have significant implications. The faker coupled with any one or more of the other negative shadow Warrior characteristics can make an organization a very difficult workplace for many people. The more anxious the faker becomes about his faking, the more probable it is that he will activate the shadow side of the Warrior.

The other side of this advancement issue comes into play when the scales tip in the opposite direction. Rather than faking it, the person who recognizes that he has been promoted to a level beyond his current capability attempts to develop and grow into the job. This willingness to learn is a Warrior characteristic of honesty and vulnerability, and implies a commitment to training and discipline. This openness to learn also solicits honest feedback on performance from subordinates and superiors alike. Witness this approach to learning in the martial arts master who has *beginner's mind*.[11] Having an open and fresh mind means taking each person or situation as though confronting it for the very first time in one's life. With this attitude comes intense focus, interest and receptivity to each thing encountered by the person. *Beginner's mind* is a Warrior quality that takes discipline, patience and much practice. A Warrior with this kind of determination understands that becoming a leader is not the result of attaining a position of power, but instead comes about through personal mastery.[12]

One cannot lead people and command their loyalty if one does not possess the attitude necessary in order to grow beyond one's current competence. To cast light on our Warrior shadow is to commit to developing an interior life that balances the energy and explosiveness of action with grace, and tempers insight with humor. As mentioned earlier, a warrior in Celtic Ireland patrolling the borders of the kingdom had to be capable of reciting a poem or dancing as well as fighting with a sword. The samurai balanced sword training with meditation, calligraphy and writing poetry. The discipline of the Warrior power in all martial arts is to attack and kill only as a last resort. All defensive effort is made to stop an aggressive situation by skill and cunning, and to prevent the situation from reaching the point of killing. These attitudes require a commitment to a fundamental philosophy of life and continual practice in situations that challenge and test one's interior power of resolve as well as one's outer capability for action.[13] We need to reclaim these positive characteristics of the Warrior's Intention and integrate back into our life the negative

ones that have emerged. Let us turn to some of the issues of shadow
Warrior behavior and the means to resolve them.

Defending Against the Shadow

The shadow Warrior, with all his compulsiveness and impersonal
attitude toward people, has run rampant in today's organizations. This
is a symptom of the imbalance between his outer aggressive actions
and his interior perspectives on what drives him and motivates his
behavior. The positional power of supervisors, managers or presidents is not a license to abuse people. Yet, all too often, put-downs,
power trips, intimidation and relentlessly pushing people regardless
of the toll it takes on them are all accepted standards for "getting
things done." Managers confronted about their behavior during
coaching sessions find it difficult to see the effect they have on their
subordinates. They are blind to their own power and often unaware of
their abuse. The shadow Warrior's first step toward integrating his
shadow is making the choice to become aware of the underlying
causes of this abuse in his life.

To come to terms with one's shadow Warrior is to come to terms
with and become aware of the wounded part of oneself that is never
satisfied with one's accomplishments, and is always driving one to do
more, to be better and to act more perfectly. Depending on how each
of us has suffered deep hurts or wounds, we will develop some
mechanism to compensate for that suffering. If our self-esteem and
intelligence have endured attacks from family or friends, we may
compensate by attaining a Ph.D. to prove how smart we are. Or, we
may compensate by receiving a promotion to prove how hard we
work. When our psychic wounds remain unconscious in us, the
power of those wounds drives us not only to compensate for having
suffered the wounds, but also, when put into a position of authority,
to project those wounds outward and drive other people to do as
much, be as good and act as perfectly as we do. The value of achieving one's highest level of incompetence lies in the exposure of those
wounds, to others as well as to oneself. Each of us must take several

steps in order to begin to work with the shadow Warrior wounds. The basis of all these steps is the pursuit of the fundamental injunction of all growth and change: Know *thyself*.

The first step toward activating awareness of one's wounds is to become willing to face the extent of one's compulsive shadow Warrior patterns. To take this first step is to confront oneself as an addict. This admission requires accepting that despite all one's capabilities and efforts, something isn't working. Yet, sometimes one cannot see that it isn't working until a boss, friend or outside "messenger" points out the problem.

The first step, mustering the willingness to look at and confront our shadow Warrior behavior, is often the most difficult to take. As with any addictive pattern, it is hard to accept that what initially brought us success is now impeding our success. Many individuals in organizations must "hit bottom" and be on their way out before they truly see themselves. At other times, the individual has become so bound by his perceptions, so overinflated by his own self-importance, that he can neither listen to anyone, nor see the truth about himself. Breaking through one's own defenses is a painful first step, which often begins a long and fruitful journey of growth and change.

The second step is to listen—to seek and be receptive to feedback from the people one manages or leads. If one takes the first step and confronts the existence of one's shadow Warrior, the most useful way to discern the shadow's power is to ask those one has interacted with about how that interaction has impacted them. Through their stories, one will hear the ways in which one has pushed and pressured them, and come to understand more clearly the characteristics of one's own driven and wounded personality. As a result of that speaking and listening, a healing can take place for all concerned. Others' fear, anxiety and anger toward one as a leader reflect the depth of these same feelings in oneself—the feelings one tries to cover up with compulsive Warrior behaviors.

Part of what drives shadow behavior are the fear and anger within oneself, which one projects onto others. A willingness to listen to one's subordinates requires a great deal of vulnerability and openness on the part of the leader. Many times someone, such as a consultant, needs to act as the "fair witness" between the leader and subordinates so that honest communication can take place. Without a neutral person present, neither party feels safe enough to face the vulnerability that honesty and receptive listening demand of them.

For example, a director of manufacturing for a high-tech company had all his managers and their staffs in rebellion because of the stress the director's unrealistic demands created. This director had answers and reasons for all his actions. When questioned about the reasons for his department's hostility and anger toward him, he could offer no explanation. He was an individual driven by data and information, so the logical approach was to survey and interview his people about the situation, and about their perception of his thinking and behavioral styles as well as those of all his key reports. The results of this data would provide a starting point for attempting to work out the situation. The director agreed to the procedure. Only after confronting the interview and survey data did he begin to "listen" to what his individual subordinates had tried to tell him for months. The steps between beginning to listen and actually changing formed a long and difficult road for him. As with any compulsive person, he was defensive, attempted to deny the information, and became very frightened at the prospect of confronting his negative behaviors and their effects on people. To his credit, the positive Warrior characteristics of persistence and determination enabled him to remain open and work through the problems.

If the Warrior is willing to confront his shadow by listening to his followers, he can begin to open up to new information and insight about his interactions. A behavioral model from the social sciences can give some clues as to how leaders and followers can relate more effectively by means of integrating the shadow.

Joseph Luft and Harry Ingham developed a relationship model called the Johari Window.[14] This graphic model (see below) helps people assess how they present and process information in their relationships.

The model is made up of two axes. One axis is feedback, and the other is exposure. Feedback represents the degree to which we are willing to solicit information from others about ourselves. Exposure is the initiative we take to reveal our thoughts, feelings and emotions to others.

These two axes create four possible regions in the model. One region is called the *arena*. This is the space where mutual understanding and shared communication occur between ourselves and another. This arena will grow in size as we actively solicit feedback and initiate exposure. For the shadow Warrior, the arena tends to be relatively small, resulting in controlled and limited communication.

The other three regions in the model point to where the Warrior must explore the shadow blocks to his relationships. The region where others can see the negative aspects of the shadow Warrior, but where

The Johari Window

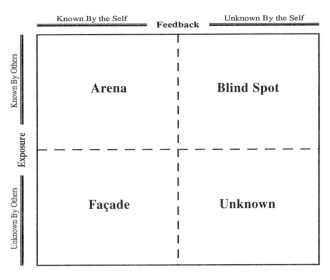

Self and Others – Pertinent information known and unknown by self and others
Exposure – Open and candid expression of feelings, knowledge, intuitions
Feedback – Active solicitation of information others may have about oneself
Arena – The interpersonal space devoted to mutual understanding and information
Blind Spot – The interpersonal space known by others, but unknown by the self
Façade – Information known by self that gives a protective front for the the self
Unknown – Contains data which may become known as interpersonal effectiveness increases

the Warrior is unable to see himself, is called the *blind spot*. For example, as followers, we see the verbal abuse, but the leader thinks he is "just talking firm" and doesn't see the negative impact on his people.

The region that will tend to dominate the shadow Warrior is called the *façade*. This is the area known by the Warrior but hidden to others around him. Here exposure is dominant because the Warrior is controlling what others see about him. The leader only exhibits the qualities, behavior or emotions that he wants his followers to see. The façade is the protective front from which the shadow begins to emerge in a Warrior leader. It is by means of the construction of the façade—the front—that the shadow comes to dominate the actions and behavior of the leader. "I am the boss. Do what I say or else" becomes the "tough guy" façade. Or, it can be the public façade of the religious leader who preaches morality on Sundays but hires hookers on Saturday nights.

The last region is called the *unknown*. The unknown represents potentials and possibilities known by neither the shadow Warrior *nor* his followers. The unknown enables the development of a new quality of relating in the shadow Warrior. Having the courage and honesty to listen to the feedback of followers and sharing one's own shortcomings and needs open the door to discovering the unknown, and release the potential for improved relations between the leader and his followers. This initiative of exploring together the potential of a different kind of relating between leader and follower expands the arena in which they can reestablish mutual trust. Exploring the unknown is the means by which the Warrior can heal his work, sexual or other shadow addictions.

The third step in addressing the shadow Warrior is to change the messages that guide one's compulsive patterns. Often what one's intellect says it is important to do and what one's emotions determine and play out in daily action become disconnected. One's current inner self-talk and messages developed at an earlier time when they helped one survive. But now that those threats no longer exist in the same ways, one no longer needs those same messages.

Those messages are very powerful, and they carry voices that are difficult to release. It may be a father's voice saying, "You'll never amount to anything unless you get all As," a frightened child's voice saying, "No one will like me unless I do it perfectly," and so on. A leader needs to expose to himself these fundamental conditioning messages because the emotions behind these messages drive his behavior and release negative shadow power when he is in a position of authority over others. Committing to work on oneself, to reflect, to probe with a neutral party the patterns that drive one's behavior create an ultimately lifelong journey of self-awareness and self-development. When the shadow emerges, it offers the opportunity to work on those destructive behaviors. Coming to terms with the addictive quality of the shadow Warrior demands the same kind of persistent Warrior discipline one exerted in other areas of life and which enabled one to achieve work success.

The fourth step is to ask for ongoing support, help and feedback from someone who will be honest and supportive. This needs to be a person who will alert one of lapses into old patterns of behavior, and offer support and encouragement when guilt and self-punishment attack one for his failures. All of us need a "training master," and as one's authority and power increase, it becomes harder to find people to fill that role. But, as we each work with the shadow sides of our personalities, it becomes increasingly important to have someone like this to warn us of the potential traps or help us find a way out of them when we become caught. The value of a training master lies in his ability to help one continually rework the fundamental purpose and meaning of one's life as one goes through difficulties and growth cycles. These difficult transitions can help one develop the moral, spiritual and pragmatic values needed in one's daily work and personal life. They can help one discover the positive motivation for one's actions, and help determine the best regime for one's emotional and physical health.

A training master isn't some wise person who knows all the answers. Rather, it is someone who "sees into" and acknowledges another person's potential for growth and improvement. A relationship with a training master is one of commitment both to each other and to oneself. The relationship involves love, appreciation and the distance required for the training master to remain objective and candid. A training master is not a spouse or a buddy. Usually, a training master's personality differs vastly from our own. The master's difference from us, and that person's ability to maintain distance and objectivity, make the training master helpful and useful to us.

The fifth step is to acknowledge a "power" greater than oneself. This is one of the basic premises of the Twelve-Step programs for addiction problems.[15] At some point, the four previous steps lead the individual to evaluate his beliefs and examine them in terms of how they relate to some larger purpose, meaning or mystery in his life. Research on belief patterns of successful leaders clearly demonstrates that the way to balance the negative shadow side of the Warrior, or any other shadow aspect of oneself, is to acknowledge, and have some type of direct experience with, a reality far greater than one's own ego.

In a study of sixty-five senior executives, Warren Bennis lists seven beliefs common to all of them.[16] The primary belief was that "everything happens for a reason and a purpose, and in some way the situation serves us." Another was that "it's not necessary to understand everything to be able to use everything." Regardless of their personal religious or spiritual views, these two beliefs clearly imply that these leaders relinquished a certain amount of rational control over their worlds and trusted some power greater than themselves.

The second step of the Twelve Step program encourages this surrender of control. At this stage, participants acknowledge that they have "[come] to believe that a Power greater than [themselves can] restore [them] to sanity."[17] In his book *Work Addiction*, Bryan Robinson comments on this step as it applies to coming to terms with the shadow Warrior within each of us:

As you let go of your control and perfectionism, you start to view your life differently. . . . This is the beginning of surrender. You realize your way is not *the* way and that only a greater source can restore your sanity. You reinterpret some of your old behavior patterns of over-doing, over-committing, over-compensating and over-controlling. . . . Realizing your own human limitations and imperfections awakens the need for help from a Power greater than yourself. . . . Your willingness to let a Higher Power guide you through your inability to control excessive work habits will also carry over into other areas of your life. . . . attempting to control other people and situations only creates stress, frustration and further unmanageability.[18]

Final Thoughts About the Warrior and the Power of Intention

To heal the compulsive actions and abusive behaviors toward other people that lie at the heart of the shadow Warrior wound is to develop what Donald Michael calls the *new competence*.[19] In his book *Leaders*, Warren Bennis provides an example of this competence. In a study of ninety leaders, Bennis found the following characteristics common to the majority of them:

- Acknowledging and sharing their uncertainty about situations with others
- Constantly reexamining current assumptions and priorities in their lives and businesses
- Using their interpersonal skills to encourage others to join in the search for new ideas
- Seeking to understand their own limits and biases by testing their views against those of knowledgeable colleagues and outside experts
- Becoming experts by continually learning within the context of their own organizations[20]

These characteristics reveal the results of working to integrate the Warrior shadow. It is difficult for a Warrior to admit his weaknesses or mistakes. The authenticity of a more integrated Warrior manifests in his humility. Humility combines honest self-appraisal with the strength necessary to admit one's needs and limitations. These characteristics prevail among leaders who have confronted the shadows of their own Warrior arrogance. As a result, these leaders have developed the power of Intention that leads them to challenge old forms of behavior; probe deeper into issues within their own lives; relate to their own responsibilities; test their own perceptions; and let their own organizations mirror what they need to see at any moment in time.

The Intention of the Warrior's strength focuses on the end results of the company's, organization's or community's success. The power of the Warrior's Intention depends on the clarity of his purpose and mission. If a Warrior does not focus his Intention in a clear direction, with clearly defined standards and values, then shadow material becomes activated very easily. Strong Warrior leaders need to cultivate the powers of the Sovereign in themselves. The Sovereign power of Presence—the state of *being* the vision rather than just enacting the vision—balances the shadow Warrior's tendencies to operate and behave compulsively.

Strong Warrior leaders lie at the core of our entrepreneurial philosophy. Too often, the larger purpose, the transpersonal ideals of these leaders, becomes lost in the rush to grab the golden ring that will earn them millions of dollars. As in the old Warrior traditions, strong contemporary Warriors need to dance and sing, reflect, and balance work time with time spent with friends and family. Boards of directors, senior executives, peers and subordinates all can help shadow Warrior leaders rebalance and strengthen both themselves and their organizations.

As with anyone who faces the shadow of addiction, the shadow Warrior must be confronted. Those codependents who have enabled the leader's shadow behavior must also face their own shadow victim.

The activation of a Warrior leader's shadow is unique in its takes-two-to-tango nature. Shadow Warrior behavior grows out of codependency. Therefore, both parties must face their shadows in order to break the addictive patterns and help each other first to control, and then to eliminate, compulsive behavior.

While working to integrate the shadow, one needs to refocus the power of Intention. Insofar as commitment, discipline, focus and sacrifice are intrinsic to Intention-shadow integration, one needs to establish a new set of priorities and a new direction that leads the heart toward loyalty and the mind toward integrity. Positive commitments to work with shadow compulsions give wounded organizations the chance to once again blossom and become vibrant communities for both leader and followers. Confronting shadow wounds allows both leader and followers to refocus their intention upon the enterprise. It also provides them with the opportunity to create the larger transpersonal purpose that satisfies the highest ideals of the Warrior.

THE MAGICIAN
THE POWER OF WISDOM

THE MAGICIAN AS TRANSFORMER

The classic Disney movie *Fantasia*[1] features "The Sorcerer's Apprentice," a segment with Mickey Mouse as an apprentice to a powerful sorcerer. Mickey's job is to tend the fire, clean the sorcerer's castle and learn magic by watching his master. When the sorcerer leaves for a while, he warns Mickey not to touch any of his magical accoutrements: wand, book of incantations, sorcerer's hat, etc. After the sorcerer leaves, Mickey continues his chores but decides that "a little" magic could help him finish the job faster. So, Mickey places the sorcerer's magic hat on his head, and uses the wand and book of incantations to command his broom and bucket to finish his chores. All goes well at first. By using the magic wand, Mickey clones his broom and bucket, and at his command, the brooms march with the buckets to the well to bring in water to wash the floor. Mickey's only problem is that he doesn't know the incantation to stop the buckets and brooms from bringing the water into the castle. Soon the dungeon is flooded as a result of hundreds of brooms continually dividing and carrying water into the castle. Mickey is frantic. He doesn't know what to do to stop the flow of water. The situation is out of control. Suddenly, the sorcerer appears, and, in an angry burst of magical words, disperses the water instantly.

Like Mickey, most of us wish we could employ a little magic to finish our work sometimes. However, like Mickey, our attempts to find the right "magical formula" to be successful in our career and relationships is difficult and challenging. What passes as magic seems to be only hopes and wishes rather than some force over which we have control. Yet, within our organizations there are magicians, sorcerers, shamans and wizards who seem to be able to do magical things. The most common term used to describe these special leaders is "wizard." Such individuals inspire comments such as "That guy's a wizard to get it solved so quickly" or "The way she got that project completed was pure magic. I don't know how she did it. She's a wizard."

The power of the Magician archetype lies in several distinguishing characteristics. In order to isolate, define and analyze these characteristics, we must first study the origins and evolution of magic. Understanding how magic has evolved will help us appreciate both the power of this archetype today as well as the power of the Magician leader.

Magic, as separate from religion or science, has been practiced for probably forty thousand years.[2] Anthropologists have indications that shamans engaged in ritual initiations in the great caves of Europe twenty to thirty thousand years ago and can trace the rites people throughout the world still practice today to ancient shamanic traditions. The purpose of the shaman was not to propitiate the gods through sacrifice or preside as priest of some religious ritual. Shamans were, and are intended to be, directly connected to the spirit world. This connection provides them with the skill and knowledge required to travel that spirit world, wherein they are able to heal individuals as well as their communities. Shamans, like all magicians through the ages, focus on the basic steps toward becoming one with the cosmos as the source of their magical powers.

The Magical Person

The shaman, then, is our core image of the magician throughout history.[3] The shaman was not a priest who demanded compliance from tribal members because he possessed some special conceptual belief or faith in which the tribe was to trust. Rather, he was someone who actively and directly experienced the sacred by exploring various realities and dimensions of existence. He became a cartographer of sorts, charting his own psyche, as well as other planes of existence. The path of the shaman, alchemist, magus, sorcerer or wizard was always a lonely one. Although members of the community valued the gifts of the shaman, their fear of his capabilities and his different lifestyle isolated him. Generally, shamans lived alone at the edge of the community. People projected onto the shaman both hope and fear: hope that the shaman's honored power might protect and heal them, and fear that the exercise of the power might destroy them. His knowledge and powers enable the shaman to help and to hurt, to heal and to kill.[4]

Magic Becomes Science

Magic, as it has come down to us over the millennia, engenders in us both attraction and awe, as well as fear and avoidance. We hope that through magic we can manipulate the world and obtain what we want. The famous nineteenth-century magician and occultist, Aleister Crowley described magic as "causing change to occur in conformity to will."[5] What shamans, magicians, alchemists, scientists and technologists all have in common is using their will to create change in the world. "Magical" power, whether used by a shaman or scientist, has as a fundamental purpose the intention to solve human problems, both personal and collective. Shamans and scientists seek knowledge in order to obtain tangible results, and they develop and practice the skills of their "trade" in order to acquire technical expertise. Common to both shamans and scientists is the use of ritual. Ritual uses words, symbols and materials in a particular order and sequence to achieve reliable and repeatable results. Whether it is using complicated chants or advanced mathematics, a magician learns the ritual tools that help him discover the source codes for manipulating the seemingly mysterious unseen.[6]

It was the alchemist of the Middle Ages who began to separate the magical worlds of the shaman from the scientist.[7] Alchemy heralded the onset of modern science on the one hand, and the reemergence of the sacred rites and mysticism of transformational magic on the other. For the original alchemist, the transformation of lead into gold was an outer act of an inner psychic and spiritual transformation. Alchemy revived secret, magical shamanic practices in ways that the Church at first accepted. The Inquisition drove into secrecy the psychic/spiritual part of gnosis, the search for true knowledge. As the humanism and rationalism of the Renaissance arrived, alchemy lost its transformational intention. Chemistry lost all the spiritual magic of alchemy and evolved rapidly into an exploration of physical, rather than psychic, matter. Chemistry centered on transformation for strictly scientific purposes, as opposed to alchemy, which approached transformation by integrating science (physical matter) with magic (psychic and spiritual forces).

Today, we generally think of magic in terms of the stage magician. Stage magic creates illusions that seem to control energy and paranormal forces. In actuality, this pseudomagic is a stage performance featuring a magician's skillful manipulation of objects and perceptions, with the aid of mechanical devices. In many ways, we each practice this type of "magic." When talent and skill combine by means of effort, dedication and continual practice, our accomplishments appear magical to others.

Yet, a deeper magic still exists beyond the sleight of hand of the stage magician. Both scientific research on paranormal experiences and individuals' spontaneous experiences of strange phenomena involving extranormal capabilities, physical healings, voices, visions, etc., all support the view of the alchemical vision that the inner and outer worlds of experience are really one and the same thing.

Regardless of the way in which we each personally react to the possibility of a "real" magic, the imprint of the archetype of the Magician lies deep within our psyches. Magic, as it has existed for thousands of years, has its own logic, rules and methods. Above all, it represents an arduous process of development and discipline that is as demanding as any other endeavor, perhaps even more so. Today, these principles of a magical reality are receiving increased attention, as individuals worldwide practice them with seriousness and commitment.

The Leader as Magician

Leaders who tap into the psychic power of the Magician archetype employ these timeless shamanic principles. These leaders fill a particular niche in our culture. Foremost among Magician leaders are the cutting-edge research scientist, the chief technology officer in high-tech organizations, the minister, the priest, the medical doctor, the teacher, the philosopher and the therapist. Besides these specific Magician manifestations, this archetype exists in CEOs trained as engineers, presidents of nonprofit environmental or relief organizations, entrepreneurs of start-up companies, inventors and political leaders. The Magician lends savvy, visionary idealism and innovation to the leadership roles described, with profound results.

When the Magician archetype becomes fully activated, the leader seems capable of accomplishing feats that subordinates and onlookers consider impossible. But, upon deeper probing of the leader who demonstrates this power, we find that his "magic" stems from common beliefs that most Magician leaders recognize and then integrate into their behavior. Common to these Magician leaders is the ability to focus and concentrate deeply, maintain consistent discipline over long periods of time, maintain commitments in the face of adversity, and have a conscious experience of an inner life of the mind, spirit or soul (whatever each might call it).

Whether they work as scientists, technologists, inventors, doctors, teachers, priests or consultants, all true Magicians share similar personalities. Their common characteristics are cool, often aloof, demeanors, strong analytical minds, introverted natures and impersonal interaction styles. These Magicians may have the social skills to interact with people, but they prefer to be alone and go it alone. Although not necessarily apparent at first, an iron will and strong opinions clearly drive the Magician. He clearly expresses his intention to control and manipulate situations in order to achieve his ends. The wisest Magicians have learned that personal ethics, clear morals and commitment to professional standards safeguard them from becoming involved in "black" magic.

The late Buckminster Fuller exemplifies the modern Magician.[8] The range of his ideas, inventions and theories was staggering. Most people know Fuller for resolution of the mathematics and construction of the geodesic dome.[9] Yet, few people know about the struggles he endured while discovering his many magical ideas and inventions. As occurs with all great Magicians, Fuller experienced his own "death" initiation. As a young man with a wife and children, his attempts to create a business failed, and he ran out of money. At this point, when he could have fallen into depression and reacted from fear, Fuller made a strange decision. He decided that he would stop talking and simply listen to his own mind. The wisdom of his higher self was telling him that he had to turn inward to discover the direction of his life, rather than outward according to cultural cues. For three years, he remained in this state of silence, recording his observations, ideas and intuitions. This extreme behavior created great financial hardship for him and his family.

At the end of that three-year period, he had accessed his inner world, along with the abundance of creative ideas and insights that inner world held. As he began to formulate his ideas and attempted to build and discover new applications for them, he also began to practice a basic principle that he would continue to employ throughout his long life. This principle was that whenever someone publicly refined one of his theories or inventions, he knew it was time to stop working with that idea and access a new one from his inner world. Basically, the more knowledge he gave away, the more new ideas would come to him.[10] This principle illustrates true magic at work, for it is by accessing our inner worlds that we acquire true Wisdom.

The Nature of Wisdom

Wisdom is the power and ultimate expression of the Magician archetype. Wisdom becomes truly magical because it enables individual Magicians to control two domains. The first domain is that of outer, or exoteric, magic. In this domain the Magician applies a combination of knowledge, skill, practice, experience and artfulness to categories of activity such as medicine, engineering and project management. The second domain is that of inner, or esoteric, magic. In this domain the Magician learns that magic is not about doing anything, but about embodying and *being* that which he intends or envisions. This means *knowing not only how to manipulate the principles of space, time and energy, but also how to allow those same principles to manipulate him.* Moreover, these three principles have always been the key objects of learning for all shamans, alchemists and scientists. In this inner domain, a second set of ideas exists, and the Magician must master this set in order to explore these three principles. *This set consists of control, motivation, purpose, intensity, secrecy, transparency and transformation.* In this second domain, the Magician possesses unlimited access to all types of power. Such power ranges from the traditional shaman's changing the weather to the modern scientist's unleashing atom bombs. This second set of ideas embodies the methodology that Magicians employ. Understanding the two domains of Wisdom is integral to understanding its function as the Magician's power.

The derivation of *wisdom* further clarifies the way in which these two domains compose the Magician archetype. Wisdom derives from two separate root words. The first is *wis-*, which means *"to think, to suppose, to imagine."* The second is *-dom*, which means *"state, condition, power"* or *"judgment."* Wisdom is a state of being. Wisdom is a state in which one makes manifest what one imagines or thinks is so. Wisdom entails acting from one's being. The magic (the manifest, the creative, the newly invented) arises from what one is, not from what one does.

Wisdom is the action that results from the inherent quality of the human ability to create. Wisdom is not the "tricks of the trade" or the "sleight of hand" developed through years of experience. It is the manifestation of the Magician's natural state of being. Expressions like "That's like magic—how did you do that?" describe witnessing Wisdom in action. Wisdom appears magical because it combines the skill and knowledge of a subjective activity that, through much experience, has moved from practice to art.

The final key to understanding Wisdom's power is recognizing that the source of magic is secret because it comes from the unrehearsed, spontaneous, transparent part of the individual. The Magician could tell you *what* he did to achieve his desired result, but the consummate Magician will remain silent as to the mystery of *how* he achieved it. Even though one may not be able to describe how one achieved the magical results, to master any art means to gain a certain level of control and to be able to use one's mastery to transform situations.

The Practicality of Magic: Knowledge and Understanding

Magic is fundamentally a performance art. In *The New Magus*, Donald Tyson argues that magic, in its traditional sense, was neither "science poorly understood nor a superstitious form of religion. Magic [was] a separate tool for acquiring and using knowledge."[11] Knowledge has both an inside and an outside; the former signifying wisdom, and the latter, understanding. In Tyson's view, the *practical* art one must learn is to bring together the inside of knowledge and the outside of knowledge. The Magician's journey consists of the long and difficult process of learning to combine the wisdom that comes from experience with the understanding that develops through skill and competence, through learning to internally control one's mind, emotions and body. This power of control enables the Magician to manipulate and make manifest that which is essentially invisible and indescribable.

This combination of knowledge and understanding developed by means of inner control defines the "expert" in any field. The expert is the individual who knows how to control the systems and flows of energy within an organization or field of activity as they pertain to his knowledge base. The magic of the expert comes through this combination of understanding and knowledge, and shows itself as "thoughtful judgment," or Wisdom, that is useful in a variety of situations.

On the one hand, if one uses that knowledge, that expert power, for the benefit of the community, organization or company, the magical power will grow in its capacity to effect positive change and growth. On the other hand, when one uses that expert power for personal gain, it can become a destructive force that brings down people and organizations. Consider the example of the destructive force that brought down Milken, Boesky and large brokerage companies such as Drexel Burnham Lambert during the Wall Street insider-trading scandals of the 1980s. This example illustrates the disastrous repercussions that can result from the illegal or unethical use of expert knowledge.

Another way to perceive knowledge and understanding is to see these characteristics of Wisdom as components of an interactive process. To understand something is to "stand under" it, or to know it by being one with it. That is, to inherently know the object of experience, one becomes a part of it. For the Magician, learning is not just a left-brained, rote or didactic process. Rather, learning is deeply rooted in feeling and intuition. Consider the alchemist, with his chemicals, who absolutely needed his female counterpart to create

the energy needed to effect both the physical and psychological transformation. Their relationship created the marriage, or *conjunto,* of
spiritual and psychic transformation. The man and woman engaged in
alchemy understood that each would become more individually complete and transformed as a result of the experiments they engaged in
together. The essence of Wisdom, then, lies not in any one of its parts,
but in the sum of its parts, and in their cohesive integration.

Modern Magician leaders need to unite their male, left-brained,
rational parts with their female, right-brained, intuitive, feeling parts.
This union enables a process that will transform the Magician, his followers and their shared environment. Many entrepreneurs of start-up
companies are more fully in contact with their intuitive sides. Without
the external assistance and organizational structure, these individuals
effectively solve problems by "pulling ideas out of a hat," doing things
at just the right time to attract investors, or having technical hunches
that pay off in product breakthroughs or new market directions. These
innate abilities reveal the most visible embodiment of the Magician's
power: the manifestation of transformation and change.

Transformation and Change

The medieval practice of alchemy used fire as a central ingredient for
attaining knowledge. The alchemist used fire to heat up his chemicals in
order to bring about transformation of the physical elements. Watching
this physical process was a "meditation" method, designed to focus his
concentration, to "heat up" the psychological and spiritual "matter"
within himself. To appreciate alchemy is to understand that the manipulation of physical matter, with heat and chemicals, was essentially a
psychic/spiritual technique designed to purify and change the forces at
work in the mind and soul. Intensity, heat and passion, manipulated in a
controlled environment, provided these explorers of human consciousness with the key to decipher the secrets of this hidden psychic/spiritual
knowledge. Deciphering these secrets enabled the alchemist to enter
the psychic/spiritual state necessary to manipulate reality. This type
of transformative manipulation is the Magician's primary passion.

The heat and intensity of desire must be strong in the Magician, but the cool control of discipline must be equally strong in him. The secret of the Magician lies in constant repetition—the continued practice of the language, tools and formulas of his particular art or field of knowledge. As with any practice, competence must grow, capability expand, and understanding deepen through the repeated exercise of one's craft. This repetition also cements the relationship between the craftsman/Magician and his craft. This practice entails the same requirements as does building a company, solving seemingly insurmountable problems, bringing a product to market or launching a worldwide sales effort. These requirements include the key Magician characteristics of inner motivation, strong communication skills (the magical language) and practiced competence (knowing how to access the essential knowledge that produces the right result every time). A leader who does this consistently creates pure "magic" for his employees, customers and shareholders. One may or may not agree with the business practices of Bill Gates and Andy Grove but must concede that these men "magically" produce the right results consistently.

Modern organizational Magicians receive the nickname of "wizard" because of their ability to achieve results that change situations in ways no one else proved capable of effecting. At the core of wizardry lies a leader who has access to some form of psychic (or inner) power. The people around this leader can feel this power emanating from him. This power to change the status quo ranges from transforming the culture of a company to completing a "monster" project on time. Regardless of the "nerdiness" that Bill Gates seems to project in public, both within his company and at industry conferences, people describe the brilliance of both his vision and his analyses of technological and business issues.

Magician leaders are able to consciously reflect and "travel" to some inner place in order to maintain personal balance. Above all, they constantly develop methods that help them understand the context, in addition to the content and process, of the projects or decisions on which they are working. Central to this contextualizing is understanding the status and conditions of a project or decision at any point in time—bogged down, speeding up, facing obstacles, etc.—as well as the condition of the team and other environmental factors. The Magician leader's prime responsibility is to monitor a process, decision, activity or project by watching the reactions, feelings and intuitions inside himself as a reflection of outer conditions. In other words, if he observes an out-of-control feeling in himself, he knows he may need to work with some out-of-control feeling among the members of his team. For example, if the Magician leader notices his own energy "sinking," he may observe the overly long work hours that are causing team members' energy to drag. The Magician leader knows he must adjust project schedules, find a way to move people into more energizing and satisfying roles, or simply "huddle" the team and discuss how to readjust the work pace. The Magician employs these and many other magical "tricks" in order to maintain energy, balance, motivation and enthusiasm for himself and his team.

The best Magician leaders never seem to work hard at leading. Most of them do not even think much about the "how's" or "what's" of leading. Rather, they operate fluidly and spontaneously, so much so that they seem to effortlessly transform both their work and their lives into art.

Artfulness and Spontaneity

Seeking to know or understand something as an end in itself does not fulfill the basic needs of the Magician. The traditional shaman and medieval alchemist wanted the direct experience of change and transformation. In short, they wanted physical results. They wanted to be able to influence the weather and save the crops. They wanted to heal the dying baby and supply game for the tribe's winter provisions. Magicians today want to achieve the same ends, but in more contemporary terms. They are experimentalists and pragmatists by nature. What they learn in their private experimentation they want to test and apply in the world. But, like any creative person, they want more than just the result. They want to practice their magic with grace and artistry. Artistry embodies the spontaneity sought by the Magician. Any artistic action appears easy and effortless. The artistry of the Magician lies in integrating into one's feeling and intuition the experiences and skills acquired as a result of years of practice, and then spontaneously bringing that integration into the world in creative and innovative ways. The true Magician's sudden and spontaneous behavior, combined with his ever-present air of artistry and beauty, may surprise and even frighten us when we see him in action. For when the Magician acts spontaneously, he is always unpredictable and uncertain.

Hermes (or Mercury by his Roman name) is the ultimate Magician. He is the one god who travels between the worlds of Hades (darkness) and Olympus (light), among the gods of both realms. Yet Hermes is also the trickster, unpredictable and cagey in his actions. As the Magician, Hermes often brings unexpected, unfamiliar wisdom to his action. His unexpected, unfamiliar, spontaneous behavior terrifies us. However, the power of Wisdom lies in its uncannily correct effect on us, its unerring accuracy in bringing about changes that we often do not even recognize as necessary until Wisdom "magically" effects them. Wisdom's uncanniness—its magic, its spontaneity—while it is precisely what astonishes and terrifies us, is also what makes it indispensable.

From this perspective, both the needs of the community and the Magician's great desire to learn the secrets of the world motivate his ability to change and transform. Tyson describes the traditional Magician as the artist who "manipulates forms and materials at the direction of his spiritual insights."[12]

The story of the Cathedral of St. John the Divine, located at the edge of New York City's Harlem, provides an example of the transformation of physical matter through spiritual insight. A massive stone cathedral, St. John the Divine rivals the grandeur and beauty of Chartres and the other great Gothic cathedrals of Europe. Although started in the 1950s, it is still not complete. During the 1960s, with the decay of the inner city, and Harlem in particular, spending money on the construction of a massive stone church seemed inappropriate. The construction of the cathedral stopped, as did the impact of the church on the surrounding community. But during the 1980s, construction resumed because of the insight of the dean of the cathedral. He recognized that resuming construction of the cathedral could give hope to the community. This was his spiritual insight. He also recognized that recruiting workers from Harlem and teaching them the traditional techniques of stonemasons, like those who worked on the great cathedrals of Europe, would not only create jobs, but also bring the surrounding community into the energy of building the church. This was his practical insight. The magical skill of the dean was his Wisdom: He transformed need into opportunity. He was able to provide a larger context for the community by reviving an old tradition that fulfilled a modern need for jobs.

Transparency

One of the significant characteristics of the Magician is *transparency*. Transparency is the quality that enables the magic to seem effortless. In simple terms, the Magician works his magic, and we experience the results; but, we do not see the tools, knowledge, skill or process that brought about the result. It takes much time and effort for the Magician to reach the point where his actions are transparent—where his result appear effortless, spontaneous and truly magical. This quality of transparency best characterizes the unique power and effect magic has on us.

Fundamentally, the Magician's objective is to convert knowledge into insight in order to change and transform himself, his immediate followers and the larger community. The Magician must complete four traditional steps in order to access the power that will eventually produce the quality of transparency.

First, he must *locate the boundaries of the knowledge to be gained.* For the alchemist this involved changing a base material, such as lead, into a refined one, such as gold. Simultaneously, he psychically transformed his base ego into a refined and fully developed human soul. Second, he must *determine his primary objective—the goal, the vision—he seeks.* The alchemist's objective was not creating gold, but rather manifesting in himself the philosopher's stone—lapis lazuli— the symbol of the highest expression of knowledge within the soul of the alchemist.

Third, he must *accept the task of learning a set of practical disciplines* that will enable him to practice the inner magic. For the alchemist, this was working with various chemistry apparatuses as a means of working on his inner state of knowledge. His external experiments in transformation caused the internal metamorphosis of his consciousness.

Fourth, he must *directly apply the technology of his craft to a problem or situation.* The classic problem of the alchemist was to discover ways to attain longevity or physical immortality through the elixirs he developed in his laboratory. This outward search for health and long life was the means to experience the eternal and continuing nature of life.

For a leader to apply his craft, he must learn its language, manipulate its tools, study its theory and philosophy, and gain competence in applying the technology of the craft in many different situations. Modern leaders may not follow this exact model, but they have evolved their own similar process for achieving transparency.

For example, a general manager of a $450-million division of a Silicon Valley high-tech company struggled to access his Magician qualities in order to solve a critical problem within the marketing operation of his division. His struggle went on for several months. Meanwhile, the competition was destroying his marketing strategy. Although he thought he had no solution to the problem, his discussions of it indicated that, in fact, he had come up with a rather innovative and simple resolution. Nevertheless, somehow he had not become conscious of the steps necessary to *recognize* the solution. He had found a solution that could transform the direction of his division, increase revenues and gain a keen edge on the competition in his product sector. Once he realized that he had found a solution, he became very excited. But he also realized that he needed to develop an understanding of the process that enabled him to reach such a transparent and easy solution.

For the Magician, the process of cultivating transparency is as important as achieving any given result. Insofar as the Magician works inwardly to produce outwardly, he must create an interior platform from which he can access intuitive knowledge and insight. The GM observed that to arrive at his solution, he had been practicing four principles that enabled him to access knowledge and understanding daily. He described these four principles as *attention, concentration, focus* and *insight*.

Attention. His practice, he realized, was to pay particular attention every day to those issues that either impeded or furthered revenue, profitability and growth for his product line. Further, when he identified a strategic problem, he knew that unless he solved it, his business would change negatively in some fundamental way. He spent some quiet time every morning before going to work, thinking about these strategic issues. However, his "thinking" was not a linear, step-by-step problem-solving process. Rather, he simply considered the issue from a point of awareness, observing its various elements from many directions. By approaching the issue in this way, without trying to "figure it out," relevant images and thoughts would enter his consciousness and enable him to focus his attention positively on the matter at hand.

Concentration. Throughout the day, the GM would concentrate on those thoughts or images he had in the morning. He would take these thoughts into his meetings, conversations and technical reading. The more he practiced this concentration, the clearer and easier it became to effectively answer the questions and address the concerns others raised about the issue.

Focus. The more the GM concentrated on the issue throughout the day, the better able he felt to "drill down" into it. For him, focus was a laser that penetrated through obstacles, to produce change, improvement and success. Day after day, he would practice these three sequential steps of "being with the situation" until, finally, insight emerged.

Insight. Insight occurs when attention, combined with concentration and focus, produces knowledge that emerges into a wider, more complex understanding of the situation. Insight enlarges the context, shifts the construct and opens the doors of perception. Insight enables a simultaneously complex and all-encompassing understanding of the situation. Insight left no doubts in the GM's mind. Once he achieved insight, he implemented it. To those around him, the solutions—the implemented insights—appeared obvious, simple and just "the right thing to do."

Additional analysis of the GM's daily inner practice revealed a complementary outer process through which he applied his inner method. He realized that this outer process grounded and made practical his inner method. The outer process, more linear and structured than the fluid and intuitive inner practice, consisted of five steps:

Observation. Observation is the practice of watching, noting and recording with full attention. For the GM, observation entailed constant scanning and filtering through as many layers of information as he could access. After observing a conversation with customers, he said to his staff, "We talked products, assuming certain customer needs. The customer was really talking to us about a new set of needs." This observation gave him the initial clue he needed to solve his marketing dilemma.

Realization. Realization is full understanding. As the GM continued to validate the knowledge he gained from various sources, it became clear that the marketing strategy was out of sync with customers' needs.

Synthesis. Synthesis is the union of two or more things, to create either a larger or an entirely different whole. From his observation, the GM synthesized a new and improved strategy that addressed and defined characteristics of the gap between his division and his customers. The synthesis provided a means to bridge the gap.

Drafting a proposal. A proposal puts forth an idea, a set of actions or a plan to address the conditions defined in the gap. As such, the proposal contains what is necessary to actually bridge the gap. The GM used proposals about the issue to stir up creativity and discussion, and to align his management team in order to change and transform their difficulties with customers into successes. His proposal for the new marketing strategy included insights as to what other companies outside their product sector were doing. The GM was not tied to his proposal. Rather, he used the proposal process to shift perceptions of both how to look at problems and possible solutions.

Incubation and testing. Incubation involves sitting on something, heating it up and giving birth to it. Testing involves proving the value and ascertaining the validity of something. A true Magician patiently waits to see whether his proposal passes the test of challenge, examination and pressure. For the GM, the proposal was the instrument around which people could align their commitments to a plan of action. The GM would circulate the proposal, hold meetings, and seek modifications and counterproposals until, magically, the proposal that had everyone's commitment and consent "popped out" fully formed. At this stage, everyone had become a Magician by means of creating something that generated new energy, enthusiasm and commitment.

Being the Magician Leader

The chief characteristics of the Magician leader are knowledge that deepens into understanding and insight, practiced skill, vast experience, proven competence, intense control, and the ability to render the mechanics of magical work transparent so that it appears artistic and spontaneous. A Magician leader employs a combination of transparency and secrecy (effortlessness, sleight of hand) that can transform one thing into something else. Wisdom allows the actions of the Magician to appear natural, obvious and effortless. True Wisdom enables leaders to know that no matter how long and hard they worked to access their magic, their single life's purpose is to be the conduit for the magical result. The greatest part of the Magician's preparation is to experience and understand the vastness and power of these magical forces, and his limited capability to control them. Humility is the cornerstone of Wisdom in the leader. Often, this Wisdom comes only as a result of personal sacrifice or years of anguish. Magicians like Albert Einstein, Robert Oppenheimer and the other atomic scientists suffered this anguish after they unleashed the destructive force of the atomic bomb.

For the Magician, each situation or event becomes a new opportunity for learning how to channel creative power. Instead of predicting and controlling outcomes, the Magician moves with the process, responding intuitively at each step, risking immediate action without hesitating. He completely trusts that the power of the process will yield its own results. This is the Wisdom of being alive, of letting go of each situation and person in our lives so that the natural mystery and wonder of the world reveal themselves. The Wisdom of the Magician leader helps us find our way out of this destructive, machinelike world that we have imagined and created together. Our leaders have come to dominate the natural state of the planet through their arrogance. Arrogance is the sign of the shadow Magician emerging.

THE SHADOW MAGICIAN

In his foreword to the book *Ritual: Power, Healing and Community*, by the African shaman Malidoma Somé, Robert Moore observes, "The culture of modernism with its attendant secularization and de-emphasis on the role of ritual in human adaptation has been dominated by the archetype of the magician and its show of dysfunctional forms. One might say that our culture is 'possessed' by the immature shadow-magician."[13]

The twentieth century's two world wars and hundreds of regional wars demonstrate the destructive power of shadow Magicians. The arrogance that precipitates the desire to control and dominate land and people constantly appears in our leaders. The only way for the Magician to remain positive and humble in the midst of this tendency toward destructiveness is to work with ritual. The Magician remains positive by finding a consistent process to guide his power toward Wisdom. Using a ritual process to access Wisdom provides a safe conduit for channeling this mysterious power that can both heal and destroy.

The Power of Ritual

A ritual is a system that consists of particular acts and procedures carried out in a set framework and sequence. Ritual provides the structure that safely contains magical power. Ancient rituals provided special rooms, temples, groves of trees, rings of stones or inscribed circles as the physical container in which to create the magic. Within these sacred spaces, the magicians and shamans sang and danced, told stories, and acted out myths. All these rituals took place on special days of the month and at precise times of the day or night. During these times, they performed rites and ceremonies in order to bring about initiations, healings, resolutions to disputes, rain for the crops and all things necessary to bring balance to the community.

Much of modern daily life involves ritual structure: morning exercises of stretching and then running, washing with a particular brand of soap, drinking black coffee, leaving for work at precisely 7:15, taking a particular route to the office, listening to NPR during the drive home from work, watching the same TV program every Thursday night, and on and on throughout the day, every day of the year, year in and year out. These are some of the innumerable rituals that we unconsciously construct and practice throughout our lives. Although these behaviors have become largely unconscious and routine for us, when we first began to practice them, they held meaning and purpose in our lives. As such, they are rituals.

Rituals must retain their meaning and purpose for the Magician. In order to become a competent Magician, certain rituals must not only remain conscious but become imbued with intent and purpose. These rituals must be practiced regularly with a particular intent and purpose in mind. Witness the example of the GM whose daily practice of attention, concentration, focus and insight was, in essence, a ritual. What sets conscious ritual apart from routine are the elements of time and space. The GM set aside a specific time to reflect and think each morning. He had a particular room at home in which he reflected each day, and he understood that the larger sacred space for his four-part ritual practice was the company building where he worked. Time and space always define the structure of ritual magic.

The Magician, by working with conscious ritual, learns to become the *witness* of the results of the power that the ritual allows. The Magician is not the source of the power. Rather, ritual practice teaches him how to gain knowledge of the power, develop experience with using the power, and learn the artistry of manipulating power for practical and useful application. The value of ritual practice lies in its ability to help the Magician develop the skill needed to direct power toward some intended purpose. This focusing of power through the structure and practice of ritual enables a Magician leader to experience power working *through* him, not originating *from* him. A true Magician serves the power. Most important, the power he channels touches and changes the Magician. The Magician's illumination, generated by his witnessing power, in turn generates the humility and Wisdom he needs to treat power as both sacred and dangerous.

The Rise of the Shadow Magician

The emergence of the shadow Magician signifies that somehow the Magician has failed to mature and open to humility and Wisdom. As Moore said, when dysfunctional forms emerge in a leader, "an immature shadow Magician" possesses him. The shadow emerges when ego consciousness, rather than the higher self, tries to contain a complex of energies.[14] When the shadow Magician becomes lodged and ingrained within a person, that individual believes the power comes *from* him. When this occurs, we say that the person's ego is inflated or dominating the individual. The shadow Magician believes that he can control, manipulate and predict the outcome of the power to satisfy his own desires and needs.

Instead of walking the long path of inner development, caution and reserve, the shadow Magician takes the short route of tricks, grandiosity and self-aggrandizement. By taking this short route to power, the shadow Magician denies responsibility for his actions. Because shadow Magicians have not developed an inner discipline, they pretend to possess "secret" knowledge when they really do not. They have practiced and acquired enough magic to access some power, but like Mickey Mouse as the sorcerer's apprentice, they don't know how to sustain it or even how to stop it when it begins to overwhelm them. In short, the shadow Magician will have gained enough knowledge to manipulate people and events for his own gain without regard for morality or ethics.

In our modern age, three shadow Magicians loom large on our historical horizon. Stalin, Mao and Hitler all used the Magician's power to twist, rationalize and deny the evil of their actions. Each of these leaders caused the intentional and wanton deaths of millions of innocent people. All three of them used death as a form of experimentation. Hitler stands monstrous in his pseudoscientific annihilation of six million Jews. James Hillman placed Hitler in the "bad seed" category. He wrote in *The Soul's Code: In Search of Character and Calling,* "Hitler knew the shadow all too well, indulged it, was obsessed by it, and strove to purge it; but he could not admit it in *himself,* seeing only its projected form as Jew, Slav, intellectual, foreign, weak and sick."[15] This refusal to admit wrongdoing, this denial and lack of any moral standard of behavior signify the tragedy of the shadow Magician's influence on mankind.

This tragedy still exists today. Contemporary daily life surrounds us with the harmful effects of shadow Magicians from the world of advertising. If denial and manipulation without regard for moral consequences are the key characteristics of the shadow Magician, then Madison Avenue casts a twenty-four-hour-a-day, seven-day-a-week shadow across our lives. For years we recognized the hypocrisy of the surgeon general's warning on tobacco products while tobacco companies' ad agencies tacitly encouraged kids to begin smoking. In addition, tobacco company scientists promulgated "research" that "proved" cigarettes were not harmful to our health. In each case, the Magician scientists and ad agencies were playing the dark trickster role. They deceived us and manipulated us into doing what we shouldn't do. Whether it is a Hitler, a research scientist, a tobacco company executive or our boss at work, two common characteristics exist in shadow Magician leaders, and we must watch for them, both around us and in ourselves. Robert Moore and Douglas Gillette, in their book *The Magician Within*, contend that the shadow Magician exists in two forms, each the polar opposite of the other.[16] The first is the shadow Magician who appears unconscious of his power and denies his effect on others. Moore and Gillette call this shadow the "Innocent One." The polar opposite is the shadow Magician who consciously uses power to manipulate and control others. This type of shadow Magician they call the "Trickster."

The Shadow Magician as the Innocent One

The primary characteristic of the Innocent One is his passive/aggressive employment of his dark power. The Innocent One appears naive and ignorant of what he does to others. However, this "innocent" front hides a cunning, manipulative and aggressive drive to control. This passive/aggressive behavior can defend its innocence with surprised looks, rages of denial, verbal abuse or intellectual one-upmanship. The apparent innocence and denial of the shadow Magician can be both subtle and very destructive when projected onto others.

Consider this example of the Innocent One in action: a battle between two Magicians at a high-tech company. The CEO of the company was the Innocent One. The other Magician was a senior VP and general manager of one of the company's operating divisions. Each was in his fifties, each had years of engineering and management experience. As an experienced Magician, each believed that he alone possessed the magic that would produce the right results. The CEO had earned his stripes by climbing the ladder of a multibillion-dollar company. The GM had been the CEO of two smaller companies. Each was a technical Magician, with knowledge, skill and experience in the marketplace. Each also had strong Warrior Intention and a great deal of practical business wisdom as a result of his experience.

The problem between them was the fundamental opposition of their magical Wisdom. The shadow part of the CEO's magic emerged in the secretive means he used to achieve his desired ends. He would tell the GM one thing to his face, then go behind the GM's back to berate him to the COO and undercut him with the chairman of the board and other executives so that the GM had little or no support when he would make proposals for his business unit. Without the support of upper management or his colleagues, the GM was publicly forced to accept the CEO's solutions to all his business issues. The GM would try the CEO's strategy, demonstrate its insufficiency and propose an alternative conceived by his team. The CEO would listen to it during executive staff meetings, ask some questions and tell the GM to try his proposed alternative. All the magic the GM tried to exercise within the organization in order to activate his proposals was in vain. The confusion resulting from the CEO's publicly supporting him but secretly trying to destroy his credibility blocked the GM's magic.

The CEO staged this public/private battle with the GM, so it would seem, to prove that the CEO's technical ideas were the best approach. When the GM saw the pattern of the CEO's passive/aggressive behavior, he confronted the CEO with it. The CEO seemed shocked and dumbfounded, and told the GM that he must have totally misunderstood what he, the CEO, was trying to do. Within his feigned display of innocence, the CEO professed feeling wronged by the GM, when he, the CEO, was only trying to help the situation.

The confrontation clearly proved to the GM that the CEO wanted only his own technical solution. Six months later, after many similar inconclusive battles, and with his business deteriorating more and more, the GM inadvertently learned that the CEO had initiated a search to replace him. Being a cunning Innocent, the CEO had planned to keep the replacement search a secret until he found the new person and could fire the current GM. Within weeks of his accidental discovery, the GM accepted a position with another company. The CEO was outwardly surprised and hurt by the GM's departure, and publicly made the GM out to be the "bad guy" who left the company. Within months, the technical solution the CEO tried to force upon the GM died a quiet death, laid to rest among the many other technical approaches that hadn't produced good business results.

The Magician whose knowledge is not tempered with an understanding of people becomes an expert separated from the community. When one uses magic to pursue pet ideas and private ends, rather than improve the organization or community as a whole, it will result in manipulation and cynicism. When the Magician works alone and in secret, the negative aspects of his unpredictable and uncertain nature become dominant. This hidden, cunning, manipulative character of the shadow Magician frightens and repulses people. This is why Magician leaders who are strong, opinionated entrepreneurs, often in denial of their own power, can destroy companies so easily. This capacity for destruction is intrinsic to the shadow Magician's other aspect: the Trickster.

The Shadow Magician as Trickster

The Trickster,[17] unlike the Innocent One, is neither unconscious of, nor in denial of, his power. The Trickster directly and aggressively controls and manipulates others to achieve his own ends. Moore and Gillette point out three distinguishing characteristics of this type of shadow Magician.[18]

Detachment. Trickster Magicians separate and detach themselves from the needs, concerns, suffering and general welfare of others.

These Magicians often become cruel and sadistic. Hitler, Stalin and Mao kept themselves separate and distant from the people. Hitler had a compulsive preoccupation that kept him detached from interpersonal relationships. His great passion, throughout the war and right up to his death, was monumental architecture. He would constantly pore over architectural designs and assign people to massive building projects. Apparently, he wanted an empire so he could build big buildings for himself as a substitute for having relationships with people.

Deliberate cruelty. The Trickster is very conscious of his ability to use and manipulate people, and he delights in using these skills to play sadistic games at the expense of others. Concentration camp commandants illustrate this characteristic.

False bravado. The Trickster cons people into believing the lies he presents to them about himself and his effectiveness and power as a leader. The Italian Fascist leader, Mussolini, deceived his people, convincing them that he was a strong, effective leader, when in reality Hitler controlled him.

To place the Trickster in a contemporary business context, consider the CEO who was the ultimate entrepreneur, having parlayed his business into a publicly traded multibillion-dollar company. As he raised millions of dollars each quarter to augment the company's growing investments, he increasingly assumed an aura of egotistical arrogance. He saw the success of the company and the ability to raise millions of dollars from investors as his personal achievement. He thought he was the smartest and most savvy deal maker in the business. However, industry analysts continually criticized that although he was a good deal maker, he ran a one-man show, and couldn't build the strong management team necessary for a large company because working for him was so difficult.

His narcissistic belief that he was the sole power source in the company led him to take others in the organization for granted.

Publicly he appeared cool and detached in his interactions with staff, but, behind the scenes, he destroyed people by demeaning their positions and capabilities as compared to his own. The most disturbing aspect of his manipulation of people was his habit of making promises that he never intended to keep in order to appease people so they would agree with him and do as he said. He also habitually lied to people in order to appear more capable and more insightful than anyone else in any given situation. Even when people caught him lying (as his board of directors and management team began to do), he merely told another lie to remove himself from the predicament.

At the core of this CEO, and of most shadow Magicians with Trickster characteristics, is a ruthless disregard for integrity and lack of concern for the welfare of others. Sadly, this CEO's narcissistic need for total control and power over people destroyed his basic Magician power. His inherent capability to create and build a truly successful enterprise became lost within his egocentric perception of himself. This narrow-minded view of himself as the only valuable member of his company essentially prevented his business from expanding beyond its current level of success and becoming a more efficient and more productive company. His own arrogance and unrestrained control caused his board to rebel and force him out of his position. Even after that action, he still believed he was superior to everyone else and that he was the victim of erroneous judgment.

Another similar, but smarter, Trickster is Wall Street trader, convict and philanthropist Michael Milken.[19] This creative Magician crossed the line into darkness when he consciously manipulated huge stock transactions that, in 1986 alone, earned him $550 million. Milken created the junk-bond industry. At the heart of every Trickster is some form of criminal or immoral conspiracy. Milken's trial, conviction and incarceration revealed the professional and personal corruption in all his dealings. He emerged from prison a billionaire, but the company he worked for, Drexel Burnham Lambert, went out of business.

Nevertheless, those who dislike, and even hate, Milken grudgingly acknowledge his brilliance, creative insight and business acumen.

Ironically, Milken, a former convict, remains a high-priced consultant, masterminding big deals like the Time-Warner merger and Rupert Murdoch's takeover of the Fox Network.

Out of prison, commanding multimillion-dollar fees from the same moguls he advised during the 1980s, and now battling prostate cancer, Milken still tries to convince everyone that he is powerful, good and effective in all aspects of his life.

When he found out that he had only three years to live, he set up a project called CaP CURE, a private venture to raise millions of dollars to fund a cure for prostate cancer. This highly visible endeavor, plus other philanthropic activities, represents Milken's drive to convince everyone he can that he is not a sinister character and that he can use his "special magic" to change the world for the better. His new enterprise is the Knowledge Kingdom, which intends to capture the multibillion-dollar education and training industry. In all his endeavors, he constantly works toward reforming his image by participating in such activities as teaching inner-city kids math and donating to charities. In direct opposition to this public community service image, he threw an expensive fiftieth birthday bash for himself at his $42-million vacation home. Milken wants appreciation, glory and, perhaps, even immortality to be lodged in everyone's perception of him. He is still a great Trickster at work.

CULTIVATING THE MAGICIAN WITHIN

Gandhi said, "The only devils in the world are those running around in our own hearts. That is where the battle should be fought." For the alchemist, for the shaman, for the CEO, for any person of magical powers, it is easy to lapse into an abuse of power.[20] One of the mottoes of alchemy is the practical antidote to shadow Magician behavior: *solve et coagula*. The connotation of this phrase is: "analyze all the elements in yourself, dissolve all that is inferior in you—even though this dissolution may destroy you as you currently exist—then, with the strength acquired from the preceding operation, congeal into a finer form." This ancient formula finds its modern equivalent in social scientist Kurt Lewin's process for producing change and learning. When a person has unexamined attitudes or behaviors, he must first "unfreeze" them, or open them up to the light, produce change through learning about the inferior or negative parts of himself; and then "refreeze" himself around the core of new attitudes or behaviors that are more appropriate to being a container of Wisdom. More succinctly: analyze, dissolve, congeal.

Alchemy as a Metaphor for Shadow Work

At the heart of alchemy lay a twofold purpose: the physical transformation of lead into gold and the simultaneous psychic trans-formation of the sacred personality from the profane. The ultimate purpose of alchemy was a profound and magical transformation of all matter (inert and alive), symbolized by the philosopher's stone—the perfect transcendent image represented by the blue lapis lazuli gem. Blue, in most esoteric traditions, represented the healing, transforma-tive power of love. The physical steps of working with the chemical apparatus were the alchemist's external focus point for the inner soul work that he had to do. The various steps of the alchemical process provide some useful insights for working with the shadow Magician.[21]

The first principle is heat. The precise amount of heat, externally under the retort (the glass container for the materials to be heated) and internally in the heart/mind (the inner container) of the alchemist, was required in order to start the transformation process. As examples of leaders who activate their shadows have shown, the activation comes most often as a result of the challenge of a new position, added responsibilities or a business opportunity larger than the leader had confronted before. It is the intensity of this newness that "heats up" the leader's life. The shadow, for all its negative impact, is also the doorway to a more profound and sacred place in our lives. This is the place within us that humans have searched for and explored since the beginning of our journey on this planet. Confronting the darkness

and finding the right heat to illuminate its inner and outer manifestations have been our constant endeavor. Heat that will also illuminate
is our eternal quest. For us, the "heat" in the shadow gap begins to
"burn" the shadow's profaneness and provides an opening to a deeper
awareness of life than we've ever known. Consciously becoming
aware of and owning our shadow parts is our way of turning up the
heat on ourselves so that we can achieve the ultimate knowledge and
awareness: Wisdom.

The second principle is repetition. Transformation does not
come from a single experiment. The alchemist had to repeat the
experiment over and over. As a result of repeating the formula and
procedure, his concentration became focused and refined. Generating
more and more concentration as he performed the experiment many
times, in turn, developed precision. These repetitions also forced
impurities out of the chemical solution in the retort. Inwardly, this
repetition refined and condensed the mind and heart to achieve what
Chinese alchemists called the "golden nectar." It was this nectar of
the heart that brought illumination and spiritual development. The
transformation of the baseness of our shadow material demands
constant and concentrated practice. That alone can transform the
shadow into golden nectar.

The third principle is distilling, purifying, dying and birthing.
This principle is the crucible of transformation—the vessel of death
and rebirth, crucifixion and resurrection. As the heat intensifies, more
and more impurities rise to the surface; the elements in the retort
become more refined; the volume of matter is reduced through
evaporation; and at the critical point when everything seems burned
up, a chemical reaction takes place and "gives birth" to a different
substance. In an instant, one thing magically becomes another. Of
course, the change really wasn't instantaneous. Just as the chemical
composition slowly transforms in the retort, so the distillation process
of working daily with shadow material slowly changes us until that
moment when we seem to suddenly burst forth reborn. At that
moment, we recognize that we have reached the threshold of true

transformation, and a sudden insight and change in attitude come to us. For some, the purifying practice is a long and difficult challenge. When the transformation happens for these individuals, it seems the natural outcome of a long process. For these people, joy is the natural result of the long night of rebirth. For others, if the death and rebirth come suddenly, this moment can be mind shattering because of the manner in which it expands the perceptions and the array of choices in one's everyday life.

The fourth principle is containment. The size of the retort determined the speed of the transformation and, indeed, whether or not the matter in the retort would ever transform at all. But beyond the retort's serving as a holder of the outer and inner material, containment provided the level of secrecy and inner purification that the alchemist needed to have in order for the experiment to work. Containment in this sense requires discipline, consistency and self-commitment to a singular purpose. As a practical principle for shadow work, it entails finding the right therapist, coach, workshops and books that can help contain the energies one feels when working with the shadow, and, thereby, help one understand them. But, most important, is the real containment of finding a daily practice that can hold the fear and terror that arise when a form of psychic death approaches. This death must occur for inner transformation to take place.

The fifth principle is synthesis. Synthesis is both the merging of opposites and the alchemical death of ego consciousness. In alchemy, synthesis was called the *conjunto*, the marriage of opposites in us. The transformation of the Magician leader qualities shows us how to access the other three powers of leadership, for the Magician energy is the integrator of all Four Powers. The Magician brings into us the power of psychological, spiritual and intellectual transformation that we need in order to become people and leaders who can bless, create, commit and transform all they touch. Many thinkers have observed that our modern technological age is the Age of the Magician. By developing and integrating the dark, shadow parts of the Magician, the promise for new leaders can arise.

A Practice for Containing Our Shadow Energies

Of the five principles of alchemy, the one most useful and practical for working with shadow Magician material is containment. Finding a daily practice to contain shadow energies and transform and integrate them into our lives is fundamental to leader development. Concepts and techniques of ancient meditation systems offer some simple ideas and practices for achieving containment. A very pragmatic system that can be used by most people comes from Buddhism.

Buddhism has two traditions. The tradition most of us know in the West is the religious one that centers around beliefs like *reincarnation, karma* and *nirvana*. The other tradition practices the original observations of a man called Siddhartha Gautama. His observations focused on the painful shadow condition of our lives, and he taught ways to remedy and change this condition.

Siddhartha was part of the Shakyamuni clan, which resided in an area of present-day Nepal approximately twenty-five hundred years ago. After his own alchemical process of transformation and illumination, some wandering ascetics asked him who he was. In the ancient language of his day (Pali) he said he was *buddha*, a word that meant "awake." This man became known as the Buddha—the Awakened One. As a great Magician, the Buddha's methods provide a practical, experiential means to transform the shadow material in one's life.

What particularly pertains to the power of the Magician archetype is that this Awakened One did not say "believe something, and you will be different." Rather, like all developed Magicians, he said: "Don't believe anything I say. Test and try for yourself what I've found. Be a skeptic, be an agnostic and simply explore the path I discovered that can end your suffering and let you awaken fully to your own life." His method was that of a doctor with a patient: "Let me give you a diagnosis of your condition and then the prescription that I've found for the healing. Test the diagnosis against your own observations and experience, and see if the prescription works."

When leaders face and admit to their shadow behavior, they confront quite deeply the guilt and pain of the suffering they've created for other people. But more profoundly, they experience deep suffering in themselves, and often hopelessness, because they can't do anything about the suffering. The therapeutic setting becomes an important healing step for most of these shadow-weary individuals. Even in addition to their personal healing work, these individuals need a practice to contain the daily material of their lives and work. Both therapy and a daily practice provide the means to awaken one from shadow suffering and pain.

The Four Facts of Life

Most of us have heard of the Buddha's Four Noble Truths. But, as Stephen Batchelor points out in his groundbreaking book on Buddhism for Westerners, *Buddhism Without Beliefs*, Buddha, in his Four Noble Truths, gave us not beliefs to struggle to understand, "but challenges to act."[22] In other words, the Four Truths provide a practice (a container) to help us awaken from our "sleep of existential confusion." Batchelor indicates that the Buddha was a pragmatist, a person of action; he therefore states the Four Truths as courses of action:

Understand our anguish. This is a call to embrace the fears and worries relative to our life and its conditions—particularly sickness, aging and death—which cause our suffering.

Let go of the origin of our anguish. Craving and desire provide the source of our existential pain. Craving shows up in terms of wanting and not wanting; in pulling things toward us and in pushing things away. Craving creates a constant dis-ease and drive to satisfy the impossible in us. Letting go doesn't let us bury our head in the sand, but rather, challenges us to let whatever exists in our lives just be as it is, without doing anything about it. When we let something be what it is, it naturally will evolve and change into its next condition. Like any good magic, the act of letting go in our lives is not about sacrifice or denial, but rather, about accepting conditions in our life and circumstances just as they are now with attention and focus.

Realize *that the suffering can stop and the craving will cease.* Letting go provides the gap for insight to emerge. In Buddhism this is called *emptiness*. It is not the emptiness of a vacuum, but the fertile ground of creativity and becoming. It is the open and noncraving place in which we realize or glimpse who we really are and know the potential of being alive and having genuine compassion for ourselves and others.

Cultivate *a path that continues to increase understanding, letting go and realization.* As Batchelor says, there is "nothing particularly religious or spiritual about this path. It encompasses everything we do. It is an authentic way of being in the world. It begins with how we understand the kind of reality we inhabit and the kind of beings we are that inhabit such a reality."[23] The last of the Four Truths represents a promise that the individual can find a way to live. It promises that within each of us (not through someone or something else) there is a path of growth, freedom and insight that is experientially different from what we had known before.

The American Buddhist teacher Lama Surya Das calls the Four Truths the Four Facts of Life.[24] Viewed in terms of leadership these Facts affirm that the tension gap between personal and positional power is not some dark wall through which to break. Rather than breaking through a wall, these Facts help us open the door that exposes the darkness of fear, lack of knowledge and inappropriate shadow behaviors. However, we can only open the door once we have the method to find it. Opening the door enables us to discover more clearly our unique paths in life, as well as to find that others have paved the way for us. Although we each determine which door to open, a community of fellow explorers has provided guideposts and boundaries to support our journey.

Eight Guideposts for Living

From his exploration, Buddha provided Eight Guideposts for cultivating the path of our lives. These Guideposts provide the structure to unravel these Four Facts of Life and apply them moment by moment. They also serve as a developmental process for working with our shadows and for uncovering our naturally wise and compassionate condition. The Eight Guideposts fall into three categories: Wisdom Development, Ethics and Standards Development, and Meditation Development.

Wisdom Development. Wisdom is the discovery of our sanity and the ability to trust a deeper knowledge and understanding of life.

Right View or *Understanding* involves developing a clear and authentic vision as to the nature of existence.

Right Thoughts or *Intention* concerns discipline and control over our thoughts, attitudes and feelings in order to purify ourselves.

Ethics and Standards Development. This involves respecting morality, and living life in an open, honest and skillful way.

Right Speech concerns using language and creative expression (as in the arts) in ways free of deception, that produce no harm to others.

Right Action means living our lives as an art form and developing appropriate responses for all situations.

Right Livelihood entails engaging in vocations that don't harm life and through which we can express our caring for the world.

Meditation Development. Meditation is a way of living consciously and being fully awake to life at every moment.

Right Effort involves making the commitment to do our inner work with total dedication and all our energy.

Right Mindfulness means gracefully and patiently paying attention to each thing we think, feel and do.

Right Concentration entails focusing all our thoughts and feelings, energy and intention in a single pointed direction.

These Eight Guideposts, within their respective three developmental categories, do not represent a sequential, linear process. Rather, each person assumes the work needed to take on and use any or all of the Eight Guideposts, according to the shadow doors that are presenting themselves to that person. The Eight Guideposts also represent a recursive process. That is, the Guideposts form a continuous spiral of development. For example, deepening one's capacity to concentrate will enable one to hold clearer knowledge and awareness of one's life and responsibilities. Awareness, in turn, deepens mindfulness, producing integrity in our communication. Honest communication and discipline over our thoughts deepens our caring and compassion in the world. Ongoing effort toward developing one's wisdom, standards and meditation capacities in the context of daily leadership activities provides the container for shadow material to be revealed and worked through in a conscious manner.

Most of the major spiritual traditions on the planet reflect these Eight Guideposts. Whether it is the Ten Commandments or the principles in the Sermon on the Mount, these traditions give us direction, and encourage us to practice wisdom and ethics. In addition the Eight Guideposts give us a practical set of techniques and tools for meditation development.

The right kind of effort, attention and concentration can provide a powerful containment "retort," an environment in which we can learn how to work consciously with our shadow material. The right kind of simple meditation practice will provide the practicality we need to analyze, dissolve and congeal. This simple meditation process mirrors the five principles of alchemy: heat, repetition, purification, containment and synthesis. Although meditation techniques exist in all spiritual traditions, the following methods seem the most accessible to Western thinking and lifestyle.

Insight Meditation Practice

The Theravadan Buddhist practice of *vipassana,* or insight medita-tion,[25] is a practical approach to letting unconscious shadow material bubble up into awareness, as well as to providing a reliable container from which to confront the outer effects of our shadow on people and situations. In this meditation form, breath, body sensations, emotions and thoughts all become the access points from which repressed material can emerge into awareness so that we can heal and integrate it.

Insight meditation is a concentration practice. The technique is easy, demanding only persistence and repetition in order to achieve noticeable results. The practice entails a half hour to an hour, and daily practice yields the best results. Its long-term benefits include increased awareness and mindfulness of all our behavior, the focusing of our *monkey mind*—the thinking process that involves constantly jumping from one thought, image or sensation to the next—into a state of quiet-ness that holds the promise of direct knowledge (insight) of ourselves and our life circumstances. The technique is as follows:

> Find a comfortable place where you can sit with your eyes closed. Use a chair or sit on a cushion in a quiet room. As with any ritual practice, establish a place and time for the meditation, and adhere to them. Following the same routine conditions the mind/body to ready itself for the practice each time you do it. This regularity is also important because it prepares your motivation and energy so that you can focus your attention and concentration. Remember, Magicians work with space, time and energy. For prac-tical reasons, have a clock that you can glance at as needed.
>
> **Your breathing is the object of the concentration.** Focus your attention on your nostrils, following the sensation of your breath as it moves in and out of your body. Don't change your breathing by consciously forcing it, speeding it up or slowing it down. The practice is to simply observe the natural rhythm of the breath. As your concentration grows, you will feel the air moving the hairs in the nostrils, the warmth or coolness of the air passing through the nostrils and many other subtler sensations. The breath

provides the anchor point as thoughts, feelings and body sensations arise in your awareness. As concentration on the breath at the tip of the nose is distracted by such thoughts or feelings as planning a trip, or by daydreaming about a meeting, feeling pain in your back, or being upset with your coworker, you follow the thought, sensation or feeling until you become aware that you are not focusing on your breath. As you become aware of these types of distractions, you gently bring the focus of your attention back to the air passing in and out of your nose. This practice of observing your breath produces a subtle but pleasurable sensation of relaxation in the body. Although the concentration requires effort, the feeling of peacefulness that the practice engenders is worth the effort.

What you will find after several weeks of this practice is that the monkey mind will not jump around so much and the periods of being able to maintain continuous attention on the breath will last longer. The more you practice, the more you will find that the upsets and confusions of the day aren't as disruptive, the more easily you will sustain your concentration on problems and issues, and the more your ability to reflect and see your impact and effect on others will grow clearer.

Labeling Thoughts. Another piece of the technique that is useful for deepening the concentration is to add the process of labeling, or naming, thoughts, sensations and feelings. When you notice your mind drifting away from your breath and toward other thoughts, name these thoughts. Notice planning and say "planning" to yourself. Or notice anger, or tightness in the stomach, or judgment of a person, and name each of them. The multipurpose labels for when you are uncertain as to where your mind has wandered are: "thinking," "judging," "planning," "feeling." As soon as you name the distraction, bring your attention back to the breath. Labeling uses the distraction as an object of your concentration. Naming helps create *disidentification* from ego involvement in the thought or sensation. It creates an observer who can access both the ego consciousness and the unconscious elements of the shadow. Over time, you will notice that the labeling will allow you to catch the thought just as it is beginning to form. When this occurs, your concentration has heated up, and you will be able to gain insight into your ego and shadow.

This labeling and observing lie at the heart of the purification process. As you simply use the breath and naming, you will notice the diversity of the weird, hateful, lovely, perplexing and confusing elements of your life coming to the surface of your awareness and then disappearing. As this repeated distillation of thought arises, as self-acceptance grows through the realization that everything in you comes and goes like the tides, the ego inflation, the shadow projections and the fears begin to die. In their place come moments of deep clarity about yourself and others, acceptance and understanding of unresolved issues, recollection of buried memories, and humorous recognition of your personality foibles.[26]

Becoming the Meditation

As you continue the practice over a period of months and years, you begin to recognize the shadow and light of your personality, and they, in turn, begin to blend and individuate you as an ever increasingly unique person. You will know when this occurs because people around you will seem changed and transformed. They have not become different; but *you* have. Your perceptions have transformed them. They still exhibit the same troubling behaviors, still anger you in the same ways, and so on; but now you will notice that you have a choice either to react in the same way as you did before or to see them and think about them in different ways. Your recognition of this choice enables the transformation. As you meet them in the same old situations, you will notice yourself labeling and feeling anger, resentment, fear or whatever you identify. At this point, the meditation practice has naturally moved off the chair or cushion and become part of a natural meditative state within your entire life. You no longer practice meditation; the meditative state has *become* your state of being. In alchemical terms, it now contains you. In this state of being, you will discover a heightened awareness, so that you don't have to be controlled by unconscious reactions or project onto others your negative thoughts or feelings.

Although being conscious of our shadow in this way doesn't make us perfect, being in contact with both the light and dark of our lives lets us awaken more to actual reality. This synthesis expands us out of the flight-or-fight response of the ego and simply lets us be with whatever we are thinking or feeling without having to project it onto another. By letting go of projecting our shadow fears onto the world, we break the bonds of separation and alienation that lie at the core of so much of our daily longing and pain. When we release the despair and hopelessness of separation, we return to ourselves the full possibility of relationships and connections with people, nature and the cosmos. When we give ourselves kindness, forgiveness and compassion for who and what we are, not what we do, we find the true freedom to experience life as our friend and companion.

This reconnection to ourselves is meditation's promise to us. We will know the value of our practice when some of the golden nectar distilled by means of our inner work has settled in our hearts and we find we have more forgiveness, appreciation and compassion for both ourselves and others. When this happens, we will have opened another door and crossed the threshold into a bigger and more beautiful world.

Final Thoughts About the Magician and the Power of Wisdom

Both the mystery and the wonder of recognizing a path that helps us move past our shadow lead us to joy and freedom. Jesus put it simply when he described in metaphor the vastness of inner reality. He said, "In my Father's house are many rooms. Come. There are rooms prepared for you." [27] We learn as leaders that opening a door to our inner room is a stage of growth. The seeming gap between uniting personal and positional power is no longer the real issue. Rather, we understand through practice that the real gap lies between a closed, limited ego-conscious perception and an expanded conscious awakening. This closed, limited ego-consciousness traps us in the personal suffering of our shadow powers. Once we commit to understanding, letting go, realizing and self-cultivation, the dark shadow powers of the Magician, or of any of the other three archetypes, will no longer dominate and control our lives. The Buddha, the Awakened One, put it to us very clearly. He said, "Day and night the person who is awake shines in the radiance of the spirit. Be quiet. Do your work with mastery. Like the moon, come out from behind the clouds! Shine." [28]

THE ARTIST
THE POWER OF COMPASSION

THE ARTIST AS INNOVATOR

One of our most impressive contemporary world leaders of Compassion is the Dalai Lama.[1] Most of us know something of the Dalai Lama's life from news accounts and the two movies that depicted his early life and escape from Tibet when the Chinese invaded and took over the country. His tireless travels around the world, his teaching of Tibetan Buddhism and his continuing commitment to find a peaceful solution to the cultural destruction of Tibet by the Chinese earned him the Nobel Peace Prize in 1989.

Whether in private conversation or in public appearances, the Dalai Lama exhibits a gentle humor, a grace of expression in both his body and speech, and a relaxed and humble manner when interacting with people. Engaged in conversation, the Dalai Lama gives his total attention to the conversation. He approaches all with a warm smile and takes both hands of everyone he greets in welcome, paying great attention to others' personal lives. He is not hurried or impatient and does not find questions intrusive. He is authentic and humble, treating everyone as his equal. The Dalai Lama's name is Tenzin Gyatso. It means "Ocean of Compassion." Those who meet him describe just such a feeling washing over them when in the Dalai Lama's presence.

The purpose of the Dalai Lama is to be the spiritual and temporal leader of the Tibetan people. But his core expression in these two roles is to be the embodiment of Compassion. His official title is "The Compassionate Holder of the White Lotus." Compassion, for this man, is very simple. He has said many times in public, "My religion is kindness." Care and concern for others is at the heart of the leadership power of Compassion that he embodies. He is not innately compassionate as a spiritual leader. Rather, he has made the commitment to live from Compassion. The Dalai Lama once said, "I don't know why people like me so much. It must be because I try to be compassionate, to have . . . the aspiration of compassion."

None of us is always loving and compassionate, spontaneous and joyful, or heartful and empathic. Our fear and guilt tend to cover these qualities. Often, we become self-protective and self-defensive. Our fear of being hurt, and of being too vulnerable in the presence of others, prevents us from acting with kindness and compassion. Yet most of us desire to overcome our fear and resistance, and aspire to open our hearts in compassion, both to ourselves and others. In Pali, the ancient language that Gautama Buddha spoke, the word for "compassion" literally meant "the trembling or the quivering of the heart."[2] To feel with our hearts is the work of cultivating compassion.

The Power of the Artist

Compassion is the power of the Artist.[3] The Artist archetype is also known as the Lover,[4] because it embodies characteristics of feeling, sensuality and passion. These characteristics are very different in tone and style from the other three powers.[5] In the most explicit sense, the Artist energy represents the "soft" side of leadership.[6] Or to put it another way, *the Artist is engaged in doing the work of the heart.* To understand this power in leadership is to first understand the word *compassion.* Compassion literally means having passion *with* someone or something. The Latin *com-* means "with," and *passion* comes from *passur* or *pati*, "to suffer." To suffer in this sense means to "tremble with the heart." In other words, to feel deeply about the conditions of people, or to feel deeply about some work or activity, so that the passion of that feeling drives one to act with creativity and spontaneity.

The Artist has sympathy—he suffers *with* people and situations. In his sympathy, the passionate Artist tries to interpret deeply felt experiences through some creative medium of expression. Our personal experience of the Artist energy occurs when the power of passion takes hold of us. In this highly energized state, we become compelled, even obsessed, to create or make something happen. Immersed in this energy, we "suffer" or hold artistic tendencies, expressing excitement, ardor, zeal, devotion, affection and love for people, events and things. We may seem a bit "on fire," a little strange or weird, probably intense; but, generally, positive and perhaps even funny.

This intense quality of artistry, of compassionate "fire," gives the leader warmth and approachability. By contrast, the Artist's opposite, the Warrior, may appear cold, calculating and separate. The Warrior needs his sharp blade at the ready to attack or defend, whereas the Artist lovingly splashes paint on a huge canvas. This fire of Compassion produces spontaneity, humor, creativity, innovation, heartfulness and joyful activity. Compassion provides a context of values that emerges from some spiritual center in the Artist leader.

Compassion acts as an integrator of the other three archetypes. The Artist's *enthusiasm* (meaning to be "god-filled") infuses the Warrior with ardor, intensifies the Sovereign's relationship with his followers, and includes the concerns of others, so that the intuitions and insights of the Magician truly serve the realm with a larger purpose and vision.

The power of Compassion tends to be the least manifested of the Four Powers in most leaders. Generally, men have greater difficulty accessing this power than women do. The Artist archetype is more right-brain oriented. The Artist focuses on emotional feelings, whereas the Warrior brings forth the quality of physical sensations. The Sovereign is mental, and the Magician more intuitive. Because of its strong emotional quality, the Artist power demands a release of control, an emphasis on feelings, an openness and vulnerability to people and situations. The Artist power fosters creativity and spontaneity and, as such, needs to access the intensity of the Warrior, the transforming power of the Magician, and the ambition and vision of the Sovereign to create true innovation. The spiritual and heartful aspects of the Artist create the context for values, purpose and meaning in the enterprise, organization or community. Leaders who strongly inspire others through this spiritual context combine the affirmation of blessing from the Sovereign with the empathy and joy of the Artist. Compassion is the power source that generates values and purpose, emerging from the spiritual center of the leader.

Compassion is the key to mature leadership development. In our culture, it is the most difficult archetype to bring out and develop. However, if a leader truly commits to developing the characteristics—spontaneity, creativity, empathy, heartfulness, joyfulness and spirituality—the impact it will have on people and the "bottom line" is immeasurable. Or to put it another way, the artistry of this power is very measurable in the quality and performance of the organization and in its constant ability to change and transform itself. Because the power of Compassion does not readily manifest itself in leadership, it is instructive to see some of these Artist leaders at work. How these leaders embody the Artist archetype can give us insight as to how we each can open the qualities of Compassion in ourselves.

Compassionate Leaders

The truly great leaders of history who have left an emotional mark on the world embody this quality of compassion and demonstrate the empathy and creativity of the Artist. Lao-tzu, Confucius, Moses, Buddha, Jesus, Muhammad, Socrates and many other spiritual leaders dedicated their lives to the same truth: Compassion and love for others and ourselves is the greatest purpose and value we can hold in life. A leader's commitment to this fundamental principle challenges the daily experience of living. The great Sufi teacher and ecstatic poet Rumi describes the experience of those who have embraced the Artist archetype and submerged themselves in the energy of its powerful love:

> Love opens my chest, and thought returns to its confines.
> Patience and rational considerations leave. Only passion stays, whimpering and feverish.
> Some men fall down in the road like dregs thrown out. Then, totally reckless, the next morning they gallop out with new purposes.
> Love is the reality, and poetry is the drum that calls us to that.[7]

Like Rumi, leaders who have changed the course and direction of our world during this century left the safe and rational to embrace the actions of love. These leaders combine a commitment to open-hearted love for their enemies, with an abandonment of old forms of confrontation and violence, and use a style of poetic speaking that moves millions of people to action. To the modern public mind, what these leaders undertake seems irrational and reckless, and rooted in some other reality than our everyday experience.

Mahatma Gandhi, who in his simple but clear creativity marched to the Indian Ocean and said he would no longer buy salt from the British, ended the rule of an empire through the principles of nonviolence. Martin Luther King Jr., who inspired a nation to give up the last traces of slavery, enabled the equal status of African Americans by using the same nonviolent methods as Gandhi employed. Mother

Teresa, who felt the pain and suffering of the world, called us to serve and heal the poorest of the poor. Burmese Nobel Peace Laureate, Aung Ian Suu Kyi, who quietly sits in her home under house arrest, demonstrates force of character and a deep resolve to use compassion and nonviolent methods to stop the oppression of a military dictatorship. Vaclav Havel, president of the Czech Republic, poet and writer, in his speeches and writing expresses a more profound challenge to our democratic process. Mikhail Gorbachev, with uncommon vision and commitment, stopped the destructive forces of dictatorship and brought down the walls that separated the world for over fifty years, and today continues to promote peaceful change through his "State of the World" forums. The Dalai Lama tirelessly practices forgiveness of the Chinese, hoping to stop the destruction of the rich and unique Tibetan culture.

All these individuals' actions came from a personal, spiritual, empathic, creative, heartful and often spontaneous center in their own lives. Beyond these world-renowned names exist hundreds of thousands of women and men who have acted from this same compassionate center in themselves, changing for the better the prevailing circumstances. This same creativity, empathy, heartfulness and passion exist in many of today's current business leaders.

Fortune magazine featured a cover story on America's most admired companies. In the same magazine, Thomas Stewart wrote a companion piece, "Why Leadership Matters."[8] In it he describes CEOs like Welch of GE, Kelleher of Southwest Airlines, Grove of Intel, Gates of Microsoft and several others. He concludes the article by saying, "There's one more item on our list of Things Leaders Must Do, and it's just what your broker says Investors Must Not Do: fall in love. There are CEOs who slash and CEOs who fix and CEOs who safeguard and CEOs who build. The great ones do all these things too, but first of all they love. Passion, commitment, ferocity—the traits of lovers are in these leaders."[9]

Of particular interest was Stewart's description of Herb Kelleher, CEO of Southwest Airlines. In this smart and savvy businessman dwells the soul of the Artist. His spontaneity is expressed in dressing up like a chicken, loading baggage with the handlers or jumping on one of his planes and serving peanuts to customers. His joyfulness comes out in his kissing and hugging people; his heartfulness comes out in the company's ticker symbol, LUV; but his true Artist flair manifests itself most clearly in the company's mission of making flying fast, cheap and *fun*. When asked about how he likes his job as CEO, Kelleher says, "I love it, I love it—I sure as heck do."

Kelleher's love, fun and sheer joy impact Southwest's business. In *Fortune*'s list of the one hundred best companies to work for, Southwest Airlines ranked number one in 1998. As Southwest spreads out in air routes across the country, the amount of traffic they can create goes up dramatically, as do the profits. Kelleher attributes both to the employees. Most airlines take an hour to turn around a plane. Southwest takes twenty minutes. Kelleher says, "We pay just as good wages and benefits as other airlines, but our costs are lower because our productivity is higher, which is achieved through dedicated energy of our people. It's sheer willpower—no mechanical tricks."[10] Kelleher is an Artist primarily, not a Magician. He *feels* how people feel about themselves and their experience flying, and this means he feels how both his employees and the customers feel. He constantly stays tuned in to people's wants and needs. It is not something intellectual that he knows or analyzes; it comes from his heart, contained within his joy of having fun and doing his best for others. All the great teachers cited above spoke one truth: Love for oneself and others is the great law. It made Kelleher's company the number-one place to work in America.

Learning to understand this power of love, passion and commitment is one of the great mysteries of leadership. Pierre Teilhard de Chardin, Jesuit priest, paleontologist and philosopher, said, "The conclusion is always the same: love is the most powerful and still the most unknown energy of the world."[11]

Spiritual Leadership

A strong example of the Artist leader who embodies these Compassion characteristics of spontaneity, humor, creativity, innovation, heartfulness and joyfulness is a man by the name of Cliff. For thirty-five years Cliff has been a Presbyterian minister, a workshop leader and a worldwide inspirational speaker.

Cliff is an interesting example of the Artist archetype because his Artist powers fueled his Warrior to build organizations, inspired his Sovereign to empower others, and deepened the insights of his Magician to embrace a worldwide vision of emotional and spiritual healing. But even with the clear dominance of the Artist archetype driving his life, many of the shadow characteristics of the Four Powers blew as a terrible, dark storm through his life, battering him mercilessly. Through difficult self-confrontation he survived his shadow obsessions, deepened his capacity to integrate his ego-consciousness, and cultivated and matured his natural gifts as both a man and as a leader.

When a person naturally and strongly expresses the characteristics of Compassion, he draws people to him like moths to a flame. Cliff was just such a "flame" to the "moths" of his audience. He was a gifted speaker and storyteller; he could entertain, tell jokes, point out the humor in situations and make people feel comfortable and joyful. He was a poet and writer, and could sing and chant with great grace and beauty. He could speak to thousands of people, lead the prayer on the floor of the U.S. Senate, feel comfortable in the home of the president of the United States, travel the world talking to peasants and kings with equal caring and humility, and sit for hours playing with children. But he did not use his talents to make people view him as exclusive. He expressed his gifts in such a way that, rather than intimidating people, his gifts inspired people to see themselves in a positive way. His artistry encouraged others to participate and express their own talents. His Compassion challenged people to break free of their self-imposed limitations so as to be better people and do more with their lives.

Cliff was a leader who naturally embodied the power of Compassion, to the extent that the various characteristics of this quality became the primary focus of his life and work. Cliff highlights the six characteristics, which, although lacking in many leaders, are essential to the individual's providing "spiritual" leadership to an organization or community. These six characteristics of Compassion are: empathy, spontaneity, creativity, joyfulness, heartfulness and spirituality.

Empathy

Empathy comes from the Greek *em-* and *pathein,* and literally means "to feel or suffer in." The Greek *empatheia* means "passion with affectionate feeling." *Empathy, then, is the opening up of one's feelings in order to be receptive to the emotional state of another person.*

In this receptive state, one feels what the other is feeling. When empathy is strong, we have the capacity not only to understand what another is feeling or thinking, but also to experience the very same sensations that the other person is having. If the person we focus on is emotionally upset, we can feel that same upset feeling in ourselves. If the other person's stomach is hurting, a highly sensitive person feels that the individual is in some physical distress. At an even deeper level of empathy, an individual can completely identify with a person and actually assume the physical pain or spontaneously replicate in his own body the same physical condition as the person who is suffering. People who replicate in themselves the same emotional and physical sensations of another are known as *empaths.*

The extreme example of the empath is the individual who exhibits the *stigmata.*[12] The stigmata replicates in a person the physical wounds Jesus suffered during his crucifixion. Bleeding will occur at the forehead where the crown of thorns pierced Jesus' skin, at the hands and feet where he was nailed to the cross, and just below the ribs where he was pierced by the spear. During Easter, these wounds will often appear spontaneously among individuals who are deeply devoted to Jesus and deeply identify with his suffering. St. Francis of

Assisi is the first documented case of the stigmata in the West. From St. Francis through the twentieth century, 330 documented cases have occurred. Twenty stigmatics are still alive today. Stigmatics are not just Christian believers. They come from all beliefs and walks of life.

One well-documented stigmatic was Padre Pio.[13] Padre Pio was a Catholic priest who bore the wounds of Jesus on his hands, feet and side for fifty years. Padre Pio first manifested the bleeding in September 1918. He continued bleeding daily until several days before he died in 1968, when all evidence of the wounds disappeared. For fifty years he was photographed, medically observed and sought out by pilgrims for blessing and healing. The research done on stigmatic empaths seems to indicate that these individuals so deeply identify with Jesus' suffering that they actually feel the same pain Jesus felt, and through the power of their minds, they manifest the same physical symptoms.

A VP who reported to a CEO offers a contemporary and more mundane application of empathic abilities. This VP was very sensitive and empathic, while the CEO was completely left-brained thinking and nonfeeling. The VP had observed over the years that he possessed a strange and, at times, difficult ability: He could enter a room to attend a meeting and immediately "feel" the condition of each person in the room. With some, he could feel their fear; others, their tiredness; and still others, their intensity or resistance. When the CEO would ask questions, criticize, judge or exhort individuals, the VP would feel each person's reactions to what the CEO was saying or doing. For many years the VP had confused what he was picking up from others as being his own feelings. After several years of therapy, he learned to recognize the difference between the two and began to use this "gift" in his professional dealings.

One way to use his gift of empathy was to support the CEO, who was a very rational, analytical, nonfeeling person. After one senior staff meeting, the VP had a one-on-one talk with the CEO. The VP asked the CEO if he had picked up on the reaction that two of the other executives in the meetings had to one of the CEO's proposals.

The CEO had no idea what the VP was talking about. When the VP explained the other executives' reactions and how negatively they felt about what he wanted them to do (but of course didn't admit to the CEO), the CEO was amazed by the observations and insights the VP was giving him. When the CEO inquired how the VP knew all this, the VP told him about his empathic abilities and how he had learned to trust and rely on them over the years.

The CEO was so impressed by the VP's insights, and the implications they held for both his own leadership and the good of the company, that he asked the VP to be his "feeling" eyes at many meetings. When they attended meetings together, the VP would debrief the CEO after the meeting as to what he picked up from the people who had attended. In this way, the CEO gained a deeper understanding of what transpired during the meeting than the mere content of the discussion provided. Interestingly, over time the CEO began to pick up some of the feeling clues that the VP was naturally teaching him to recognize when he gave the CEO his impressions. This CEO teaches us that "nonfeeling" leaders who are willing to try and who have the right intention can begin to learn to open their feelings and, thereby, perceive other people's feeling states. Empathy is a leader's radar screen for registering what transpires in both the individual's experience and the organizational environment.

Spontaneity

The word *spontaneity* comes from the Latin *sponte*, meaning "of one's free will." To be spontaneous is to act from a natural feeling that is not premeditated, compulsive or contrived. Spontaneous artistic Compassion is the capacity not to judge, but to see clearly and act directly. This clear seeing creates the honesty and courage necessary to express ourselves with unexpected and joyous abandon.

When spontaneity is present in a leader, vitality and energy exist among his followers, enabling them to accomplish things they couldn't do on their own. Consider the way a project leader energized her team. The team was meeting at a downtown hotel for a planning meeting. A fundamental problem with their product had stymied them for a couple of hours. They seemed unable to come up with a consensus on the right specifications. The team's arguing and defensiveness with each other was destroying the group's ability to function. The project leader acted spontaneously. She brought the team out of the hotel and onto the downtown streets. When they reached a busy intersection with a lot of sidewalk traffic, she told the team to start asking people on the street how to solve the problem that had created the impasse. The team members were reluctant and uncomfortable at first, but they saw their team leader jump in, asking people questions, bringing two or three people together on the street to discuss the problem together, and then moving on to other people. The energy and enthusiasm of the leader encouraged the whole team to begin interacting with people. They spread out and went from talking to people on the street to entering businesses, where they received remarkably sympathetic and interesting responses. After two hours, they came back to the hotel conference room excited, energized and full of ideas.

The comments they received from people they interviewed were not important. The act of spontaneously asking questions and explaining the problem over and over in different ways freed their "stuck" thinking. Within another hour, they had not only figured out their problem, but also created a new and original set of specs for the kind of product they actually should have been building all along. People loved this leader, and throughout the large Fortune 50 company where she worked, people knew her as the leader with whom everyone wanted to create new products.

Spontaneity and creativity are interconnected. When our behavior is not contrived, we can be original; we can be our natural selves. In this natural state we do not think and then act. We simply act.[14] Most artists don't like to comment on the meaning of their work. Similarly the project leader wasn't interested in talking about the techniques she used to create successful teams. She said that the ideas that come to her to create a product with one team don't work with the next team. The fun was to make it up as she went along. To figure out the work, to explain it, was to lose its original spontaneity.

To put this in another context, for a person to view a work of art, without the meaning of it spelled out for him in advance, permits that person to spontaneously encounter it. The work can surprise or open him, or make him aware of different perceptions. Spontaneity is being in the moment, being fully present with the experience as it is happening. Spontaneity carries with it freshness, delight, wonder and a sense of *flow*[15] and creativity. When spontaneous creativity emerges from a person or group, more energy is present and available for everyone. Artistic performances of spontaneous originality generate great amounts of energy both for the performers as well as the audience.

In a work setting like the project team in the last example, spontaneity speeds the process, accomplishes things more quickly and creates a more efficient operation. For individuals or teams who work with creative spontaneity, mistakes become learning experiments that those individuals or teams digest and integrate into the creative process. Talking with all the people on the downtown streets and in the businesses for two hours could have been a waste of time. Rather, it was fun, engaging and stimulating, as well as far more productive in positive results than struggling to analyze the problem over and over again. The leader who embodies this quality of spontaneity within the Artist power genuinely cares for his people and cares about the work. That caring engenders significant results.

As described earlier, the Zen tradition calls spontaneity the *beginner's mind.*[16] Leaders who encourage people to think out of the box, who are not afraid of being diverted from the original intent, and who do not control the focus and direction of a conversation have beginner's mind. Those who encourage diversity and multidimensional thinking, who relax and "go with the flow" with the groups they lead have this fresh perspective. These leaders will see old issues in new ways, be surprised and delighted by different viewpoints, and have a wellspring of energy to meet challenges and problems as true learning experiences. Some of the best creative technical people in organizations have beginner's mind. They treat each encounter or meeting as though it were their first. They come to conversations with an open mind and don't assume anything. They look for the simplest and most elegant answer or solution. When they find it, they become as delighted as children. In addition, their insights are penetrating, profound and original.

Thomas Edison had beginner's mind. Electricity had been around for a long time. It was known that it could produce light. The problem was that every material that inventors had used to try to produce the light burned up. All these other attempts to produce light focused on reducing resistance to the electricity. Rather than following the same logic, Edison went in the opposite direction. He began to experiment with materials that would increase resistance and finally found a carbonized element as the means of conducting electricity into light. Fresh eyes, fresh thinking, trusting intuitions, playing with a problem because it is fun to explore and discover—these are key to being spontaneous.

Creativity

Creativity comes from the Sanskrit *kar*, meaning "to make, to originate, to bring into existence." Creativity is the act of accomplishing, producing and bringing into being—the act of pure inventiveness.[17] Creativity is about making up the world as we go along. Creativity is about exploring as an end in itself, being interested in the unassuming, paying attention to the strange and the weird, not intending to produce any particular result, but delighting in the process of exploration.[18]

Creativity is about innovation.[19] The word *innovation* comes from the Latin *innovare*, meaning "to renew, to alter, to make new." Innovation is about changing the established order of things. An innovator is one who experiments and introduces the truly novel. Constant innovation lies at the heart of the quality movement. The quality movement has most effectively worked and sustained itself as more than a fad only when the leaders involved were interested in more than just the bottom line of the process. Leaders who encourage quality improvement are creative and they like innovation. They like learning and they like when things change and become different. They like the creative challenge of the problem and the fun of solving it.

This is what Peter Senge describes as the core of the "learning organization" in his book *The Fifth Discipline.* "In a learning organization, leaders are designers, stewards and teachers."[20] Senge makes an interesting point about leaders as designers. Asking senior managers to describe their roles as leaders, he told them to imagine that their organization was a ship. If the organization were a ship, he asked, what role did they have? He received the following answers: captain, navigator, helmsman—all controlling and directing roles. Others said the engineer for energy and the social director for communication. The neglected role was designer of the ship. Designers are the Artists, the creators of organizations. Their primary function, according to Senge, is integration. Integration is the artistic vision of the whole system, the creativity of fitting things together, of creating new containers. Senge calls this activity the creative "quiet design work of leadership."[21]

To be creative is the act of pursuing the novel, the paradoxical, the mysterious. To be creative is to not know that you are creative. One exists outside of time and it becomes engrossed and obsessed when in the activity of creation. Creativity is not singular or individual. It may start with one person, but it becomes geometrically and increasingly dynamic when it includes more people in the process.

To live at the center of creativity is the consummate gift and skill of the leader. The French philosopher Henri Bergson said, "I believe I experience creativity at every moment of my life." The challenge of the Artist power is to live and demonstrate this quality from moment to moment.

Business is a "game" in which the rules are constantly changing, constantly challenging leaders to be creative, in order both to survive and design the "world" in which these leaders want to live and work. Creativity is discovering new possibilities among growing complexities and uncertainties. Creativity amazes us because it mirrors so fully the nature of existence. However, most of what goes on in organizations feels like a test to us, something we have to "get through" and finish: make the quarter's numbers, move the next product out the door, do the next deal, solve the latest HR crisis. When the focus is always on the dilemmas, we put down our heads and just try to "plow through" our work and our lives. To work successfully, creativity needs messy experimentation, positive tension and the vision that lifts our heads above the mundane. Positive tension fuels the mission of creativity. Without it, vision and experimentation will not yield the desired outcomes.

Consider, for example, the CEO of an Internet-related start-up company who challenged his team to create a new product category. Following the ideas of Jeffrey Moore in *Crossing the Chasm*,[22] this team struggled to convince early retail adopters to try the product, as well as to convince enough major telcos and computer companies to act as original equipment manufactures (OEMs) for this product. The product itself was an innovative and creative solution enabling small businesses to use the Internet, but the start-up was unable to gain the momentum to create a successful business. During the many months of helping his team try alternative strategies, and facing discouraging sales results and pressure from his board, this leader came to recognize the problem. His design work lacked neither experimentation nor a strong, clear, compelling vision; but it did lack positive tension.

Robert Fritz, in his classic *The Path of Least Resistance: Principles for Creating What You Want to Create*, calls this *structural tension*.[23] Structural tension has two elements. The first element is current reality. This is what is actually happening right now. The second element is the result you want to create. This is what Fritz calls vision. The difference between current reality and vision creates structural tension. Structural tension demands resolution. We either change current reality to move closer to the vision, or we change the vision so that the modified vision corresponds more closely to current reality. Creative leaders consciously design, create and manage this tension.

Visualize the process of managing structural tension as the leader stretching a rubber band between his two hands. One hand is vision, the other is current reality. A leader designs the situation so that if the vision is stronger, it will, like the tension in the rubber band, pull the current reality toward it. If the leader creates too much tension by pulling the hand of vision too far from the hand of current reality, the tension can overstress the system, even destroy it. If, however, the leader keeps the two hands close together, little tension develops and the natural pull of the rubber band won't be available to produce change. Managing this change-producing tension is one of the most critical activities of creative leadership.

In the case of the CEO of the start-up, the vision he created didn't match current reality structures. The reality was that their product was ahead of the market by a couple of years because they designed it in a way that customers didn't need or want. After they recognized that their reality didn't match their vision, their first step was to redesign the strategy using the same product, but with a different vision deployment. In addition, they were running out of both time to market (other competitive products were appearing) and start-up capital. The CEO designed a very simple structural tension between their current reality and their vision. This current reality was a great product with too little sales, rapidly decreasing capital to run the business and a short period of time to establish themselves in the market in order to go public. The new vision was to get a "break-away" (a sudden and rapid explosion of sales) in both retail and OEM sales, and work current OEMs through a direct customer marketing program to create product recognition. The tension between the two was expressed in the CEO's constant mantra: "Work the sales [they had created a new marketing plan], increase revenue by 20 percent each month and watch budgets [manage costs daily]." This creative tension was not about creating a "cool" product, but rather, about creating a new market category. The difference between creating an innovative product and creating a market produced a great deal of tension that challenged the team to discover new and creative approaches.

Fritz speaks eloquently of the power of creativity. "Once you know yourself on that level, you begin to build the new structure of the creative orientation, in which reality is not a threat but a welcome experience and vision is not pie in the sky but the concrete expression of what most matters to you."[24] Leaders who enable us to achieve both creative vision and meaningful reality lead from true Compassion and appreciation for what is most important and worthwhile in our lives.

Joyfulness

The word *joy* comes from Latin, *gaudium*, meaning "pleasure, gladness and happiness." The Latin derivation *gaudia* also means "jewel." Joy, like a jewel, is multifaceted. Joy comes to us in varied and unexpected ways. Its inherent nature is one of sudden surprise. Joy, again like a jewel, shows many sides and arises as a result of both internal and external stimuli. Joy is both a physical sensation and an emotional feeling. We can weep in response to pain as well as joy. Joy is what causes us to tremble with sweet pleasure when we view a magnificent sunset, and to smile with deep satisfaction when we fondly recall a dear friend. In other words, joy arises in us as feelings of happiness, accompanied by great pleasure. When we experience joy, we feel contained, complete and whole in the moment.

When we experience joyfulness, we are satisfied with things as they are. Many things can stimulate joy. Joy can come from watching our child at play, our dogs romping in the park or a friend fulfilling a lifelong dream; joy also can come from completing a project with beautiful results—the sources of joy are infinite as we open to it. In *Finite and Infinite Games: A Vision of Life as Play and Possibility*, James Carse writes, "The joyfulness of infinite play, its laughter, lies in learning to start something we cannot finish. . . . We laugh not at what has surprisingly come to be impossible for others, but over what has surprisingly come to be possible with others."[25] Joy deepens our relationship with individuals, with our work and with our community. When we lose any of these, our capacity for joy diminishes. Leaders who embody the joyful aspect of the Artist's Compassion possess an energy that gives followers hope when challenges are great, when fear is overpowering and when the future seems dark and uncertain. As Carse suggests, joy creates possibility.[26]

Leaders who ignite the joyful aspect of the Artist energy in themselves and their followers make work into play. Herb Kelleher of Southwest Airlines has created a company that runs on "fun," while generating $3.8 billion in revenue and being rated the number-one company in the country by *Fortune* magazine. Albert Michelson was the first American to receive a Nobel Prize in physics. When he was very old, someone asked him why he continued to work with his team, figuring out new and different ways to measure the speed of light. Michelson replied that he did it because "it was so much fun." Joel Slutzky, chairman of Odetics, Inc., put it simply, "I think it's important for there to be an element of humor, laughter. It adds to the company. It's one more thing that makes you want to get up in the morning and go to work."[27]

Leaders who exhibit joyfulness work at mastering the following disciplines in their daily lives:

> They don't take themselves seriously as *the* leader. They publicly poke fun at their own foibles and mistakes. They are humble and grateful to be doing what they are doing.

> They practice centering, meditating, relaxing and turning off the analytical mind daily. They make it a priority to practice such techniques for at least an hour a day.

> They participate in more than just work, involving themselves in community affairs and challenging, exciting hobbies.

> Their relationship with their spouses and children are top priority.

> They exercise for pleasure, not to keep off weight. They garden, walk, practice yoga, ride bikes, swim, hike, pump iron—all for the fun of it.

> They don't do the same thing all the time, but vary their activities.

They don't overschedule themselves. They have open time during the day to do the unexpected and the spontaneous.

When leaders live joyfully, they appear centered, relaxed, approachable. But more important, they create an example for their followers to emulate. All the studies on peak performance in athletics and with work teams show that an atmosphere of fun and joy makes people more productive and creative, and helps them achieve results faster.

For instance, consider Ric, the COO of a 500-million-dollar-a-year technology research institute. Over the years, Ric built into his life this capacity for joyfulness. He built the first twenty years of his career on the powers of the Warrior and the Magician. Long hours, intense focus and magical skills produced results. But, ultimately, he could never make the changes in the organization that he knew would make it world-class and competitive in a rapidly changing global market. As an executive VP, he had a shot at the CEO position when the CEO and chairman retired. But he knew that another executive VP was better suited to the job. The other VP could be the company's "face to the world." Ric knew his job was to remain inside and help shape a creative organizational culture that would contribute significantly to the future technology needs of the world.

When Ric became COO, he was also actively involved in chairing local community programs and serving on nonprofit boards. He began the day at 4:30 A.M. with his daily practice of meditation, yoga, inspirational reading and aerobic exercise. He spent time with his wife and son every day, no matter what his schedule of evening meetings or travel demanded. Ric remains open to constant growth and change. He constantly solicits feedback, reads, seeks out people to coach him and attends development programs that will shift his perceptions and encourage him to change and grow. People like Ric because it is easy to be around him. People enjoy him because he is happy.

However, this was not true during the early days of his career. As a Warrior, he demanded a great deal, did not countenance failure of any kind, and angrily exploded and "dumped on" people. His own development work began to show him his shadow in action. Over time, as he slowly integrated his shadow material, he transformed his anger into genuine joy for his work, for people, for the possibility of what seemed improbable. Most improbable of all was seeing a conservative, analytical community of technical people become customer-responsive, entrepreneurial and excited about their collective vision.

When Ric took on his position as COO, he knew his number-one responsibility was to support the vision and direction of the CEO. As they grew into this partnering relationship, their mutual trust and respect became a model for the organization. Together, these two leaders developed the sharp focus necessary to create a vital organization, based on an openness to learning and on development. The work of change is the combined effort of these two leaders. Ric has his daily challenges and a packed schedule, and he tires like the rest of us. Yet, in the course of a couple of years, the CEO and he led the company to totally reorganize its business structure so that it would be customer-responsive, and he created a framework of values and practices focused on commitments, results and a more efficient decision-making process. As a result, their creations and accomplishments excite, inspire and surprise people. They are experiencing the elements that must cohere if joy and vitality are to enter the work lives of employees.

Heartfulness

Malcolm Forbes defined heartfulness in leaders when he said, "At the heart of any good business is a chief executive office with one." Sadly, many CEOs today lack the kind of "heart" referred to by Forbes. Heartfulness in people is not something that we can easily define. We know it when it is present in a person. And we *really* know it when it is absent. Heartfulness is something we directly experience when we are with a person. The following paragraphs describe some of the characteristics observed in heartful leaders.

Heartful leaders deeply appreciate the work they are doing and feel grateful that they can serve others by completing the task at hand. For them, work is an act of the heart that inspires and energizes them, not an act of "gutting out" something that tires and debilitates them. Horst Schultze, COO of Ritz-Carlton, says, "You are nothing unless it comes from your heart. Passion, caring, really looking to create excellence. If you perform functions only and go to work only to do processes, then you are effectively retired. And it scares me—most people I see, by age twenty-eight, are retired."[28]

Heartful leaders possess a great capacity for tenderness. They give comfort easily, and they are receptive and approachable. People feel comfortable and natural in their presence. Mary Kay Ash, founder of Mary Kay Cosmetics, is renowned for her support of women and encouragement of self-esteem in others. It is not the pink Cadillac that she gives to successful saleswomen that fosters the enthusiasm of her company; rather, it is the invisible message that she reads in each person that says to her: "Make me feel important!" Treating others with tenderness simply requires focusing on them—their needs, their value, their worth independent from their appearance—and acknowledging them for who they are, not just for what they do.

Heartful leaders' minds are very expansive and open, not judging or closed. They entertain many viewpoints, but exhibit a remarkable stillness of mind. Turmoil does not agitate them. Rather, they remain still and unruffled in the midst of turmoil. They take seriously the situations facing them, but they have a sense of humor and remain lighthearted when tackling difficult challenges.

Heartful leaders remain closer to the present moment. They are less preoccupied with other matters and are very present when they engage with people. They both acknowledge people and see into them, recognizing and perceiving what others often miss. For example, the Dalai Lama has a remarkable sense of being totally present with people. Other noted people also have this sense of just *being* in the moment. Heartful leaders affirm and accept others for who they are, not for what they do or do not do. This affirmation does not need to come in words. Heartful leaders acknowledge by paying total attention to the other person.

Heartful leaders respect the natural world. They spend time in nature. They don't walk, run or hike just for exercise, but to connect to the natural world, and allow nature to nourish them. They love beauty and find it exists most in nature. They perceive themselves as both part of nature and responsible to be its steward. They love and have natural affinity for animals, plants and children. Heartful leaders don't generally talk about business first. Their interests range from the blueness of the sky and the terrific lightning storm the night before to the conversation they had with their child.

Finally, heartful leaders possess consistently positive attitudes, and exhibit bright minds and happy outlooks without being Pollyannas. Their eyes are soft and clear. They hold one's gaze gently without intimidation. Heartful leaders engender in others a sense of peacefulness and a depth of understanding and insight. These leaders demonstrate an unconditional giving and helpfulness that express themselves through their service to others.

Consider Bev, the chairwoman of a large county, who runs a four thousand–employee organization, in addition to being an elected official. Bev graduated from law school during the 1960s with the goal of righting social injustice and became a community organizer. During the 1980s, she saw that she could create change in her local district by running for the state legislature. By knocking on every door in her district, listening to people and telling them how she saw their mutual needs and concerns, she was elected by an overwhelming margin. In the legislature, she championed social causes related to children, housing and the poor. Although she was at the more liberal end of the political spectrum, she was known for building consensus, respecting others' views and holding her principles with integrity, but not self-righteously.

Her step up to chairwoman of the municipality was a whole new challenge. She was no longer just a community organizer or a political advocate, but the leader of a huge bureaucratic organization.

Bev's gift to the organization was her heartfulness—her focusing on the present, appreciating people and encouraging government officials to produce real results on behalf of the citizens they served. To make practical her intentions to change the way county government responded to the citizenry, she initiated a "Results" program of benchmarks in every department of the county to bring about positive customer responsiveness. Bev is not a great orator, but when she speaks, people feel her honesty, her openness, her inclusion of them, her passion for the needs of people in the community. Her leadership moves and inspires people. Cynicism is rampant in a large bureaucratic structure that has seen politicians come and go. But slowly, she has learned to translate vision into results, to establish performance-based management, to develop initiatives that actually change the way things work in the municipality. Employees have come to believe that Bev is committed to what she says. Government officials with genuine heart and integrity, such as Bev, offer hope for the future of our country.

No one leader necessarily embodies all the characteristics of heartfulness. But when you are around heartful leaders for a while, you sense that many of these characteristics run like a thread of gold through their lives. We encounter leaders like this in all walks of life.

Princess Diana had the captivating quality of deep heartfulness, evident in her service to children and to those suffering. This quality seemed to grow as she exorcised her own inner fears and demons. Oprah Winfrey seems to maintain her audience loyalty by the genuineness of her caring and appreciation for people and causes. When Jesse Jackson speaks, whatever one's political views may be, one can see in his consistent caring for what he advocates an expansive leadership in the midst of great challenges. As earlier descriptions in this chapter indicated, the Dalai Lama embodies many of the characteristics of the heartful leader. He communicates with thousands of people with a stillness of spirit, a bright and expansive mind, and a delightful self-deprecating sense of humor.

Spirituality

Spirituality comes from the Latin *spiritus*, meaning "breath, courage, the soul, life," which in turn derives from *spirare*—"to blow, to breathe." Spirituality represents the intangible, higher aspirations that expand both thinking and feeling, intellect and emotion to more refined, even sublime, levels of experience. Spiritual leadership is the capacity to generate for followers the conditions in which they *together* (both leader and followers) experience a feeling of connection, rapport and mutual identification with some transcendent purpose. The leadership of spirituality helps communities and organizations "breathe" together. The simplest way this "breathing together" starts is by a leader helping people identify significant shared values. Understanding how to create shared values is the first step toward spiritual leadership.[29]

Values are always present and expressed when two or more people are together. We learn from each other what our values are by observing and experiencing the behaviors, attitudes, responses and practices that naturally arise during our interactions with people. Generally, we don't talk about our values until they are in some way jeopardized or threatened. When we don't feel safe, when we feel something important in our life has been violated, when we are not clear on how to do things with each other or when living and working are not good, we become very conscious of, and focus on, our values. Values set the boundaries, agreements, commitments and frameworks for being and working with others.

Within organizations, leaders and managers can focus on the kinds of values that they want individuals to follow, in order to shape the organization's efforts to perform in certain ways and achieve desired results. This value-focusing process lies at the heart of spiritual work. Spiritual leadership entails teaching and training individuals— through classes and one-on-one coaching and feedback sessions—the important behaviors, attitudes and ethics that will further the purpose, vision and mission of the company. Values, then, become the context, the atmosphere of people in various kinds of organizational structures. At a more subtle level, values are the intangible connections that make people feel safe, included and part of something larger than themselves.

Strategy development is one of the key areas where values can have strong impact. Often, leaders focus on the values component of strategy, that is, the "desired" list of values that the organization wants to ensure it does not violate—these are the "good things" that leaders want to preserve and not lose in the rush of organizational activity. This "desired list" of values includes such things as respect for the individual, honesty, good customer service and ethical behavior. Things we don't want to "get lost in the shuffle" include, for example, clear communication, good teamwork and collaborative problem solving.

When developing an overall strategy for an organization, these desired and preferred lists don't necessarily support the strategic challenges. The values leaders need to articulate, teach and use to solve problems need to be built into the organization in a conscious way. If a company's strategy diagnosis, as well as attitudinal and organizational surveys, indicate that leaders and staff communicate well, it is probably not necessary to isolate communication as an important value to discuss in the organization. However, if that company's strategy indicates the need for more innovation, visionary leadership and customer focus in order to be successful in the marketplace, then its leaders need to do more than put some words on a wall plaque. They must have a process to ensure that those needs are translated into implemented values.

Values that can change the spiritual and strategic climate of an organization need to fulfill the following criteria:

> Primary values should focus on the characteristics that are not fully present in the organization, and that the leaders need to build into every part of the organization in order to achieve the leader's and the organization's vision.

Leaders must behaviorally define values in order to effectively communicate them and use them to coach, manage and change behavior.

Each value must be practical enough to provide such things as:

- Boundaries for action—what we permit to happen/not happen
- Agreements for performance—how we will do things with each other
- Commitments to stretch and grow—promises of what we will/will not do
- Frameworks to create context—the conditions we set for being and working together

The value statement must be broad enough to be meaningful to every function within the organization.

One should be able to answer the following questions about the value statement affirmatively:

- Can leaders teach it practically, clearly and easily to all members of the organization?
- Can it solve problems?
- Can managers use it to coach and develop people?
- Can people outside the organization clearly understand the fundamentals of the company culture or strategy when they hear/read the value statement?

Within organizational and business culture, value statements fall into the following categories:

- Behaviors/work attitudes/ethics/performance
- Relationships/individual and group interactions
- Customers and vendors
- Standards and quality
- Financial perspective
- Development and growth of people and the organization

A single word or phrase used to communicate a value is generally not enough to achieve these criteria. Terms like *innovation, customer responsiveness* or *ethical behavior* do not adequately express the important behavior or attitude that leaders need to build into the organization. Take, for example, the value of customer responsiveness. To give it more behavioral focus and a boundary for action, one can state customer responsiveness as: "We will anticipate and meet customer needs beyond what the customer seems to want from us."

A manager in information services, for example, could use this value statement to teach his team what "anticipating and meeting customer needs beyond what the customer seems to want" means for employees of the organization. If one of his subordinates was not meeting customer needs, the manager could point to the value statement and coach the person based on the meaning of "anticipation" and "beyond." He can also coach based on a clarification of the boundaries inherent in "what the customer seems to want from us." The manager can teach and manage behaviors that not only fulfill the value proposition for his group, but also promote a spiritual climate that supports the overall company strategy.

In summary, values create both tangible and intangible links within an organization as follows:

Values represent the social agreements we make consciously or unconsciously within a human structure.

Values are the bonds that hold an organization together—they inspire and encourage.

Values set the boundaries that give us a context for safety and security in our interactions with other people.

Values are what we respect, appreciate and prize as being of primary importance to us.

Values determine our fundamental attitudes, behaviors and choices.

Values provide the basis for creating meaning and purpose in our individual and organizational lives.

If leaders learn to consciously incorporate the value process into their organizations, reaffirming, emphasizing and making it primary, then they build into their organizations a spiritual context, in which people will feel safe, open and willing to take risks. From its very inception, Hewlett-Packard focused on creating a conscious value structure of interaction, communication and collaborative decision making within all aspects of the organization. Every year, all managers in the company attend a program on "Managing the HP Way." Every year, old concepts and values are reinforced, while new, evolving ones are brought forward. This constant training and emphasis on building a culture of respect is a significant part of HP's decades of success and its leaders' ability to continually reinvent the organization.

As author Terry Cole-Whittaker says, "Spiritual values and ideals give us a space in which to grow. Each of us is a divine seed and when nurtured and empowered, we grow into ourselves."[30] Using values as the spiritual atmosphere in which we can "grow into ourselves" is the key work of the spiritual leader.

The following paragraphs outline some of the most significant characteristics of individuals who practice spiritual leadership.

Success and prosperity are balanced between work, self, family and community. There is never a perfect balance between all of them at any given moment. It is more like a pendulum that passes through all these. Emphasis moves from one to the other, as needed. When challenges exist at work, the emphasis moves in that direction. If opportunities arise for service in the community, the emphasis moves in that direction.

Spirituality is inclusive of all experience. Existence is viewed as a continuum on which everything is energy, from more refined to more base. Spirituality recognizes that this common energy imbues everything with life. For example, the notion that "work is love in action" represents the spiritual insight that what we do—our livelihood—is as much a part of our spiritual practice as prayer, meditation or a ritual service at a church or synagogue.

Wealth and material things do not constitute the goal of life. Rather, they serve to complement life, for they can come and go, depending on circumstances. Entrepreneurs often make and lose millions of dollars in the course of their careers. For these individuals, ultimately, it is not devotion to the material world, but devotion to an inner spiritual inspiration of challenge, risk taking and the opportunity to create that drives them.

Rather than forcing things to happen, spiritual leaders trust the timing of events. They have the intuition, knack, instinct to become the intersection of the manifested and unmanifested nature of events. They trust that they can sense what isn't apparent to others. If they are patient, they can be the midwives who bring the unseen into existence.

Spiritual leaders are proactive rather than reactive. They maintain a state of anticipation and readiness for the unexpected, and they move with it when it occurs. They have great timing and act with confidence as events are developing.

The spiritual leader does not force things to happen. There is time in their schedule to observe, reflect and contemplate situations and events that are unfolding. The genius of spiritual leadership is the ability to pace and move with events as they happen—making decisions and proposing strategies—rather than pushing and forcing change indiscriminately. When observed, these leaders often seem to be doing nothing. They are in accord with the Taoist principle of "doing nothing, everything gets done."[31]

James Dixon illustrates this principle well. He became president for San Francisco start-up Cellular One and is now executive VP for Nextel Communications. Jim has worked with a colleague and friend, Chris Thorsen, who uses the principles of the martial art aikido to help develop leaders and teams. In an interview, Jim described the effect of these Taoist principles of nonresistance on his leadership. He began to understand through the principles of aikido that "Inspired leadership has the quality of a master sitting in the center of the cyclone. . . . [It was] my willingness to not know what to do that allowed others to create what needed to be done. There is power in silence, and one question out of the silence can move something with very little effort. My direct reports followed my modeling by being willing to 'not know' when they found themselves in tough situations. This really gave people a chance to take more and more power in the organization and, ultimately, to produce extraordinary results."[32] Extraordinary results provide the cornerstone of spiritual leadership. Spiritual leadership isn't about making people feel good. But people do feel good, happy, positive and productive when the spiritual aspect of a leader is fully present.

In the light of the nature of spiritual qualities, the challenge for the leader is to develop an inner life that provides the ground from which to cultivate and grow all of one's powers and capabilities. Within the Artist, the power of Compassion is where inner life grows and develops. Lao-tzu, in the *Tao Te Ching* ("The Book of How Things Work"), one of the oldest records of humankind, gives a sage's advice to leaders. "The wise leader," he writes, "models spiritual behavior and lives in harmony with spiritual values. There is a way of knowing, higher than reason; there is a self, greater than egocentricity."[33] The integration and growth of the ego-centered self into this greater Self of knowing is the practical work of inner development.

The Artist power of Compassion is the most difficult leadership power to develop. And it is the power that brings to the leader and his followers the most human and satisfying experience. Growing into the characteristics of Compassion takes a lifetime for anyone, including a leader. The ground in which a leader consciously cultivates them is the darkness of his own shadow.

THE SHADOW ARTIST

Carl Jung described well the tension between the positive and negative aspects of the power of Compassion. He said, "Where love

rules, there is no will to power; and where power predominates, there
love is lacking. The one is the shadow of the other."[34] Compulsive/
obsessive love or suppressed/depressed love are the two shadow
reflections of the Artist. Robert Moore characterizes the Artist/Lover
shadow as the shadow manifestation that moves between the poles of
being addicted or being impotent.[35]

A leader caught up in his shadow Artist loses focus, balance and
intensity in decision making. Powerless to act, he has difficulty committing to a plan or strategy. Overcome by self-indulgence and self-
interest, the addicted shadow Artist leader will focus more on his own
activities—like golf or sailing—than on leading and guiding others.
The addictive behavior can also come out in spending too much
money and time on pet projects or continually beginning new projects
without ever completing unfinished ones.

The shadow material of the Artist manifests itself in other aspects
of Compassion as well. The Artist power of empathy can become the
shadow of sympathy and pity for others. The shadow Artist's attach-
ment to a special few supplants the authentic Artist's genuine caring
for the well-being of all employees or followers. Instead of a
true Artist fostering creativity and innovation, the shadow Artist is a
dilettante "playing at" innovation. Finally, the addictive quality of the
shadow Artist tends to be codependent, and manifests itself in the
lack of an adequate value structure, with little or no emotional or
sexual boundaries between him and others around him.

For instance, one pioneer of Silicon Valley, who drove his company
into the ground, was creative but also an alcoholic, incapable of differ-
entiating between his own feelings and those of people around him.
Followers loved and hated him, but in the end he was unable to make
the hard decisions that would keep the company successful. A deep
codependency that excused the alcoholic's behavior and rationalized
his "crazy ideas" as the brilliance of a genius developed between this
leader and his close followers. When he was drinking, he was playful
and fun to be around, and made the working environment different and
interesting. But the playful environment could just as easily turn

ugly and brutal when a dark rage would take hold of him and he would verbally tear apart people around him. This complicated shadow behavior so cast itself over the organization that employees could not see their own part in their self-destruction.

The shadow of addictive self-indulgence can show its face in many different ways with leaders. Some leaders, like the creative alcoholic in the example, are easy to spot. In line with Jung's comment that where there is all love, there is no focused power, this type of leadership-addiction produces great damage to an organization. Over the years one observes good-hearted, well-intentioned engineers try to start up companies, and fail because they couldn't stay focused and produce results in product development. They were people who had very creative ideas, innovative approaches to solving technical problems and the vision of how these innovations could change things in the market. Yet, for all their good artistry, their executions were impotent. Artistic power, without the self-discipline drawn from the Warrior's energy of Intention, cannot focus a leader's artistic Compassion in constructive ways. At a more subtle level is the seemingly "good" leader who can demonstrate caring but has a shadow addiction of self-indulgence that prevents him from accessing open-hearted Compassion.

Shadow Artist Characteristics

Looking more closely at the characteristics that make up the Artist/Lover shadow, Moore and Gillette note some of the following:[36]

Shadow Artists become caught up in the pleasures of their own feelings and sensations.

The shadow Artist is restless, always searching and looking, and in the search loses the sense of what he originally wanted.

The shadow Artist becomes overpowered by and caught up in the fantasy of his own inner world.

The shadow Artist can't tolerate limits and loses all sense of boundaries and proportion in his life.

If the shadow Artist begins to feel impotent and incapable of action, he can become unfeeling, bored, depressed and alienated from others.

Finally, the shadow Artist can confuse sexual drives for genuine feelings of caring and compassion.

In summary, the constellation of characteristics common to the activated shadow are: becoming lost in sensual pleasure, restlessness, fantasy, lack of personal boundaries, feelings of boredom, depression and confused sexual impulses. All of us can identify with some of these characteristics at different points in our lives. All good-hearted people become lost in their shadows at times and fail to recognize that the shadow is alive in one's daily life. Add to these characteristics a strong compulsiveness or a strong suppression of these feelings, and one finds oneself possessed and seemingly controlled by one's shadow.

Many of us have seen the tragedy of good-hearted, caring, compassionate people who begin to become locked into the shadow of being either compulsive/obsessive or suppressed/depressed about their capacity to love, create and help others. We may even have felt trapped by our own shadow in this way. When we become possessed by our shadow Artist for a period of time, this twisted form of energy turns back onto us in some destructive way.

The Arch Shadow: Adolf Hitler

Adolf Hitler provides one of the most fascinating examples of the Artist shadow manifesting itself in a deeply obsessive and destructive way. Most Westerners can conjure up images of Hitler, with his small brush mustache, standing stiff, speaking in a maniacal tone to thousands; or news clips of him surrounded by adoring German children or with his arm raised in salute as goose-stepping soldiers parade past him. The other images of Hitler are not of him at all, but rather, of concentration camps, where piles of eyeglasses fill whole rooms;

emaciated bodies stacked like cordwood lie in trenches; and living skeletons stare from behind barbed-wire fences. Many, many people have researched and studied what lay behind Hitler's madness, the inherent evil that tricked a sophisticated, cultured people into believing an enormous lie and conspiring to murder six million Jews, as well as another six million people from among the handicapped, the retarded, homosexuals, gypsies and political dissenters.

When facing questions of the shadow, it is useful to remember Hitler. To gain fresh insight about Hitler and understand how his shadow can exist in each of us, see James Hillman's *The Soul's Code: In Search of Character and Calling*. His chapter on "The Bad Seed"[37] uses Hitler as the case study for considering questions of evil in the world.

In Hitler's case, as in the case of many well-known psychopathic murderers such as Charles Manson, Gary Gilmore or Mary Bell, we witness the cultivation of some form of artistic interest. Many of the most evil people throughout history tapped into and accessed some aspects of the Artist archetype. Hitler, for example, painted and was constantly making architectural designs. Hitler was also noticeably humorless. He considered himself cold hearted. In his last speech to his commanders, he said, "Come what may, my heart remains ice-cold." This iciness manifests itself cruelly in the shadow Artist, in ways both large and small.

Hitler's enormous personal obsessions generated his drive to be loved and adored by thousands in a circuslike environment of big parades and huge coliseums. For example, Hitler had an obsession with wolves. At one point, he called himself "Herr Wolf." Three of his military headquarters had wolf names. He saw himself as having "wolf power." In the German tradition the wolf is among the death demons. He gave himself enemas, hated to be touched, consumed strange diets and was paranoid about personal cleanliness. Physical deformations constantly fascinated him, and he surrounded himself with deformed people who served and attended to him. These individuals included midgets, and people with one eye, one arm, speech defects, clubfeet, and the like. Six of the women with whom he had intimate relations killed, or attempted to kill, themselves. Ultimately, Hitler was a loner. He pushed himself further and further into his own inner world of strange and bizarre fantasy, and played it out in the world around him.

These strange obsessions, as well as a continual state of depression and fear, coexisted in Hitler and were so twisted together that he was incapable of responding with caring and concern for others. Relationships became means of fulfilling some unarticulated fear and compulsion to destroy. Hitler expresses every characteristic in the shadow Artist list. He lost himself in his own sensory pleasure; he was constantly restless and nervous; he was delusional; he had no personal boundaries (the world was he); he was always actively fighting off feelings of boredom; and he suffered from chronic depression that woke him up at night with nightmares about someone in his room, coming after him. Finally, confused sexual impulses resulted in his pleasure arising from defecating on women. Hitler was not your average shadow Artist. Yet, even in his extremes, he represents parts of all of us.

Hitler's story is instructive because it so clearly represents the twisting of love and compassion into their shadows of evil and destruction. Hillman's study suggests that the bad seed is in all of us. Hitlers are always present in a society, whether they be serial killers of women, or politicians who project their shadows on special groups or classes of people. Just as Compassion is one of the most powerful forces in the world, so, too, is its shadow—destruction. Both Compassion and destruction dwell in each of us.

The Need to Work with the Shadow Artist

Now more than ever, in this time so fraught with chaos, fear and uncertainty, we need leaders who will work with their shadow Artist. We need leaders who can integrate the demons of sexual and emotional compulsion and of restless and impotent depression into their lives. This is the work that we all must do with our shadow Artist.

In the most public of worldwide settings, Princess Diana embodied such integration, as she struggled with the shadows of low self-esteem and bulimia, and tried to find a focus for her Compassion by working with children and the underprivileged around the world. In the organizational setting, human resource leaders usually have huge hearts and care deeply for the people in their organizations. Yet, after years of effort, many of them fall into the emotional sinkhole of impotence, as they struggle to find a way to really make a difference.

Many of these HR executives go through the motions of creating programs, advocating change and pushing for the right training; nevertheless, they are restless and search for something more meaningful in their lives. We cannot lose these Artists to the shadows of their sense of failure. The strong Artists are few among our business and civic leaders. Many, of course, work in the arts, but we need Artist power to nurture the places where the majority of us live and work daily. We need these HR leaders to help give us the vision to build generative, creative environments for the twenty-first century. We need these Artists' creativity to guide and partner with their CEO and senior-management teams in order to develop leadership capabilities. We need these Artists within our organizations to show us the face of humanness and Compassion. The way any of us work with our shadow and the other qualities of the power of Compassion is the way to open our hearts.

CULTIVATING THE ARTIST WITHIN

To further open up the Artist within us is to access the spiritual roots of our lives as leaders. It is the Artist who longs for a better world for himself and others. He is the idealist, the dreamer, the one who gives us hope in difficult times. The Artist archetype activates the spirituality of the leader. The leader who is spiritual gives us the ability to touch the intangibles in our lives, gives us hope for something larger and better than what we can see, creates a climate that fosters interrelationships and community within the organization, and permits and encourages growth, creativity and joyfulness. The spiritual Artist knows how to help individuals "fall in love" with what they are doing. The Artist leader knows how to appreciate and include everyone's concerns and needs.

Cultivating the Power of Compassion

The modern Western tradition emphasizes the romantic and sentimental aspects of love. Love is something that is supposed to hit us like a bolt of lightning. One seeks love and knows love through physical and emotional attraction to a member of the opposite sex. In contrast, most ancient traditions viewed love relationships as something that one cultivated over time. One learned to love another. Malidoma Somé, an African scholar, says, "You in the West have the fire of love at the beginning of a relationship or marriage and then it cools off and dies away. In my tribe we have no love at the beginning, but we learn to grow it day-by-day. It takes us a whole lifetime together to build the fire of love with another."[38] To cultivate our spiritual leadership, we need to learn how to "build the fire of our love" each day.

The Theravadan Buddhist tradition describes the primary characteristics of love as the Four Sacred Homes.[39] These Four Sacred Homes are Loving Kindness, Deep Caring, Sympathetic Joy and Grounded Equanimity. Cultivating these "homes" is much like Malidoma's description of growing the fire of love over a lifetime. A home is a sanctuary, a safe place where we can be ourselves. Home is the place where our loved ones nurture us and where we nurture others. It is a place where we can practice loving and where we can cultivate a life dedicated to loving. The Four Sacred Homes describe how we cultivate the four primary qualities of love (Compassion) in our lives. Each of the Four Sacred Homes creates a context in which to deepen, grow and expand love in our lives. Cultivating these four characteristics of Compassion becomes the essential grounding that any leader can develop in order to open this power in his life.

The practice[40] that one commits to in the Four Sacred Homes is to mentally and emotionally hold the attitude and feeling of a *wish*—a wish of goodwill, a wish of concern and caring—for both oneself and others. A wish is the intent that something will happen, even when circumstances indicate it may not be possible. The purpose of this compassionate "wishing" is to open and soften the heart. The Four Sacred Homes "wishing" is a practice, and practice involves discipline. Discipline is an act of the will. Wishing is willing the mind, as well as the heart. Doing this "wishing" practice every day changes us slowly, opens our hearts and increases the capacity of our emotions and feelings.

Each of the Four Sacred Homes entails the practice of focusing the Compassion characteristic on five people. The first person is oneself. The second is a mentor or teacher, or someone who significantly influences one's life. The third is a close friend. The fourth is a neutral person—the mailman, a clerk at the checkout stand, etc. (A neutral person is someone toward whom one has neither positive nor negative feelings.) The fifth is a difficult person in one's life, even a person one considers an enemy. The practice of each of the Four Sacred Homes is to visualize each of the five people in turn, accompanied by repeating a phrase that holds the "wish" for them. One can do this practice while sitting, walking, jogging, driving—anywhere one has some quiet, private time.

Loving Kindness

The first Sacred Home in which we begin a practice of Compassion is Loving Kindness.[41] To have kindness is to be sympathetic, gentle and tenderhearted, and to treat others with affection. *Kindness* comes from the Middle English *kynde,* which means "affectionate, sympathetic, caring." In the Buddhist tradition the "habit" of being kind is the practice of friendship. *Friend* comes from the Old English *freon*— "to love." To be a friend to someone is to bring that person close to you, to be intimate, to open yourself to accept the person as he is, as opposed to the way you want him to be. In the Loving Kindness practice, you focus first on your most important friend—yourself.

The practice for Loving Kindness is to first hold a mental image of yourself, or feel warmth or tingling through the body, or an emotional feeling of peace and well-being—any positive visual or kinesthetic affirmation toward yourself—while repeating several phrases to yourself, and then doing the same for the four other individuals. You can choose phrases such as: "May I (you) be happy and peaceful just as I am (you are)." "May I (you) love myself (yourself) just as I am (you are)." "May I (you) be safe from all inner and outer harm." "May I (you) be healthy and strong." "May I (you) take care of myself (yourself) joyfully." You may make up other phrases to accompany the generating of positive physical sensations, emotions or images for yourself and the four others. After focusing on yourself, repeat the choice of image, feeling or positive regard for each of the other four people—mentor, friend, neutral person and "enemy," or difficult person. Continue doing the Loving Kindness practice for a period of days or weeks before going onto the next "home" in the Four Sacred Homes.

The focusing of affirmative visual images, warm physical sensations and positive feelings upon yourself and the other four people, as well as the use of the mental phrases, serves to strengthen your concentration. This practice of intentionally and consciously focusing your feelings and thoughts on yourself and others is like building a fire. Friendship grows as you extend yourself with positive intent. Each time you focus on yourself and these four individuals, you learn how to gain entrance to your feelings. After a little practice, you need only recall yourself or one of the other individuals, and the Loving Kindness will immediately return and grow into a fire—a warm feeling of caring and concern.

All people, even one's enemy, can be one's friend through Compassion. As leaders, we must be careful to teach our followers, as well as ourselves, to learn the deeper meaning of friendship, to be a friend to everyone, even when we may not like the behaviors or personality characteristics of an individual. For this reason, the Loving Kindness step in the practice particularly entails focusing on both a neutral person and a difficult person. By using the phrases and positive intention, one reduces the negative reaction toward the difficult person by contrasting it to the nonreaction when focusing on the neutral person. Directing our positive intentions and feelings of goodwill, concern and caring back and forth between the difficult and neutral person permits us, over time, to shift our perception away from the difficult person as, "enemy," and reduce the negative "charge" toward him.

Deep Caring

The second Sacred Home is Deep Caring. The word *care* comes from the Old English *caru*, which means "sorrow, anxiety and lament." Care also implies close attention, watchfulness and protection. Deep Caring involves confronting the pain and suffering of ourselves and others.

Physical and emotional pain are difficult for most of us to handle. We tend to avoid pain, suppress it or divert ourselves from it in some way. Many executives constantly work so as to avoid facing their own pain. Not being in contact with their own pain, they can't see the pain in others. Suffering indicates the pain we are resisting in our lives. Many leaders agonize over downsizing decisions because of the people who will lose their jobs. They genuinely suffer when considering the consequences for both the workers and their families.

Deep Caring shows us that instead of avoiding pain, we need to fully experience it and move through it—both to understand it and to release it. Pain plus resistance equals suffering. As we resist the pain (try to get rid of it in some way) we remain stuck in it. To be open to the pain, to explore it mentally and emotionally but not resist it, is to watch it naturally change into something else.

Pain can be a door to growth. Suffering puts a person in the role of victim. Suffering doesn't permit one to see that a choice exists in a situation. Working with pain develops the strength and courage one needs to see that choice does exist—one need only claim it. This courage to choose in the face of difficulty is a *resource* state, whereas suffering is a *victim* state.

When in a resource state, one experiences the awareness, dedication and determination necessary to be present in life no matter how painful the conditions. In this state, one's heart is wide open and naturally connects with others. When in a victim state, one experiences limitation, weakness, uncertainty, doubt and the inability to act. In this state, one's heart closes tight, one can be cruel to others and one's actions separate one from others.

The Deep Caring practice involves the same method of visually and kinesthetically concentrating on oneself and the four other people, as with Loving Kindness, but now one repeats a new set of phrases: "May I (you) be free of suffering and its causes." "I care for myself (you)." "I care about my pain (your pain)." Other creative phrases that affirm one's deep caring for oneself and others are just as effective. Again, practice this "home" for several days or weeks before going to the next Sacred Home.

Sympathetic Joy

The third Sacred Home is Sympathetic Joy. Sympathetic Joy is the act of taking delight in other people's success. It means one does not feel threatened or diminished because of what others are able to do. Sympathetic Joy enables one to envision Compassion as one's connection to others, and, in turn, gives one integrity and willingness to act from that vision. To be glad for others is to affirm the delight and goodness of one's own life. Sympathetic Joy means realizing that other people's happiness can potentially increase one's own. At the heart of Sympathetic Joy is gratitude. Gratitude is the deep appreciation for the people we know and the situations in which we find ourselves.

For instance, a GM spent some time every day at work walking around to extend his appreciation to people for their work, their commitments and their willingness to contribute to the organization's success. He did this by asking people about their accomplishments, their learning, their problem solving, their assisting customers and their support of their teams or work groups. He was low-key, but very genuine, in his expression of praise, congratulations and appreciation. Through his daily practice of gratitude, he created a climate of appreciation that others found easy to emulate and natural to repeat among themselves.

When a leader responds with sympathy, appreciation and delight to other people's success, like the GM, he brings people together and creates a lighter, more open climate, conducive to interaction and communication. When a leader exhibits joy, gratitude and appreciation consistently, regardless of the prevailing business challenges or circumstances, he naturally cultivates a community of mutual support in his organization. Interaction between people becomes more open and candid, and communication is able to operate in a climate of trust.

Leaders want the interactions and communication in their organizations to encourage people to be themselves (be vulnerable) and to take risks (try things out in ways they never have before). Leaders and followers both want relationships without hurt, domination and abuse. We all want to be among people with whom we feel safe to discuss issues and test ideas, without having to monitor the way we express ourselves. Honesty may create more trust in others, who, in turn, will risk opening up and expressing honesty. We've all been in groups with defensive and cautious people. One joke or candid remark is usually all other people need to hear to join in the interaction. We are all looking for the opportunity to experience relaxed and free-flowing communication. The more we model taking risks, the more others become willing to do the same. The extent to which leaders are open within a group determines the level of everyone's risk taking. The choices the leader makes create the level of trust that he and others are willing to experience.

Trust and risk taking reveal intimacy, feelings, instincts and intuitions. A deep level of trust and ease in any interaction moves one from control to flow, from predictability to spontaneity. It is this flow and spontaneity in one's interactions that produce creativity, joy and the ability to fully be oneself with others. One individual's willingness to choose to be open with another person or group of people widens the terrain of interaction, encouraging others to join in and become more open themselves. Practicing joy that affirms and supports others' success is the choice that changes the "spiritual" climate and permits long-term growth and continuous change in any organization.

The practice of Sympathetic Joy is like that of the previous two. Focus on yourself and then on the four other categories of people. While focusing, repeat the phrases "I feel joy for my (your) successes." "May I (you) feel joyful." "An ease and a flow move through everything I (you) do." Remember to start with Loving Kindness and Deep Caring phrases for a short while at the beginning of the practice, to deepen concentration and create a feeling of well-being, and then spend the rest of the time on the practice with Sympathetic Joy, doing it for several days or weeks before beginning the next Sacred Home.

Grounded Equanimity

The fourth and final Sacred Home is Grounded Equanimity. *Equanimity* comes from the Latin *æquanimitas,* which means "evenness of mind," or a composed, balanced mind. In this sense, equanimity is balanced calm. *Ground* comes from the Old English *grund* and means "something that serves as a base of support." To be grounded is to be in touch with the reality of a situation through physical sensations or to grasp the implications of the situation through understanding or knowledge. Grounded Equanimity is accepting situations and people as they actually are, rather than as what one wants them to be. Equanimity is a tricky concept because it can lead to indifference and denial. One can appear to be very calm and to accept a situation, when, in reality, one is simply not permitting oneself to experience or "feel" it.

For the calm acceptance of Equanimity to work in one's life, one must be grounded in empathy and concern. This entails personally understanding and feeling the impact of the situation. One may feel the sorrow, the pain or even the joy of a situation but recognize that one can do little about it. Leadership in the midst of situations over which one has little or no control requires that one not be emotionally expressive and that one not act dramatically just for the sake of acting. Leadership in these "impossible" situations must demonstrate calm, balance, detached and unemotional concern, and attentiveness to one's intuition and instinct as the place from which to act or respond. This type of leadership stems from Grounded Equanimity. The secret to achieving Grounded Equanimity is to have an expansive, clear, still mind. This permits one to connect to what is occurring without being ensnared by habitual reactions such as fear, control or panic.

At the core of the practice of Grounded Equanimity lies a continual affirmation: "I take ownership for my actions." In order not to become stuck in feelings of guilt and self-recrimination, one must recognize and understand three concepts: perfection, accountability and integrity.

Many leaders obsess about perfection. In some cases, they even deny their imperfections. The practice of Grounded Equanimity helps leaders accept that "things are as they are," "mistakes happen," "life is complex," "we are all human" and "no one can ever have 100 percent control over *any* situation." The daily practice of contemplating these principles makes clear to leaders that they can treat themselves with Compassion. Many executives often find this experience liberating. One can express neither spontaneity, joyfulness nor creativity when compelled to obsessively strive for perfection.

Although no one can be perfect, and no one should believe that he can, everyone is accountable for his actions. Releasing compulsive perfectionism does not imply ignoring one's accountability. Accountability means choosing to answer for what one commits to accomplish. Accountability differs from responsibility. Responsibility encompasses roles and job descriptions. Leaders usually delegate some of their responsibilities to others. Once the responsibilities are delegated, leaders may or may not see themselves as accountable for fulfilling the responsibilities. Leaders may say "the buck stops here" but then reprimand subordinates for "screwing up." For this reason, integrity is essential to true accountability. In order to act with integrity in any situation, both delegator and delegatee need to mutu-ally commit to accountability. In other words, when one assigns any of one's responsibilities to another, both parties must be accountable for achieving the end result. This entails clarifying each person's needs in order to fulfill the accountability. If one person fails, both fail, because their mutual commitment to the responsibility links them together. Failed accountability has no excuse because each person is responsible for understanding and carrying out what is expected of him.

Grounded Equanimity enables leaders first to release the need for perfection, and then achieve integrity and accountability in all situations. Within the context of the calming power of equanimity, accountability means simply to own the results of one's decisions, actions and communications. Integrity means that one's actions must align with one's commitments. Failure to meet a commitment one agreed to be accountable for stems from one's being "out of integ-rity." (Because we are not perfect, we will always be moving in and out of integrity.) When one is out of integrity, one can easily sink into self-judgment, rationalization, projection and other strategies to excuse one's actions. However, when one goes "out of integrity" and fails to meet a commitment, the groundedness of equanimity must be brought into play. There is a simple four-step process that permits one to use the concept of Grounded Equanimity to acknowledge that "things are as they are," when we fail our own integrity standards. For example, in an instant of failed commitment, the four steps would be:

State the *data* (the circumstances of the failure).

Provide one's *assessment* as to why it happened (in order to demonstrate the lesson one learned from it).

Express one's *feelings* about the failure of integrity (guilt, fear, anger, etc.).

Describe one's *decision* to rectify the situation (the new commitment).

Grounded Equanimity is like the rudder of a boat that keeps us steady as we move through the rough waters of daily life. Because we are not perfect we are not always accountable or operating from total integrity; we therefore need some "rudder" in our lives. Without this rudder of equanimity, we can easily slip into blaming, shaming and condemning both ourselves and others.

Consider this simple example of accountability/integrity. A management team was preparing for a weeklong off-site meeting at a conference center several states away. This event required the coordination of transportation to the facility, as well as the mutual commitment that everyone be on time at the first meeting. Being on time was important because the information presented at that first session would set the stage for the rest of the week's work.

Despite the mutual commitment, four of the twenty-five participants were over an hour late for the first session. However, in deference to that commitment, the CEO would not start the meeting until these four arrived, and he patiently waited for them. Instead of displaying anger toward them, or giving them the cold shoulder or dirty looks when they finally arrived, he engaged in a conversation with them. He used the situation as a learning venue for the whole team. He began by asking the four to present the data on what caused them to be late, then to give their assessment of what they had learned from the situation, their feelings about having held up the meeting for twenty-one other participants and their perceptions of what needed to be done to rectify the situation. Initially, the four made an excuse: One person's plane was late, so the other three could not have avoided being late as well. The CEO patiently asked them if they had met their commitment to be on time. The driver answered, "No, but . . ." The CEO asked the other three if they had kept their commitment to be on time, and he received three more "No, but" responses. This interchange proved to be very interesting because it appeared that the four had no control over being on time.

The CEO then explored other alternatives with the four. He suggested that they could have left a message for the late person and come ahead. They could have called to advise that they would be late. The four agreed that they could have chosen those alternatives, but they protested that, when they had committed to being on time, no one had told them that it was so critically important. The CEO then asked for comments from some of the participants who had been waiting for them. The comments reflected a mixture of frustration and anger regarding the delay.

The CEO stopped the discussion and asked the four late arrivals whether they were accountable for the choice they had made to be late. In other words, whether they owned the fact that they didn't honor the commitment, irrespective of their reasons. They agreed. "Integrity," the CEO said, "is often a choice between two or more commitments. The fact that you chose the delay over being on time means that you are out of integrity—out of alignment—with the rest of the team. There is no shame or blame if you are accountable for your action, but you need to demonstrate some form of restitution to get back in alignment with this group. Are you willing to do that?" After some give-and-take between the four and the rest of the participants, the four late arrivals agreed to carry golf bags during the afternoon recreation period.

Following his discussion with the four, the CEO observed to the group that failure is never final or fatal if one is willing to be accountable. Every team member operates in good faith and always has the chance to reclaim the trust of his teammates by owning his actions and attempting to restore integrity. The restoration of integrity by means of a compensating action clarifies where one's intentions lie. An act to restore integrity also removes the psychological tendency to "beat oneself up" for one's failed integrity. An action agreed upon by all parties restores alignment, reestablishes integrity, releases energy, and allows people to be present and responsive to the current situation.

As this last example showed, of all the Sacred Homes of Compassion, equanimity is the most difficult to develop. Yet it is key to developing all the others. Without a grounding in calmness, we would only make friends with those who *want* to be friends with us, and, conversely, would find ourselves caught in the shadows of projection, resentment and anger when people don't respond to us in the manner we would like. Without the clear perspective of equanimity, deep concern can easily turn into the shadow of pity, grief or even cruelty. Likewise, we would only offer supportive joy to others when we didn't feel jealous or envious.

This practice of Grounded Equanimity is like the other three. However, instead of starting with yourself, begin with the neutral person and then proceed to your mentor, your friend, your difficult person and then yourself. Because establishing equanimity is a more difficult challenge, starting with the neutral person has less emotional charge. As you visualize yourself and each person, use the following phrases for contemplation: "Things are as they are." "I (You) own my (your) actions." "I am (You are) the owner of my (your) happiness and difficulties." "I am (You are) responsible and accountable for everything that happens to me (you)." "Joys and sorrows deepen me (you), and I am (you are) peaceful and calm." As with all the phrases, try out each one and then settle on one or two that feel the most comfortable to use.

We all can incorporate these phrases from the Four Sacred Homes into the daily activities of our lives, whether by setting aside a specific time each day to practice or by practicing while engaged in mundane activities. In whatever way we integrate the practice, the Four Sacred Homes help us cultivate Compassion for ourselves and others. The practice of repeating the phrases does not create an artificial attitude that masks feelings of fear, anger or guilt. Rather, the practice provides the alternative to remove the masking behavior of the shadow from our personalities and allows the mind to naturally shift away from chronic victim patterns. This practice of the Four Sacred Homes encourages honesty and self-appraisal, and deepens the capacity of an individual to continually grow in their experience of genuine Compassion.

Learning Forgiveness Develops Compassion

In the simplest terms, the leader and his relationship with his spouse provide the container in which to work on Compassion—Compassion for oneself, for one's intimate companion, and for other loved ones, friends, associates and followers. Relationships are intense crucibles for learning the qualities of Compassion. A leader's companion can help him cultivate the qualities of Compassion by *facing, embracing and erasing* those patterns that block Compassion and caring. Both spousal partners or companions need to agree that they will remind each other of those attitudes and behaviors that remain hidden in their unconscious shadows. This entails the following:

> *Facing things as they are.* One's partner can help reduce the illusion and ego inflation that cloud reality. Honest, objective communication, as opposed to judgment or blame, is what will provide insight and understanding.

> *Embracing and accepting the situation.* One's partner can help one confront life's circumstances without self-pity. Owning one's effect on others and the results of one's actions starts the process of change.

> *Erasing and releasing shame and guilt.* One's partner can help one work with the shadow aspects of the Artist within and develop the self-forgiveness and forgiveness of others that are the key to opening one's heart to Compassion. Forgiveness is also the access point to expanding one's care and concern for others, and deepening care and concern into love and Compassion. A caring partner can help one learn to forgive oneself. Forgiveness is a practice. One needs to do it repeatedly—daily. Forgiveness is an action one applies to oneself and to others. It is not an attitude or an emotional state one merely conjures up. Rather, forgiveness is one of those miraculous gifts that, if one chooses to use it, ultimately can revolutionize one's life.

The act of forgiveness opens one to Compassion. At the heart of

Compassion is the capacity for forgiveness.[42] One can hold guilt, judgment and shame about who one is and what one did, for years. Holding onto these feelings causes one to experience difficulty feeling Compassion for oneself and others. Forgiving oneself is a conscious act that interrupts a pattern of thought and feeling. This interruption releases beliefs deeply held in one's mind. One gave oneself the guilt, shame or self-judgment at some point in one's life as a response to a person or situation but probably does not remember that event. The event most likely centered around some form of hurt or pain, either self-imposed or imposed by others. Every time one experiences anything reminiscent of that original pain, it triggers the learned reaction of guilt, shame or self-judgment. If one is not in contact with feeling, it usually means that one is suppressing and denying the original emotions. This denial paralyzes one's awareness and capacity for change and growth.

Conscious forgiveness neutralizes those hurtful, negative reactions and leads to reconditioned behavior. The guilt, pain or anger one carries from the original encounter of abuse or hurt continues to operate only because, in some way, one accepted that abuse. Accepting entails taking it in, integrating it and reinforcing that same acceptance in similar situations. When one forgives oneself, the negative reactions no longer apply and eventually cease to manifest themselves. Forgiveness of others entails consciously going back in one's mind to the time before one received and accepted the abuse from them, and erasing that conditioned response from one's mind. The mind holds the pattern of emotional reaction; therefore, only the mind can change it. As so many wise, spiritual teachers have said, if we change things in the mind, the emotions will follow suit.

The practice of forgiveness is very simple.[43] Every time a negative thought or feeling about oneself or another person enters one's consciousness, one simply says to oneself, "I forgive myself for that" or "I forgive [so-and-so]." When one asserts the phrase of forgiveness, one interrupts the pattern of conditioned response in the mind. Using the word "forgiveness" returns choices to one's life. Either one chooses to keep reinforcing the old hurtful or negative feelings and reactions, or one chooses to interrupt that pattern, begin to neutralize them and, thereby, recondition one's reactions. Claiming responsibility for one's own mind and heart in this way allows one to be responsible for one's own freedom. Compassion cannot exist in the person imprisoned by his own negative behavior and self-judgment.

Final Thoughts About the Artist and the Power of Compassion

Activating and accessing the Artist opens a leader to experience both his own core values about life and the ways to bring joy, creativity, empathy, spontaneity and heartfulness into his organization. Learning to treat oneself and others with Compassion nurtures the spiritual leadership every group of followers wants. The spiritual leader gives us hope for something larger and better than what we can envision alone. Such a leader creates a community atmosphere within an organization, a climate that permits and fosters growth, creativity, and meaningful accomplishment. The compassionate leader knows how to help individuals "fall in love" with what they are doing. He also knows how to appreciate and address everyone's concerns and needs. Accessing and using the tools of Compassion opens the door to this kind of spiritual leadership.[44]

Compassion, consequently, integrates the other three Powers, achieving a new level and quality of leadership. Compassion activates Presence by enabling the Sovereign to relieve the suffering in people's lives. Compassion renders Presence moral and ethical. Compassion activates Intention by enabling the Warrior to focus commitment creatively and heartfully. In this sense, Compassion and Intention work together: Compassion lends heart to Intention, and Intention lends focus to Compassion. Finally, Compassion and Wisdom activate each other. The Magician and the Artist are interdependent. Wisdom shows us our interconnectedness to the whole of existence. Compassion shows us that everything touches us and we can never truly stand apart. Wisdom recognizes the fragility and unpredictability of life. Compassion recognizes the interdependence of all things. Neither can exist without the other, and so, together they complete us. Compassion does not involve projecting an image, but rather, relaxing the heart and releasing pretense. The full expression of Compassion requires the leader to risk his vulnerability, to trust his intuition and to be himself in any situation. Above all, the leader must be *willing* to surrender his conception of himself if he is to embody Compassion.

THE SOVEREIGN
THE POWER OF PRESENCE

THE SOVEREIGN AS STEWARD

John Weir Perry, in his book *Lord of the Four Quarters: The Mythology of Kingship,*[1] points out that all Sovereigns are, by nature, sacred.[2] That is, in ancient tradition the king or queen was always connected to the divine—to some potent power. The Sovereign, in this sense, is one with the creator of this potent power.

To provide for the well-being of the kingdom was to ensure that the relationship between the Sovereign and the divine, as well as the alignment and commitment between the Sovereign and the people, was strong, creative and uncompromising. In this view the inverse is also true. If the kingdom (in modern times, the company or the organization) is not healthy, is having problems or is going downhill, then the Sovereign (in modern times, the president, chairman of the board, director, etc.) is not healthy. The Sovereign is not healthy in this view because he is not aligned with creation, the source of the universe, the Self or God. In ancient traditions, then, the Sovereign was the source of fertility (or, in modern terms, "success") for the realm. Kings were often sacrificed ritually to ensure the fertility of the kingdom. The ancient saying "The king is dead, long live the king" provided the ritual basis to affirm that life would continue and prosper through the sacrifice of a person filled with this great power that the community conferred on him. Today, company boards of directors will fire the CEO to save the company.

What is critical to understand about the Sovereign archetype is the notion that it claims the *center*, not necessarily the *top*, of the power structure. This is, in fact, the paradox of the Sovereign. Outwardly, in its ritual sense, Sovereign power appears to occupy the top position in a hierarchical structure, but psychically and energetically it occupies the center point. Structures and systems cohere not from a top or an edge, but from a center point. It is the cohesion from the center that gives strength, resiliency and flexibility to the whole. The power of the Sovereign is his Presence at the center. It is the act of renewal and regeneration as the center of the realm that gives freshness and reality to the charisma of Presence in the leader. Citing ancient myth and tradition, John Weir Perry points out that "Renewal . . . alongside that of the giving of order and the giving of life, was a major function of the center and a most essential rite of the kingship."[3]

In Christian theology, Jesus' death on the cross is the prime example of sacrifice of life. Jesus died a martyr so that the whole world would be renewed. The symbol of the crown on the cross in many churches is an affirmation of Jesus' kingship role as the energetic force at the center of the cosmos. This deeply held image of the Sovereign archetype within people is at the center of much of the individual and collective struggle with avoiding and desiring the exercise of power over others. On the one hand, people love the control it gives them; on the other, they fear that this same power can destroy them.

Presence is one of the most critical powers that a leader can exercise. With Presence comes the perfect blending of both positional power and personal power. People are awed by the queen, the president of the company, the chairman of the board, the general of the army or even the principal of the grade school. This awe, this timidity in the presence of an authoritative position, is real because people know the position carries the capability to exercise some kind of control over their lives. How a leader blends this positional power with his own charisma—his personal power—will determine how favorably or unfavorably followers respond to the power of his position.

When positional power begins to catalyze the Sovereign archetype in an individual, *the characteristics of stewardship, ambition, vision, order, mentorship and affirmation, or blessing,* begin to constitute themselves. The characteristics of Presence are often difficult for a person to embody successfully. Whether it is a rock star who, unable to handle all the attention he receives, goes into a spiral of self-destruction or the president of a country who believes he is above the law, constellating the Sovereign archetype in one's life can have brutal consequences on both oneself and others.

Stewardship

The prime characteristic of Presence in the Sovereign archetype is *stewardship. Steward* comes from the Old English *styward,* which means "a keeper of the pen or sty," or "one who is entrusted and charged with the care of things." The steward became the one entrusted with the management of the household, estate and kingdom. In modern terms, the leader activating the Sovereign archetype creates a center point, or focus, for his organization. He is the *presence* around which the organization becomes successful. He creates this presence by fostering creativity, fertile ideas, and an atmosphere that inspires commitment and growth in people. Through expressing basic values and the intention of how the realm or organization will function, the leader creates and embodies Presence. At the fundamental level, the stewardship role of a Sovereign is to frame the vision in which his followers can see collectively the purpose and meaning of working and being together. Donald Peterson, chairman and CEO of Ford Motor Company, describes this stewardship role very clearly:

> Identify a vision for your group. It should be something everyone can understand, relate to, and take pride in working for. Create an agenda—steps and strategies and timetables and goals for achieving the vision. Share them with the group, modify them to incorporate good suggestions, and make certain that everyone understands the final goals. Listen to the people in the group. Respect them. Give them the freedom and power to contribute. Praise them and reward their efforts. Let them know they are important to the group's success. Never compromise on integrity.[4]

In the short period of time that Peterson was chairman and CEO of Ford, he was able not only to turn around a financially ailing company, but also to reinvigorate the people at Ford with new creativity and excitement. Peterson dynamically moved to the emotional center of the organization to not only provide the focus of what to do in the "work," but to become the *psychic stake* in the organizational ground—that is, the one who established balance and freedom, and encouraged people to experiment and develop the business or organization. This quality of a leader's Presence, that which brings a company "to life," is a distinguishing characteristic of leadership.

A leader serves as a psychic stake in order to help followers find their own fundamental power and integrity. The metaphor of putting a stake in the ground suggests principles, commitments and rules that make sense. *Psyche* refers to the soul. A leader needs to "put his roots down" into the soul of the organization. A leader, in essence, embodies the soul of the organization. As such, he must make it clear that he is "holding the psychic energy" for the whole organization, and not just for his own self-interests. To do this requires maturity, a good deal of self-exploration, experience tempered by both success and failure, and a clear set of moral and spiritual values that can be communicated and applied in simple, pragmatic ways.

Order

The second characteristic of the power of Presence is the ability to provide order for the realm. The importance of order lies in its inherent growth outward from within. Order is the organic container that a leader creates for his followers to operate within as a cohesive group. The quality of order is experienced as a direct extension of the presence of the Sovereign leader. Whether or not a leader has order within his own life largely determines whether that individual is capable of bringing order to the enterprise. Order is not making things neat and tidy. Rather, order is the manner in which things naturally cohere. When a leader embodies order as an element of Presence, efficiency and effectiveness of work and activity become a natural focus of attention. Wasting time, energy, money and human resources becomes a concern of the Sovereign leader. Things fit and work together in a natural order for the situation at hand. The Sovereign leader recognizes and encourages his followers to be aware of the principle of order.

The way in which a leader develops the appropriate structure for an organization determines the quality of the order. This structure is more than just organization charts; it is the kind of atmosphere, tone or, in the broadest sense, culture that the leader establishes. The leader, by virtue of his individual style, values and attitudes, sets the order—the atmosphere, tone, culture—for his followers.

Andrew Grove, the chairman of Intel Corporation, has set a strong, positive tone of creativity and productivity, based on his own personality as a highly confrontational individual. The order that Grove sets at Intel is one of confrontation with all employees, regardless of their positions. A new manager may be shaken and intimidated during the middle of a presentation because nonmanagement employees challenge and/or confront him. Sometimes, employees even walk out in the middle of presentations. Such actions result from employees' dissatisfaction with either the person, the content of the presentation or both. The new manager soon learns that the cultural order is to engage in a give-and-take of open and frank discussion. These individuals also find out quickly that informality, rather than formality, is the order and way Andy Grove and Intel do business. Whereas many employees thrive in this environment, others find it very difficult and not to their liking, and leave.

Another critical aspect of the Sovereign power of Presence is that it *doesn't impose order from without.* A leader with the power of Presence focuses on keeping order and maintaining balance first in himself and then in all issues he confronts within his realm—that is, within his sphere of influence. He does not use violence to make things right, but, by example, demonstrates centeredness, calmness, wisdom and responsibility for the whole realm—the entire organization. A quality of presence and energy radiates outward from the leader. This radiance is part of the positional power as well as the personal power—charisma—of the individual.

Radiance evokes a response from followers. In order for members of the realm (the organization) to experience this type of balanced and centered leadership, they must be able to "view" the Sovereign. Even in modern times, the desire to see Queen Elizabeth, Prince Charles or, formerly, Princess Diana, or to stand and watch the motorcade of the president of the United States, stems from the desire to view power and the person who wields that power. Such glimpses of power respond to mechanisms within our psyche that reach out, yearning to be connected to the source of power.

Besides wanting to see the Sovereign, we want to *be seen* by him. Being recognized, acknowledged, called to by the Sovereign is intrinsic to the power of this archetype. All of us need blessing, or affirmation, from leaders. Viewing the Sovereign—seeing him, hearing him speak—inspires us. Having the Sovereign acknowledge us by name, express appreciation for our work or recognize our contribution to an idea exalts us emotionally, deepens our commitment to the company or leader, and drives us to more determined action. Being close to power stimulates us, motivates us to act and commits us to beliefs that are transpersonal and, therefore, larger than our individual view of reality.

The idea of "MBWA," or "Management By Walking Around," expressed in Tom Peters and Robert Waterman's *In Search of Excellence*[5] elucidates this significant part of the power of Presence —this need to be seen by and see the Sovereign, to feel the physical presence of the leader. This expression of our leader's recognition traditionally comes in the form of a "blessing," or affirmation, from the Sovereign.

Affirmation

Blessing, or affirmation, is a form of approval and confirmation of the follower by the leader. The Sovereign archetype functions in the classic role of bestowing a blessing when the pope, as vicar of God, confers his blessing on the people from the balcony of St. Peter's. In modern leadership, the *eye of blessing* comes when the president of a company focuses on a project team and tells them, "You did an outstanding job. You completed the project on time, within budget and according to what the customer wanted." This type of approval may be all the reward and recognition the team needs if the president gives the "blessing" before all the vice presidents, directors and managers of the company. The leader, as bestower of the eye of blessing (seeing and affirming people), when disappointed, can also "curse" (blame and condemn) the team for any failure. This public disapproval can cause a great deal of fear, not only in the team receiving the "curse," but in everyone else witnessing the leader applying the curse. Public cursing both brings immediate fear and creates a climate of intimidation in which people move from openness and trust to self-protection and defensiveness.

Blessings are very real in the human psyche. We need them, and we seek them from the significant people in our life. If we struggle to express our own initiative, creativity and success, it may be because we don't feel we've received what Matthew Fox calls the *original blessing*[6]—recognition, acknowledgment, affirmation from one's own father or mother. Because of this lack of personal confirmation from parents, many people in organizations seek the approval of a leader (be it president, manager or lead person). Unconsciously they are still seeking the blessing they never received from their own parents. There is something in us that wants the blessing of someone in authority. When we don't get it, we can turn cynical and angry; we can demonstrate the lack of that confirmation by negative attitudes and behavior in the workplace, as well as by destructiveness in our personal life and relationships.

Consider, for example, the executive who has built her organization on her continual communication to her employees of their value and worth, both as employees and as people. For her, the social and personal interaction became the prime focus of her daily work. During an extended period of time when she was extremely busy with issues that took her away from her organization, her employees became very upset because she was not available. They felt that her absence left them without the prime focus that had given them the energy and support to complete difficult tasks. Her direct reports felt deprived of the time they thought they needed with her. In general, the momentum and productivity of the organization began to decline, problems that employees usually solved easily were left unresolved, and the sense of community that she had provided as the center point of the organization began to fall apart as interpersonal conflict increased.

This leader learned many lessons from this experience. The first lesson was the critical role she played as center point for the organization. The second was the importance of her physical presence—her employees needed to see her in order to muster their energy and productivity. The third was her role in bestowing blessings. Without her confirmation and encouragement of all employees, a greater number of interpersonal problems arose. But the most important lesson was the dependency upon her that she had created in her employees. She saw the value of her leadership role but recognized that she had failed to transmit her power to her direct reports so that many centers of power could exist to motivate and support employees in the organization.

The Sovereign characteristics of stewardship, order and affirmation provide the foundation for cultivating the quality of Presence in leadership. Vision, ambition and mentorship are the remaining characteristics through which a leader builds the realm on a daily basis.

Vision

One definition of *vision*[7] is the ability to perceive something not actually visible, through mental acuteness or keen foresight ("His breadth of vision made this project possible"). Presence, in this context, entails *being the source* of vision and creativity that enables the organization to flourish and grow. At a personal level, the leader must be potent, creative and emotionally healthy. An organization is aligned and focused by the fundamental meaning, purpose and direction that the leader articulates and the visionary strategy that he formulates. The leader's focus allows everyone in the organization to collectively see the end result of their efforts. This collective view of the end result provides followers with the power to be creative, to make choices that fit the vision and strategy articulated by the leader. With this shared focus, people in the organization are able to be in alignment with each other, and to know what to do and what decisions they can make to further the overall success of the organization.

Warren Bennis and Burt Nanus, in their much-referenced book *Leaders: The Strategy for Taking Charge*, promote the importance of vision in leaders as the quality that separates leaders from managers. Their investigation of vision demonstrated an interesting contrast between the true work of leaders, as opposed to managers: "By focusing attention on a vision, the leader operates on the emotional and spiritual resources of the organization, on its values, commitment, and aspirations. The manager by contrast, operates on the physical resources of the organization, on its capital, human skills, raw materials, and technology."[8] Burt Nanus, in a solo academic research effort, *Visionary Leadership*,[9] provides another core message: that there is no more powerful engine driving an organization toward excellence and long-range success than an attractive, worthwhile and achievable vision of the future, widely shared.[10]

What is important about this characteristic of vision for the Sovereign is that it is not about the capability to perform a process or technique of "visioning." Expressing the Presence of vision as its *source* is different from being a good facilitator or articulator of a vision. A Sovereign leader, as the source of vision, may urge, encourage and even demand that other technical or organizational visionaries come forward with an articulated vision for the enterprise. The Presence of the Sovereign leader supports the vision that is the basic context in which all strategy, change and organizational health will arise. Everyone wants a context of meaning and purpose in order to make sense of life. Vision is what provides that meaning. As Nietzsche said, "He who has a *why* to live for can bear almost any *how*."[11]

Consider Mike, a newly appointed executive chairman of a recently merged $4-billion company. After months of grueling negotiations, and more months of premerger integration work by both companies, the new entity arrived at postmerger facing the prospect of creating a new seven-year strategic plan to submit to the board. The dates were set for the planning sessions, but it was clear from the management team that their idea was to put together the two existing—and very successful vision and strategy plans for the separate companies, put a little stretch into the combined plans, and get on with running the daily demands of the new company.

Mike, embodying the Sovereign power, could feel that more of the same strategy was not good enough to take the new company forward and enable it to compete successfully in the marketplace. After struggling to articulate to himself what a new company would look like seven years down the road, he decided to challenge the senior management team to envision the company in an entirely different way. In essence, the vision was to turn a United States–focused product company into a world-class, worldwide services company. For his industry and market segment, what Mike proposed was bold, scary and fraught with seemingly insurmountable problems. Yet, intuitively, everyone knew that Mike's visionary challenge was just what the company needed to survive as a competitor in the marketplace. Mike knew that his specific vision might not be the right vision ultimately. But Mike could sense that to be successful as a new company, they would have to turn themselves upside down. Mike didn't have to force his vision down anyone's throat. In presenting the vision, he laid out where all the problems and resistance would occur. He didn't have the answers to all the questions, but he was the source of the challenge to think big and bold. As one person indicated, "Mike's gorilla was so big, crouching at the ready in the center of the table, that we had to pay attention to it. But we also *wanted* to pay attention to it because, in the end, we could become the gorilla."

Ambition

Another key component of the leader's responsibility lies in fostering the organization's *ambition. Ambition* derives from the word *ambit* or *ambulate*, meaning "to walk around the realm." How far the king was able to walk around the realm represented his ambition to steward the resources of his people. For a modern leader, this represents the broad visionary perspective he assumes within the organization and the balance he provides between all the competing forces to ensure that results are achieved. But achieving the vision cannot come at the expense of blocking diversity of opinions or action within the organization. As with stewardship, ambition cannot be about the leader's personal gain or self-aggrandizement. Rather, the leader's ambition must be the wide embrace that will further the whole enterprise by ensuring that everyone realizes and actualizes his own energy, creativity and ambition.

The power of Presence, when fully expressed through ambition, shows that the leader is *not threatened by talented men or women*. Rather, he sees the potential in them and encourages that potential with opportunity and challenge. The centered leader blesses and affirms the people in his organization. This type of leader actively seeks out and knows those who have great potential for growth and contribution within the realm. He encourages them to expand and test their capabilities and limits because a Sovereign leader knows that the health and growth of the organization depend on them.

The leader with presence *holds up to public view the achievements of subordinates.* He goes out of his way to acknowledge peers, subordinates and other employees for the quality of their work, the effort they expend and the time they invest. Part of "holding up" the achievements of followers involves participating with them—brainstorming, problem solving, celebrating. This balanced availability to followers provides a center in which people can work and participate within the eye of the continuous storm of organizational life.

Mentorship

Mentor was the friend and counselor of Odysseus. Because Mentor was a wise and faithful counselor, anyone who willingly took on this role was known as a *mentor.* A mentor is a source of confirmation and approval to his protégés.

To take on the mentoring role as a leader means *not being threatened* by the insight, power and capability of others in the realm. To be a mentor means to have achieved maturity and security in oneself and to not seek to prove anything, particularly to the people with whom one is working. In a mentor role, a leader will *nurture followers and their work*, rather than merely dictate or direct work. The mentoring leader is continually interested in what others are working on, and listens to issues, encourages the work and makes suggestions when appropriate. Moreover, the mentoring leader cultivates his followers' capacity to grow, to stretch beyond their comfort levels and to confront difficult challenges.

John Gardner, in his book *On Leadership*, describes a mentor as a "grower" or a "farmer," as opposed to an inventor or a mechanic. In his words, "Growers have to accept that the main ingredients and processes with which they work are not under their own control. They are in a patient partnership with nature, with an eye to the weather and a feeling for cultivation. A recognition that seeds sometimes fall on barren ground, a willingness to keep trying, a concern for the growing thing, patience—such are the virtues of the grower. And the mentor."[12]

The eye of the Sovereign leader is focused on providing the opportunity for those in the realm to learn, test out ideas and develop capabilities. A leader in a mentor role *both inspires and criticizes a person or organization* but does so in a way that motivates change, productivity and quality. In general, the Sovereign leader is neither a judge nor jury of his followers' development, so that no one feels shamed or abused by his observations or criticisms. The power of Presence is constructive. It focuses not on personalities or characteristics, but on the actions and results of a person or group.

In *Mentoring: The Tao of Giving and Receiving Wisdom*,[13] Al Huang and Jerry Lynch describe some of the basic aspects of a healthy and positive mentoring relationship with a leader. A good mentor, they suggest, holds several fundamental attitudes about the one he is mentoring. The mentor is open, compassionate and caring in metaphorically "walking side by side" with his students (rather than posturing as the "all wise" person) for the purpose of guiding them and opening natural possibilities for them. The authors also list a number of qualities that would make up the ideal mentoring relationship:

> A mentor supports his student to "think big," and supports the student's dreams and goals by encouraging the student to test and try to make them a reality.

> The mentor creates a feeling of safety in his student, so that the student will listen when the mentor gives advice and direction.

> Honesty in feedback from the mentor guides the conversation and interaction. The mentor's role is not to make the student "feel good," but rather, to provide a mirror in which the student can see himself clearly.

A mentor increases the confidence level of the student by vocally supporting the student's talents and capabilities to others.

When the student is in times of challenge, conflict or chaos, the mentor encourages self-reliance, self-confidence and self-determination.

The mentor creates both an emotional and physical environment of learning that permits the risk of failure. When failure does happen, there is an emotional and intellectual debriefing process to explore "the lessons learned."

The mentor demonstrates loyalty to the student. A mentor will risk his own reputation to fight for a student if need be.

The mentor models by his values, attitudes and behaviors much of what the student will learn from him. It is the old adage "More things are caught, rather than taught."

For a healthy mentoring relationship to exist, the mentor must feel he is learning, growing and being expanded by the relationship with the student.

Finally, the mentor must be accountable for the relationship. Ethics, moral attitudes and appropriate behavior must be the foundation of the relationship.

The authors make an important distinction between the mentoring relationship and student-teacher or boss-employee relationships. There is an intimacy and exposure in a mentoring relationship. The point the authors make, however, is that "mentors should be accessible and open to you, yet they are not necessarily your buddies. In time, you and your mentor may become friends, but do not assume at the outset that your mentor and you will have a close personal relationship. It's not a prerequisite for good mentoring."[14]

This last point of not having to have a close personal relationship with a student is also important for a leader. A leader can perceive the talent in an individual and decide that with some coaching and mentoring, that person can develop his capacity and capability to achieve more, manage better, etc. To give the time and energy to develop a person doesn't mean that the leader needs to be a friend or even fully comfortable with the person. *For leaders mentoring is a strategic activity.* All Sovereigns who were concerned about the growth of the realm demonstrated a Presence that invited a relationship with and growth of key people. Without a leader investing time in key mentoring relationships, the growth and development of the organization is weakened. A leader's mentoring capability represents the strength of the power of Presence in his life. To mentor effectively the leader must feel self-assured, self-confident, and at the same time humble and aware of his inadequacies. A good mentor is good because he usually has his own mentor to challenge him and urge him to grow.

A Leader with Presence

Having Presence is being fully present. Presence radiates. One knows that someone has Presence when one can feel it emanating from that person. One can sense that the person is mindful and aware of what's going on, both within himself and within his environment. Presence is a quality that results when positional and personal power merge in an individual. The process of that merging is generally the result of consciously working on the six characteristics of Presence: stewardship, ambition, vision, order, affirmation and mentorship. These Sovereign characteristics challenge a leader to discover the seeds of his inner life—the seeds that lie fallow in his personality and are waiting to be watered, nourished and developed. As a leader begins to understand and practice the Sovereign archetype, personal power-drives get muted and transformed, and the needs of the realm—the enterprise and people—become of greater concern.

Instead of protecting one's personal interests, one finds that stewarding the larger enterprise automatically takes care of one's own interests. Personal ambition can never be fully realized until the ambitions of many are synthesized. Creating an ambition that is bigger than one's own ego or financial concerns provides a context for meaning and purpose that is more satisfying and fulfilling. Being the source of vision does not mean that the leader has the only vision or must create the vision himself. The leader may stimulate others to create vision, knowing as the old proverb says, that "without vision the people perish." To order something is to organize it in such a manner that it works best for everyone. A Sovereign leader is the stake in the organizational ground, the center post around which the enterprise structures itself both formally and informally. To truly bless, affirm or mentor others, one has to be able to do the same for oneself. As one grows and opens the power of Presence, one's natural response is to realize that everyone is a mirror to oneself. If one sees another's pain and sorrow, anger and despair, success and failure, joy and achievement, one is seeing one's own face. The Sovereign comes to know this because the role of Sovereign is to become the entire enterprise, to embrace all the people, to take all issues and problems inside oneself. We believe a leader when he says "the buck stops here" if we sense the Sovereign has been constellated in that person. It is not his position that convinces us; rather, it is the Presence he radiates as he says it. Power and position have merged, and we have confidence and trust in the declaration of authority.

THE SHADOW SOVEREIGN

Generally, a leader is not aware that he is manifesting the shadow side of the Sovereign. As a leader, his positional power contains Sovereign energy, and Sovereign power conveys a certain inherent "rightness" about what one does. What the leader does is deemed right by him for all kinds of self-justifying reasons, all of which boil down to "I am the boss."

This unawareness of how the positional power shadow is influencing the leader negatively is why shadow aspects of positional power are so important to understand. As Peter Nulty pointed out in his article on "America's Toughest Bosses,"[15] the "tough boss" doesn't know when he is being abusive. The positional power of the leader as the head of the corporation or organization leads that person to act in whatever way he wants, with what he believes to be justified impunity. In this view, he is the Sovereign and, because of that position, has the right to do whatever he wants. If he is successful in furthering the purpose of the business or organization, it becomes an even stronger affirmation that however many "bodies" may lie in his wake, it does not matter—so long as he "gets the job done." Positional power from the perspective of such a leader entails the privilege of having people do "what I want, whenever I want it."

Power as Abuse

Fundamentally, the leader with shadow Presence is preoccupied with using power as an agent to mask something he himself fears but will not admit to himself. At the heart of this power drive is the desire to control and treat people in whatever way he pleases. This pursuit of power for its own sake is usually in the shadow bag because of a deep sense of personal inadequacy that the individual is trying to hide from himself and others. These leaders are frustrated by a lack of creativity, and they are using the realm—the organization—for their own ends. Such abuse of power eventually results in organizational disarray. The display of power for its own sake drives these shadow Sovereigns because they've lost touch with the positive creative power that lies buried deep within the shadow bag.

A strong example of the abuse of this Sovereign shadow power is Albert "Chainsaw Al" Dunlap. Dunlap is a CEO who specializes in corporate "turnarounds." He is willing to do almost anything to increase the stock value of a company. One book reviewer labeled Dunlap's autobiography (*Mean Business: How I Save Bad Companies and Make Good Companies Great*) "Confessions of a Corporate Killer."[16] Dunlap has built a reputation for slashing costs, selling assets and laying off workers. He says that his primary allegiance is to the shareholder of the corporation, not to the management, workers or even the customers. He "rescued" Scott Paper by making shareholders a great deal of money, as well as reaping $100 million for himself. When Sunbeam Corporation hired him, the stock price went up 41 percent in anticipation of what he would do. His book reveals the essence of the shadow Sovereign: total focus on himself as hero, promotion of his own greatness as a man who has never made a mistake, abuse of and disregard for management and workers (stating publicly, "hang the prior management," among other threats), and public proclamation that his purpose in turning companies around is to create greater wealth for himself. Rather than the good of the whole realm, Dunlap takes a narrow focus that "kills" all others so that his own success becomes primary. He rationalizes this shadow abuse with "I am doing it all for the shareholders."

Dunlap follows the traditional path of the shadow Sovereign, the tyrant with all the typically associated paranoia. This tyrant leader controls a kingdom—an organization or community—in order to ward off his own fears. He projects onto others his own self-hate and self-aggrandizement, and makes the innocent his enemies in order to justify his actions. Whether it is the ancient king Saul of the Old Testament pursuing young David to kill him; King Herod frightened by the prophecy and killing all the newborn babies when Jesus was born; Hitler killing the Jews; Stalin "purging" the peasants and intellectuals; or the division manger terrorizing his sales force—each uses Sovereign positional power to control, oppress and even destroy individuals.

Shadow Fear

For the shadow Sovereign to give power to others is for him to perceive a twofold danger: a threat to himself, because he gave some of his power to others, and a diminishing of what he views as his already limited amount of power. The shadow leader believes that power will be used against him. Therefore, this leader attempts to retain and wield all the power himself. With the fear of impotency (of being fundamentally bereft of inherent personal power) at the edge of his mind, he can allow no one to be superior to him, no matter what the cost.

An example of the fear of impotency is the entrepreneur who loses connection between his positional and his personal power. It is generally the personal charisma and power of an entrepreneur that permits him to gain his initial success. He can launch companies very successfully, but he often lacks the skills needed to develop that company beyond its early stages. As size and complexity increase, the entrepreneur loses contact with the day-to-day decisions (because others are making them) and with the detailed knowledge that he had at the beginning of the venture. This loss of control over *his* enterprise creates a host of inevitable shadow-fear responses. In an attempt to regain control, he will make autocratic decisions that don't make business sense; he will forbid people more capable than him to take initiative without his absolute approval; he will pit subordinates against each other to make them weaker in the organization. This attempt to regain absolute control will begin to destroy the success that the entrepreneur created in the first place. The earliest sign of this destruction will be the resignation of the brightest and best in the organization.

Whether entrepreneur or not, the general behavioral pattern of the shadow Sovereign is to create constant chaos and turmoil, to eliminate people he perceives to be threatening, and to pit subordinates against each other. This management style is clearly authoritarian, with the leader being the only one who can make the final decision. This leader is incapable of affirming or blessing others. Rather, he feels the need to be constantly stroked and affirmed by subordinates. Instead of "lifting" up his followers in affirmation/blessing, he publicly humiliates them before their peers whenever he perceives any kind of "failure" by a subordinate. Ridicule and the threat of ridicule, as opposed to supporting subordinates and employees, and helping them save face in public, is the shadow Sovereign's normal means of exerting control and exercising authority. Al Dunlap proudly relates that he so severely reprimanded one of his most trusted advisers that the man didn't speak to him for over eighteen months, even though he still worked for Dunlap.[17]

The beginning of our discussion of the Sovereign archetype suggested that the realm reflects the Sovereign. If the Sovereign is healthy, so is the realm. If the realm is sick, so must the Sovereign be. Whatever condition the leader manifests in himself, he will project onto his organization as his shadow. In her book *Individuation*, Jolande Jacobi, a student of C. G. Jung, describes how this loss of control produces actions that arise from a power deeper than one's conscious awareness: "When we lose conscious control of ourselves for one reason or another, the qualities of the shadow appear on our own persons, in the form of blunders, asocial behavior, egoisms, rudeness, etc., which can no longer be projected and show that there are other powers in us besides the ego."[18] When the negative and dark display of shadow behaviors begins to dominate the Sovereign leader's life through a feeling of loss of control, the shadow power has taken over the personality, and the ego consciousness now rationalizes this shadow behavior as right and appropriate. If confronted with his shadow behavior, the Sovereign will deny his behavior and often simply dismiss, or "banish," the person who challenges him. When the shadow dominates the Sovereign, it will only be a matter of time before the kingdom falls into sickness or disrepair.

Victim Cultures

The level of an organization's health is directly related to the way the Sovereign power functions between the leaders and employees. What is tragic in these negative Sovereign organizations is that the employees spend their lives in these systems with increasing pain, debilitation and loss of self-esteem.

Organizations that have the so-called tough boss patterns generally lack the creativity necessary to achieve long-term success. It is impossible to balance a diverse community of people working together toward a larger vision if the leader focuses on short-term financial goals or his expression of power over people for its own sake. When a leader focuses only on the short-term financial issues without providing a broader vision of how the service or product contributes to society or providing a vision of meaning and purpose for the enterprise, a vacuum occurs in which employees feel like victims without personal power. What the shadow leader effectively does is promote the view that any meaning is short-term and, ultimately, serves his self-interest.

Viktor Frankl, in his classic *Man's Search for Meaning*, explores the vacuum of the meaningless world within which so many people feel lost. Being victimized by a lack of meaning is to perceive that one has no future, that there are no transcendent values to give hope to one's life. From observing others, as well as himself, survive the Nazi concentration camps, and from working with people who are bored, depressed and lost in life, he insists that as human beings our "main concern consists in fulfilling a meaning and in actualizing values, rather than in the mere gratification and satisfaction of drives and instincts. . . ."[19] The victimization of others into meaninglessness that shadow leaders promote reduces vitality in the organization. It also pushes people into trying to satisfy short-term needs, instead of finding genuine purpose and meaning in their work and civic life. Without a vision and purpose that satisfies the meaning and drive that people long for, they begin substituting the false illusions of pleasure that come from substance or emotional addictions. "Values," Frankl says, "do not drive a man; they do not push him, but rather they pull him."[20] And they pull one toward the spiritual, toward an understanding of suffering, toward a goal that is worthy of one. This *pull* is what creates meaning, creates tension, calls to be fulfilled. This tension toward meaning is what pulls one out of victimization and enables one to break free of the shadow Sovereign.

The shadow Sovereign leader is unable to steward a broader and longer-range view of the organization that would serve the needs of the employees, as well as stockholders and management. It is this narrow, selfish shadow Sovereign power that often drives businesses to leveraged buyouts, mergers and acquisitions.

Fortune magazine's ten-year study of mergers and acquisitions in the 1980s and Mercer Consultants' study in the 1990s both showed that 80 percent of mergers and acquisitions failed within twenty-four to forty-eight months, for the initial reasons given for the merger or acquisition. The major reason behind that failure rate is that employees were left out of the merger process. The financial reasons for a merger may look good, but leaders forget the impact the merger will have on the needs and involvement of people throughout the organizations. Without in-depth consideration of people and systems integration, and without premerger preparation or realistic transition plans that take into account people's sense of loss and change, a merger or acquisition will cost more in time, money and management headache than the merging or acquiring company ever considered.[21]

Consider the example of a large Fortune 500 company with a very rapidly growing division. This company's business strategy was to buy up small companies in their market and merge these companies into their system. This company acquired six small companies in one year. All six companies were profitable when the larger company bought them. Within nine months of the merger, four of the six were losing money. After fourteen months, only one of the six was still profitable. But beyond the profitability issue was the enormous amount of time and energy being expended to solve an array of people problems because the leaders had not considered how to integrate the people, systems, values and beliefs of these various communities and form a new, cohesive organization. The skills of a community organizer were desperately needed to bring this diversity into some common unity of form, vision and purpose.

What the president of the acquiring company clearly lacked was the will and understanding to meet the diverse survival needs of the six minicultures and to steward the needs (the different ambitions, if you will) of the employees of his own organization, who were overwhelmed by the lack of systems, structure and resources necessary to meet the acquisition challenge. In this case the Sovereign ambulated and tried to add territory to the realm. The new dominion proved too unmanageable to successfully rule because of the lack of planning and inclusion. The tragedy of the situation was that when the president's direct reports came to him with the problems in these companies, he would not listen to or counsel (mentor) them. Rather, he accused them of failing and of creating the problems themselves, and blamed them for the financial losses publicly before other company officials. Needless to say, demoralization and employee turnover increased rapidly in that organization. Merging or acquiring out of concern for survival or competitive advantage may be reasonable in some cases. But often, the shadow fear and greed that motivates these decisions serve the financial benefit of the relative few, and the decision usually fails to consider the needs of people in the organization as they cope with the loss of purpose and meaning they experience from the destruction of their organizational cultures.

The power of the Sovereign can cast an enormous shadow over enterprises and affect large groups of people. The power to be autocratic, dictatorial and abusive, the power to disrupt and control the life and culture of organizations, becomes easily rationalized in today's competitive world as the necessary "cost of doing business" and "staying competitive." In this shadow madness of fewer and fewer companies owning more and more, society may be losing the central value and meaning of work and community.

CULTIVATING THE SOVEREIGN WITHIN

Those who have experienced the rule of a shadow Sovereign leader often vow that they would be different if they were the boss. However, paradoxically, when one does assume positional power—when one becomes the boss—one's new role as leader tends to bring out the shadow characteristics that are in one's own shadow bag. As suggested earlier, this gap between assuming new positional power and the capacity of our personal power to meet the challenge of a new level of leadership activates the shadow within us. The issue is not so much whether the shadow has been activated, but whether we begin to work to integrate the shadow into our conscious life. Sometimes positional power, because it forces us to assume the role of the leader, gives the unconscious the permission to open the shadow bag and release that authority figure that one has consciously been afraid to express.

Positional power gives us the authority that our parents, teachers and bosses had over us. We will tend to act out in the shadow expression what has been acted out upon us. If parents did not permit us to be angry, we will often project our anger onto others when given the chance. Positional power, in the role as manager, president or any form of recognized leader, gives the shadow side of the unconscious permission to act out what it fears to do in other circumstances. As a leader, one is confident, because of the positional power, that one need not answer to others for one's actions, particularly if the behavior (abusive anger for example) directed toward others is justified in the name of "results," the "bottom line" or the "stockholders." Because we take on the Sovereign authority when we gain new positional power, the ego begins to justify the emergence of both subtle and obvious shadow behavior.

Alvaro Unama Quesada, former minister of natural resources for the government of Costa Rica, puts to us clearly the challenge of working with shadow power. He says: "Keep power under control and in perspective. Try to see the position with detachment and let yourself be humbled by it. Remember it is not you, it is the position. Like the entropy law, power naturally tends to corrupt. One must struggle not to let that happen. If one can reverse that tendency, power can also ennoble." [22]

The Ego Battle with the Shadow

When one is faced with one's own shadow, a number of reactions can occur:

One can be in denial and refuse to confront the shadow.

One can intellectually understand the exhibition of shadow behavior and try to implement one's best intentions to stop it.

One can refuse to accept responsibility for one's behavior and lay blame for the problem on the other person.

One can feel guilty and suffer, but not change one's behavior.

One can grit one's teeth and exert willpower to keep from manifesting the behavior.

When one first catches sight of the shadow at work in one's life, the initial reaction will be to try to eliminate it, particularly if one's moral and ethical standards stand in opposition to one's behavior. One wants to be consistent between what one holds to be true and what one does. When confronted with this discrepancy, one's rationalization is, "I am not going to do that ever again." After asserting this view, one will try to stop the behavior, only to forget and slip back into the unconscious shadow behavior once again. By experience, one has discovered that willpower and best intentions won't necessarily eliminate shadow actions.

Exerting willpower to stop negative behavior is just another form of rejecting the shadow as part of one's personality, while at the same time driving it deeper into unconscious life, a place from which it is more difficult to engage and work with the shadow. Although the shadow is described metaphorically as a bag we drag around with us, it is really not a container filled only with negative behaviors or attitudes that suddenly pop out in various circumstances. Rather, the shadow is a complex of both positive and negative energies that are expressed through a pattern of emotions, feelings and behaviors. What we see in the expression of the shadow is symbolic of the unused creativity, enthusiasm and dynamic of our lives. Jolande Jacobi describes the shadow bag as filled "partly [with] unlived psychic features which, for moral, social, educational, or other reasons, were from the outset excluded from consciousness and from active participation in life and were therefore repressed or split off. Accordingly the shadow can be marked by both positive and negative qualities."[23]

When trying to stop shadow feelings and behaviors from manifesting themselves, rationalization comes to the fore to control shadow expression. The reality is that the unconscious shadow energy is generally more powerful than one's conscious ego personality. One will have little success attempting to change its operation in one's life by trying to control or suppress it. However, one does have choices available. These choices can enable one not to be a victim to shadow impulses.

> The first choice is to accept that the shadow that has emerged is from oneself and no one else. What is hard for one to accept is the lifelong process of constantly holding a truce with shadow material as it emerges in various situations.

> The second choice is not to repress, excuse, ignore or deny the presence of one's shadow when it emerges. One must become conscious of and accept without judgment one's shadow thoughts, feelings and actions before integrating their energy into one's life.

> The third choice is to make a decision not to grit one's teeth in some supreme effort to *control* the shadow, but rather, to hold the shadow feelings and thoughts in conscious awareness without acting them out. Letting go of and safely experiencing shadow material is the key to transforming it. In the world of dark and light the key is not doing something about the shadow, but *being with* the shadow.

By knowing one's shadow characteristics, but not acting on them, one begins to transform and realign the *energy* that the shadow parts represent, rather than just stopping certain negative behaviors. These choices represent the commitment to release and integrate the repressed energy that one is not using consciously.

Working with the Shadow

Working with the shadow entails more *being* than *doing*. It is more about gaining understanding and insight than about changing behavior. To gain this insight, and actively look for the shadow in one's daily life, changes a person from a resister of the shadow to an active agent of what Jung described as the core purpose of everyone's life: the *individuation* of a human being. To put it another way, it is one's individual purpose to discover the path that leads to wholeness and integration. Jung saw the individuation process as the transformation and development of an individual "that culminates in rounding out the individual in a psychic whole."[24]

William Miller, a therapist and writer, suggests five ways to work more effectively with one's shadow.[25] These are five useful tips that are particularly valuable to Sovereign leadership, where the position of power, of being the "boss," can easily blind, and where one can stand above, separate and alone in the leadership roles:

Constantly solicit feedback from others as to how they see you.

When you become aware of shadow characteristics, explore how you project them onto others.

Notice your slips of the tongue and slips in behavior throughout the day.

Examine your type of humor and your responses to humor.

Write down and examine dreams and daytime fantasies. By doing this, you give the signal to the unconscious that you are taking the inner world seriously by trying to understand what these symbols represent in your conscious life.

Feedback. Asking others how they perceive you, both generally and in specific situations, will provide a framework for observing the pattern of how your shadow emerges in various situations. Establishing agreements in advance with peers and subordinates to give feedback when negative material surfaces during meetings or one-on-one encounters does not demand action or self-judgment. This agreement with another is as simple as having people talk about it, then listening and asking questions, and not justifying or rationalizing what they say. Working with and attempting to integrate the energies of the shadow into our conscious life is more about becoming conscious of the shadow material than doing something about it. A good clue to recognize shadow manifestation is the self-talk you use to resist or react negatively to someone's observation. The reactive self-talk can be: "I am really not that way" or "I can't believe I am that bad" or "You're as bad as I am." The intensity of the negative reaction against what the person says is a good indication that you are in shadow territory.

Projections. A concrete way to examine your projections is to list the various people you dislike and describe on paper all that you like and dislike about them. Doing a content analysis, comparing the characteristics that are similar among these various individuals will give a strong indication of your shadow projections. When noting what you project onto others, remember that the shadow holds both positive and negative characteristics that you aren't expressing. For example, if you notice in the lists that you judge people for their focus on making money as the prime motivator of their success, while at the same time you are struggling with the tendency to spend too much money and are in debt, you are probably seeing shadow money envy and fear of possessing large sums of money. In fact, many executives' difficulties in making their business enterprises financially successful stem from their blocked shadow energy related to their personal financial success. The *positive* shadow manifests itself in the repressed desire to make money, disguised under the conscious value judgment that "money really isn't important to success." The *negative* shadow manifests itself in the behavior of overspending and constant debt. Gaining awareness that both the positive and negative sides of the shadow are at work sets up behavioral tension that permits you to gain insights about how to integrate blocked personal power with the positional power you exercise.

Slips. Embarrassing slips of the tongue and behavior become signals of when the shadow is trying to emerge into ego consciousness. Most everyone has had the experience of intending to say one thing and saying the opposite. Behavioral shadow slips often come from saying one thing and then doing something entirely different.

Much of sexual harassment in the workplace demonstrates this phenomenon. Many executives who take racial, mixed-gender and sexual harassment training "preach" respect for women and all races, and then inappropriately touch or speak to female employees, or use racial epithets in the heat of anger. Such executives often are shocked and deny any wrongdoing, arguing that they were only being "friendly" and "sympathetic" to the women or the groups, when confronted with their behavior. This denial, rejection and being "caught" in the discrepancy is a sure indication of the shadow at work. The conscious ego can't integrate the behavior into the conscious value pattern in which they believe. The Anita Hill/Clarence Thomas hearing probably illustrated some of this behavioral shadow slipping. Certainly, the Bob Packwood sexual harassment case reveals a man caught between his public support of women's issues and the shadow of his personal behavior with scores of women.

The challenge in working with slips is similar to that of working with projections. Make an agreement with a friend or colleague to give feedback when slips occur. Use the slip as a metaphor for something else trying to emerge in consciousness. Write a list of slips over a period of several weeks. Observe any pattern to help gain insight as to what the shadow is trying to bring into awareness.

Humor. Miller contends that individuals "who strongly deny and repress their shadow generally lack a sense of humor and find very few things funny."[26] Most people, however, do laugh and enjoy funny stories and situations. One's shadow most often comes out when participating in cynical or aggressive humor. The sadist shadow emerges when one engages in relating or listening to cruel jokes; views slapstick comedy where, for example, the Three Stooges are hitting each other; or watches cartoons where, for instance, the Road Runner blows up or otherwise hurts and maims Wile E. Coyote. In organizational settings, gossip is more often where another person's reputation is impugned and everyone laughs at the person's perceived stupidity or inept response to some situation. The other person may even be present and may join in the laughter to cover his own embarrassment and hurt. In each case the humor is a mask for the negative repressed desire to scapegoat, hurt and abuse others. Many shadow Sovereigns use sarcastic humor to berate, control and intimidate followers by manipulating others to laugh and demean fellow workers. This type of humor becomes a telling aspect of shadow behavior for both leaders and followers.

A useful way to let humor reveal the shadow at work is to observe the kind of humor one participates in or enjoys. What is even more useful is to ask selected friends and colleagues how others respond and react to one's humor. Again, the pattern and the reactions of these people to one's humor will provide insight and understanding about the constrained energy that is being held in one's shadow bag. Consciously freeing that energy from the disguise of humor permits a more honest and genuine happiness to emerge from one's personality. For the Sovereign leader the movement away from negative humor allows affirmation, or blessing, to express itself more naturally.

Dreams and fantasies. The dark, evil or negative persons or situations in one's nighttime or daytime dreams and fantasies represent pieces of the shadow energy that are trying to bubble up into conscious life. The challenge of dream material is that the symbolic nature of the image permits one to rationalize and not accept it as part of oneself. Or, even if one accepts it as a source of information, one may simply be too confused as to what the dream is attempting to say to be able to integrate it into consciousness. The value of any image lies not so much in its content as in the way the image will trigger other associations in one's mind. Trying to interpret the meaning of the shadow dream image isn't as important as acknowledging that it is a part of one's shadow.

The dream image permits much more of the energy of the shadow to come through, particularly if one writes about it or talks about it with someone. Insight will occur by means of interaction with the image. Simply noting the levels of violence, sexual fantasy, acting out of power, desires for wealth, etc., in one's fantasies gives valuable information about one's most repressed and immediate shadow issues. Accepting them as part of one's life provides a conduit that lets their power into consciousness. Much of the frustration and tension that the leader projects onto his direct reports and other followers comes from repeated focus on his own fantasy material. For example, many vice presidents become "stuck" on the fantasy of becoming the CEO of a start-up and making millions when it goes public but are unable to demonstrate the skills and capabilities needed to build the organization for which they are responsibile. A large shadow gap exists in them and reveals how far they are from accessing the Sovereign power they would need to take on such a position.

Noting the pattern of what one repeatedly fantasizes about by writing down and analyzing the images and their contents reveals where the unconscious energy is "leaking out." Remember that the shadow bag stores both the unexpressed and unfulfilled positive and negative parts of personality. Enacting parts of the fantasy as a means to explore their intensity and reality is also a way to both discharge accumulated energy and heal unresolved parts of one's life from the past.

One senior manager had, for years, fantasized about sailing around the world. He had also been working with understanding and integrating shadow material into his life. It became clear to him as he worked with the complex of his shadow material that the power of the sailing fantasy was driving him to make continual personal and professional decisions that were not good for him. Confronting the challenge of his fantasy, he made a plan that took him a year to implement. He first bought a sailing boat and then moved aboard full-time. But then, instead of quitting his job and sailing off into the sunset as his fantasy was impelling him to do, he negotiated a three-month sabbatical to sail from the West Coast to Hawaii. If the ocean is a metaphor for the unconscious, this leader sailed into the depths of his emotions and feelings. The trip was the most difficult in his life, both emotionally and spiritually. By the end of the trip, he had resolved long-standing difficulties that he had been unwilling to face with his spouse. He now understood the pattern of escape that the sailing fantasy had represented. He returned to the mainland with the intention of moving out of his current position back into his original profession as a religious leader.

The setup line used at the beginning of the 1940s radio program *The Shadow* was "Who knows what lurks in the hearts of men? The Shadow knows." The shadow does know what is lurking—what is most ready to come into consciousness to help a person at any moment in his life. And the shadow does know what energies one wants to make available in one's life. Through seeking feedback and examining projections, slips, humor, dreams and fantasies, one can work to gain insight into the shadow energy at work in one's life. Learning to open one's own shadow bag, by consciously using the five methods described in this chapter and by understanding what one projects onto others, is a major step toward releasing the stranglehold the shadow Sovereign has on one's daily life.

Final Thoughts About the Sovereign and the Power of Presence

The key to the Sovereign's sense of positive Presence is the capacity to connect, provide and hold a larger context of direction, meaning, safety and encouragement for followers within the realm— the organization, company or community. Ultimately, when the shadow Sovereign is activated, the leader separates himself from his followers, holds himself apart as special and has followers focus their energy on him. This is done at the expense of holding up the larger vision and ambition that the leader must steward and to which he must bring structure and order. Within the shadow Sovereign there reigns a leader who curses and denies, rather than affirming and supporting. When a leader is willing to acknowledge this dark Presence, his work toward what C. G. Jung called *individuation*[27] has begun.

The integration work that is required of the Sovereign is to release the fear, victimization and blind allegiance his shadow holds upon his followers. The first step is to own the shadow projections placed on others. The second step is to see the projections on his followers as a mirror of what is inside him as a leader. Bringing one's own shadow material to consciousness moves both dark and light Presence into reality, resulting in a leader who is more authentic, approachable and capable of holding the goodwill and trust of his followers.

When a leader consciously holds the tension of both the dark and the light shadow, the power of Presence emerges, providing an atmosphere in which individuals in the organization can be themselves. Presence in leadership allows followers to make mistakes, be creative, challenge old ideas, and experience a climate of trust and risk taking that gives freedom to everyone. This context of freedom is what enables followers to discover more of their own natural states of being. This Presence also provides a field in which they can explore their own shadow material more honestly.

The value statements that most organizations place in their corporate handbooks and on the walls of their offices highly prize trust and risk taking. However, in most organizations these values remain mere words because employees know from experience that attempting to exercise risk taking gets them in trouble with their boss or peers. Risk taking needs a leader who communicates Presence in an organization. To trust others and take risks requires being vulnerable and open. Authentic Presence can create an environment in which it is possible to choose to open up, to be willing to accept the consequences of being candid with others and to risk the vulnerability inherent in being oneself within the organizational culture. When leaders work to integrate their shadow material, they provide the Presence upon which followers can model their own growth, learning and ability to accept change. This leadership effort results in a strong and vibrant organization, company or community able to weather all kinds of storms.

7

CULTIVATING THE
FOUR POWERS

Because they are ancient patterns of consciousness, the Four Powers of Leadership are deeply embedded in the psyche of every individual. These archetypes of leadership are like seeds that one can water and nurture. Once these seeds bud into young plants, one can grow and cultivate them. Even though these leadership archetypes exist in everyone, not everyone is a leader. Nor do most people want to be leaders. Some individuals don't even consider it as a possibility for themselves. Others don't want any part of the responsibility. Still others want simply to be followers, or perhaps even loners, resisting any form of allegiance to another person's guidance or direction. Then, too, there are those individuals who never gave leadership a thought but always seemed to be elected president of the class, urged to be captain of the team or, for some reason, were quickly recognized and promoted to management positions. The rarest of all are those individuals who, from childhood, wanted to run something, be in charge, to *lead*. For example, most know the story of Bill Clinton wanting to be president at an early age and planning his life to achieve that goal.

Whether one never wanted to lead, fell naturally into the leader role or consciously worked at becoming a leader, each case represents the unique circumstances and personality of the individual. Whatever one's preference—given personality, circumstances and choices—the capacity to lead lies within each person. If an individual chooses to nurture the archetypal seeds in order to begin to grow the plant of leadership, how he accesses the Four Powers (consciously or unconsciously) will largely determine the blossoming and success of that leadership.

One may give the four leadership powers different names and descriptions. But beyond any names or descriptions, the daily challenges a leader confronts force him to recognize these powers as deep structures of his own psyche. These daily leadership confrontations also awaken one to consciously perceive the positive and negative aspects of one's personality and the impact of one's personality on followers. Most important, leadership challenges reveal in daily experience the areas that need development and practice. If one acknowledges and embraces as real these powers of Intention, Wisdom, Compassion and Presence, one can begin to both accelerate the competence to respond appropriately in all types of leadership situations, and enlarge the capability to decide and act within one's realm of responsibility.

The Requirements of Cultivation

Leadership is not something one learns by going to school to obtain a degree or certificate. Education and training can provide information, understanding and techniques, but they are only *developmental* tools of leadership. As such, they have their usefulness in the cultivation process. However, leadership that grows and matures is the result of personal, daily commitment to cultivate one's inner life within the midst of leadership work. Cultivation requires the following of a leader:

To be willing to risk the exposure that being open and honest about all aspects of one's life entails

To continually participate in self-reflection

To commit to ongoing personal change and growth

To be willing to seek feedback from many sources, including followers

To assume the discipline of a thoughtful, daily practice that strengthens weaknesses, and builds new capabilities and competencies

CULTIVATING THE GAP BETWEEN PERSONAL AND POSITIONAL POWER

The place to begin practicing cultivation is the fertile ground (the gap) between personal and positional power. Use the *positional* power of leadership (the role itself) to discover more about the strengths and weaknesses of one's own *personal* power. Cultivating this gap helps one focus on what the demands of positional power reveal positively and negatively about oneself, and how to gain access to underdeveloped personal power. Much of what has been presented in this book has explored both the conscious and unconscious aspects of how one adjusts to the gap between one's personal and positional power. This gap is the fertile ground where leadership development is cultivated daily. Furthermore, this gap is home to the rocks and weeds, as well as the healthy sprouting seeds, of our leadership. If one does not actively practice some form of "cultivating," the shadow aspects (the weeds and rocks) of one's personal power can begin to dominate this ground.

In order to consider how to cultivate the personal/positional gap, one needs to understand how positional power activates the shadow parts of one's personal power. The traditional metaphors used to describe leadership positions employ vertical phrases such as "he's above us," "she's at the top," "he heads up the organization" or "move it up the chain of command." This vertical, "at the top" conception of positional power creates the illusion of exaggerated importance. It engenders in one the perception that, as a leader, "I am somebody special. But not only am I special, I have arrived at the head of the organization. I am the person with all the power." Even more seductively, it implies, "What I do is more important than what anyone else does."

This self-importance may cover up and hide for years shadow sides of a leader's personality. As the difficulties and challenges of leadership began to assault one, fear may enter one's consciousness. The frightening terror comes for many leaders when they realize that self-importance not only brings one to the "top" position, but also separates one from everyone else. If a leader probes his emotions, he often finds that he is frightened because he feels alone and lonely. Out of this fear of separation and loneliness emerges insight into aspects of one's own dark shadows of projection that have been described in each of the Four Powers chapters. When a leader recognizes this gap of separation and takes responsibility for inappropriate reactions and responses, or when he simply acknowledges that he lacks the personal power needed to meet the demands of the position, the ground for cultivation will naturally open. One of the first steps one needs to take in this cultivation process is to shift one's perception of what positional power means to a leader. This shift enables the leader to understand that the power of a leadership position moves metaphorically between the so-called top of the pyramid of power *and* what will be described as the center of the circle of power.

THE HIERARCHY AND PARTNERSHIP ASPECTS OF POWER

Leadership is both a hierarchy and a partnership: Leadership cannot exist without followers. Leading and following play equally important roles within the network of the leadership system. A leader of a company does not build, market and service a product himself.

Many other people within this sytem have leadership roles and responsibilities that allow the system as a whole to accomplish results. Like concentric rings, the success of each sphere of leadership and followership is interrelated and interdependent. The value of hierarchy lies in its ability to give the system a clear structure for efficient actions, decisions and timing. All organic systems have some form of structure that promotes efficiency. Efficiency is a mechanism in and of itself. In the most expedient and simplest way, it connects parts and pieces of the whole system—the company, organization or community—and unifies them into a fully functional whole. For example, the brain becomes one control mechanism for coordinating the efficient working of the many other systems in the body. The leader as "brain" does the same. But, practically speaking, when the leader functions strictly as the brain, he serves only one part of his purpose. Cultivating leadership begins to teach a person that he must balance being *efficient* with being *effective*. In other words, *hierarchy* must be integrated with *partnership:* vertical (hierarchy) and horizontal (side-by-side partnership) must complement one another in order to achieve true, effective leadership.

Partnership is an invitation by a leader that is, in turn, accepted by followers, to "hold the rim together." Together, leaders and followers create standards for effectiveness of behavior and work. They develop conditions for establishing trust and initiative. They build relationships throughout the organization and community, and, most important, together they create a structure of mutual regard and support. Leaders who understand that partnership is as vital as, if not more so than, hierarchy practice *being at the center* more than at the top. This is the *circle of power* referred to earlier. It is the place from which a leader must operate in order to cohere all parts of the organization and ensure that they work together effectively. In any system, the center is the point of cohesion. Cohesion brings *focus, competence, creativity and purpose* to the whole system. These four characteristics of leadership cohesion match the Four Powers of Intention, Wisdom, Compassion and Presence.

For a leader to be at the center more than at the top, he must envision and practice a more integrated and balanced purpose for his leadership. Every part of a wheel—the hub, spokes, rim, tire—serves the wheel intrinsically. The wheel could not be a wheel with any part missing. The leader as *hub* provides cohesion to the organization. The leader as *head* provides guidance and direction. Different conditions demand the leader to function in different capacities. It is *purpose* that balances the choice of which capacity. Whether the choice needs to be power or partnership in any given situation, purpose provides the lens of judgment. *Purpose* keeps the center balanced by focusing on critical results; weighing issues by virtue of values, boundaries and agreements; reevaluating conditions for success; managing the dynamics of change and growth; and maintaining common intent to affirm unity between vision and action. When a leader changes the *self-importance* quotient attached to his leadership and sees his role as a piece of the whole system, he usually develops humility. When a leader does not see himself as part of the whole system, he will tend to see himself not just as indispensable to the organization, but as the reason for the organization's existence.

Cultivating Humility

Great leaders are most often humble, and serving as both power source and partner humbles them. To see oneself as part of a living system—interdependent upon it, rather than separate from it—is a major step of cultivation and in itself generates humility. Genuine humility indicates that a leader has worked to integrate his shadow projections. When a leader recognizes that he projects his grandiosity—his overinflated self-importance—onto the organization or community, and, most important, when he reclaims that grandiosity, he becomes able to affirm others more naturally (Presence), to be more empathic toward others (Compassion), to better understand the needs and potential of the entire enterprise (Wisdom) and to dedicate himself to the enterprise with a clear focus (Intention). When he eliminates his own grandiosity, a leader gains the proper perspective of himself: He is nothing more *and* nothing less than one aspect of a vital community. With this perspective, the leader is better able to handle both the positive and negative aspects that his followers project on him.

For example, despite his followers' constantly projecting a divine image on him, the Dalai Lama continually affirms that he is nothing more than a simple Buddhist monk. His daily practice of meditation and study, his lighthearted yet dedicated attitude toward his secular and spiritual duties as the leader of Tibetan Buddhism and of the Tibetan government in exile indicate the seriousness of his assertion and his ability to work with his own challenges of grandiosity.

REEVALUATING THE LEADER'S IMAGE OF LEADERSHIP

As part of the cultivating process, besides shifting one's perception to the leader's role as the center of power, one must also reexamine one's inner images of what it is to be a leader. These inner images have been built up over a long period of time and have been tested against people whom one regards as leaders. These images arise out of the deep strata of archetypes in the human unconscious that have been activated by fairy tales, stories, movies, TV and unique encounters throughout one's life. One tests these leader images in daily reality by projecting both positive and negative aspects of them onto parents, teachers, ministers, bosses, politicians, generals, athletes, entertainers, etc. As one unconsciously projects these images onto real people, one judges these individuals as positive or negative leaders based on how they match or don't match one's images.

For example, if one positively regards strong, objective, direct leadership (Warrior), one may dislike any leadership behavior that shows too many collaborative, inclusive, intuitive qualities (Artist). Or, one may be attracted to the calm, stable, affirming, visionary leader (Sovereign), and reject the secretive, manipulative, creative, innovative leader (Magician). Of course, the images of leadership one holds are more complicated than these one-dimensional distinctions. The images of leadership that one develops for oneself and attempts to embody when in the leadership position oneself hold positive and negative characteristics that combine aspects of all four leadership archetypes.

Over time, one's projection of positive and negative attitudes changes as one encounters different types of leaders. These projections represent, on the one hand, the need to have another person provide, in a positive way, what one finds difficult to provide for oneself—such as purpose, motivation and challenge. Or, on the other hand, the projection can represent a negative attitude that resists anyone else's influence on one's life. If these images remain unconscious, they will drive one's reactions and responses to leaders in several different ways. One may reject some leaders outright, while others may seduce one into giving time, money or effort to their business, project or cause.

However one plays out leadership images, this testing between inner image and outer person illustrates how one will act as a leader oneself. One will tend to do what one admires, and avoid what one dislikes, in leaders. As pressures build in one's leadership position, the negative characteristics in others that one vowed never to manifest strangely begin to appear in one's own behavior. Over time, as one commits to working with one's inner leadership images, one may begin to understand that any leader upon whom one projects is simply another human being who is also struggling to make sense of his own life. When a developing leader acknowledges that one's attitude toward other leaders comes from one's own inner world, and may have nothing to do with those individual leaders' personalities or behavior, more fertile ground for cultivating insight and learning emerges.

A useful exercise for clarifying one's leader projections is to pick a leader one strongly likes and a leader one strongly dislikes, write out all the positive characteristics of the leader one likes and all the negative characteristics of the leader one dislikes. One then takes both lists to two or three trusted friends (and, if one is brave enough, to subordinates and colleagues) and asks these individuals for their feedback as to how they see these positive and negative leadership characteristics manifested in oneself. This exercise provides fertile ground for matching one's leadership self-image to external reality.

REFLECTION TOOLS FOR CULTIVATING

Assessments

Another more formal process for tilling the leadership ground is to take a series of leadership, personality and behavioral assessments. Many of these assessment processes include a variety of self-reflection instruments. An example of one assessment process has a leader take sixteen to twenty assessments profiling five areas. The first area, *the physical body*, contains assessments in brain orientation, negative stress patterns, information gathering, processing and expressing. The second area, *the mental domain*, includes instruments assessing one's approach to framing situations and problems, sequence of thinking, problem solving and decision making with groups, and modes of responding to conflict. The third area, *the personality characteristics*, assesses personality typology, interaction behavior in groups, interpersonal relationships and emotional reactions. The fourth area, *the characteristics of leadership*, has instruments that examine a leader's use of power, leadership effectiveness, interactions with subordinates, peers and superiors, and leadership typology. The fifth and final area of this particular assessment is a *summary snapshot* of the individual's current behaviors, based on attitudes, values and key stressors.

A 360-degree assessment review by subordinates, peers and superiors (CEO, chairman or board of directors), evaluating one's leadership characteristics, is another useful method to provide feedback and a multidimensional view of a person's leadership competencies as they are experienced by others in one's work world. All leadership assessing is designed to help the leader reflect back to himself his own leader image and compare it to an objectified reference.

The purpose of taking a *variety* of assessments is to help the leader form a picture of the pattern of his entire life. For example, understanding from assessments how negative stress patterns drive behavior and how one makes decisions may provide insight as to how one interacts with both spouse and subordinates. The strengths and weaknesses of behavior, as well as the positive and negative characteristics of personality style, provide an individual a lens through which he can become more conscious of himself in all types of daily activity. These assessments provide a framework for engaging in a series of in-depth explorations, reflections and exercises that can increase a leader's ability to determine the next natural step of his growth and development.

Journaling

Daily journaling and monthly review of the journal can also provide a real-time snapshot of the patterns within which a leader is operating. Contemplating the patterns of decision making, employee interaction and intuitive thoughts and hunches can provide clues to which of the Four Powers one needs to cultivate in order to achieve the most effective leadership one can.

"Elder" Counselor

Using an "elder" counselor as a reflection partner is another way to assess areas that need cultivation. An elder counselor is not necessarily someone of advanced age. Rather, "elder" denotes someone with experience, insight and wisdom regarding those leadership issues one is working to master on a daily basis. Each of us needs a wise person in our life, someone who can provide an objective reflection when we need it. Most leaders find that they can't talk about certain issues with people inside their organizations. They need to find someone *outside* the organization, yet familiar enough with it, to listen, evaluate and give useful comments when needed. Leaders who are seeking growth know that they need an elder partner in their lives.

Peer Group Support

Some individuals use leadership organizations like a TEC Group or Young Presidents as peer sounding boards for their thoughts and concerns. This type of group provides peer discussion as well as regular one-on-one coaching from the group facilitator. Other individuals engage a personal leader-trainer—a coach who specializes in leadership development. Still others have a trusted friend who simply listens and mirrors back, through dialogue, what he hears the leader saying.

Whatever one's choice, leaders need someone outside the organization with whom they can confidentially discuss problems, strategies and ideas for leading their organizations. This dialogue needs to include both the personal issues of leading as well as the critical demands of the enterprise. Experience suggests that leaders should commit to a standing appointment of once every couple of weeks or once a month if they are serious about reflection. The elder counselor needs continuity and regular time with a leader in order to see the patterns within the daily changing issues. If a leader only seeks out an elder counselor in times of crisis, he limits the ability to see a crisis in advance and act on it before it becomes serious. Also, regular contact with an elder counselor prevents only putting one's best foot forward in conversation. A wise elder will read between the lines when presented a situation and be able to give the issue context and perspective from previous conversations in order to aid a leader in his development process.

The value of an elder counselor lies in his assisting the leader to think through current issues and their implications for the organization, as well as their implications as to leadership competence. In all these discussions, both the elder counselor and the leader need to keep their attention on understanding the patterns, the organizational dynamics, the business strategies and the leader's personal power—both the positive and shadow characteristics—in order for the leader to learn to be more self-reflective and aware on his own.

Cultivating Each Power in Its Own Time

No one person, at any given time, accesses all Four Powers equally in his leadership. The learning of each Power comes at different times in one's leadership life. The integration and synthesis of the Powers take a lifetime; the leader is never really "done." The personal/positional power gap provides ground for cultivation, as do changes of business circumstances, major organizational problems or interpersonal conflicts related to one's leadership position. Any of these situations, alone or in tandem, may activate shadow material and other unconscious behaviors. These difficult situations help one understand which of the Four Powers one needs to be actively cultivating. *One of the primary rules of thumb for cultivating leadership is that external difficulties and challenges mirror the place of growth and development within a person.* C. G. Jung's notion of individuation acknowledges that our inner world knows when it is ready to work on integrating and developing new aspects of the personality. Difficulties provide the message that cultivation is needed in a new field of growth.

The Purpose of Cultivation

There is no end to leadership learning and development. Many spiritual and psychological traditions affirm that the more one learns and experiences, the less one truly knows. These traditions suggest that as the ego structure (the structure that keeps one unconscious and bound to shadow behaviors) shrinks, one awakens and so becomes more conscious of the deeper patterns of reaction and fear that are part of the ego structure. What emerges as one confronts these deeper patterns is the conscious integration of the ego into a larger container within one's psyche called the *Self*. The Self is the most basic and central archetypal structure of a human being. The goal of the Self is to bring wholeness and unity to the human personality. The development of one's unique ego personality emerges out of this larger Self. The effort to find differentiation as a unique human being apart from parents and siblings is the struggle to separate from the Self. At a further point in life, one's psyche is set up to begin to release this highly constellated, unique ego structure back into the wider dimensions of the Self. This is a process of letting go and of integrating one structure—the ego—into another structure—the Self.

Many people live their whole lives without ever consciously confronting this very natural process. Those who don't confront this integration feel the emergence of the Self but connect the grandeur of it to their egos, becoming self-inflated by their perceptions of themselves as godlike and superior to others. Others may react in the opposite manner and be overcome by the Self's approach to the ego. Consequently, they come to feel small and weak—victims of some large and incomprehensible force. Still others take this onset of the Self's presence as the manifestation of God and they worship the Self as such. Jung in fact, suggested that the Self does hold the God-image for us; yet, the Self is not God. Many people, leaders included, often erroneously confuse their Selves with God.

Those individuals in leadership roles find this tension between the ego and the Self to be a growing presence in their lives. The more a leader learns about his ego, the more cultivation he needs to integrate it back into the more encompassing Self. This journey of awakening to the Self provides the true integration of not only the four archetypes of a leader, but also the integration of a wide variety of archetypal patterns that an individual needs to embrace in order to become fully human and humane.

As with any garden, the purpose of cultivation in a leader is to stimulate healthy, productive growth. A leader's garden is the organization, his followers or a cause to which he is committed. The way in which a leader views himself in this garden is *his* reality. Reality, whether it is viewed scientifically, metaphysically or personally is the basic organizing structure that makes sense of the world and gives it meaning. One experiences his own reality by the type of energy it has. Energy is a descriptor for how things move, change and transform. Energy either expands or contracts, grows or recedes. Cultivation is consciously using energy to keep one's reality living, growing and expanding.

CULTIVATION REQUIRES AWARENESS AND PRACTICE

The four archetypes provide the source of a leader's energy. Conscious, daily cultivation through awareness and practice is the means to grow and expand these powers. There are three things to keep in mind in order to learn to cultivate consistently and to foster healthy, productive growth.

First, in small and large ways, learn to *surrender the ego and let go* on a daily basis. Remember the principle of equanimity: Things are as they are. One can do little to influence and change most things. Resistance only creates frustration. Letting go creates the openness and space within one's consciousness that one needs in order to perceive things differently. Seeing people and situations differently provides a greater freedom for responding and acting. Letting go is a fundamental challenge for a leader because of the built-in need to control that is part of the responsibility and accountability inherent to positional power.

One COO created a time map for a week, month and year that reflected work, family, community and personal life, with time goals for each segment. His elder counselor would periodically challenge the COO by examining the percentage of time given to the various categories. Invariably work would begin to dominate the time map, sneaking into evenings, morning breakfasts and weekends. After reworking the commitments and issues that were causing this time imbalance, the COO would take a minisabbatical. He would take a sabbatical from the area that was dominating his time and give that time for the next several weeks to the segment that had been receiving the least amount of time. Letting go of control where the most time had been devoted was both scary and challenging for him. The letting go of control let the COO learn to trust his subordinates more, integrate some shadow material into his life and reaffirm relationship priorities.

Second, decisions are a leader's number-one job, and *pattern recognition is his key.* To be effective at making optimal decisions, a leader needs to keep his attention on the larger pattern shaping the decision, not the particular issues at hand. It was said of Napoleon that he didn't answer any of his mail for three weeks. His reason was that the immediate issues and concerns that people were bringing to him would generally be solved within that three-week period. He had discovered that if he responded immediately to a request, he usually made the situation worse. Time and changing circumstances gave him more perspective. We don't all have three weeks to make a decision, but Napoleon's principle of using time to achieve a wider perspective on how things fit together is a useful notion for leaders.

Learning to shift perceptions is the key to pattern recognition. To learn to see from different viewpoints, one CEO would have workers on the assembly line and clerks in the offices periodically attend senior staff meetings to give their viewpoints on a particular business issue. A CFO would regularly call an analyst who was opposed to the company's strategy, respectfully listen to the analyst's negative comments and ask for suggestions. This was very risky for a CFO of a public company, but in the end, for this leader it paid off in understanding some basic flaws in the company strategy that no one on the management team or in the analyst community were seeing.

Shifting perception provides contrast between one's old reactions and new responses to people and situations. A common challenge for a leader is to learn not to view subordinates and followers according to an initial interaction, actions they've undertaken or hearsay. If the view of someone is negative, one has difficulty seeing beyond that filter. "New eyes" require a leader to make the effort to shift perception and see, hear and interact with this person in different ways. One executive routinely had one-on-one skip-level meetings with employees who tended to complain or be resistant to a company policy or strategy. He would not talk about the issue or complaint; rather, he would talk about the employee's family, personal interests and career aspirations. The executive was not interested in learning about the issue or changing the person's views. What the executive wanted was a chance to *see* the person outside the context of his complaints. A leader doesn't have to like everyone he leads, but all leaders need to see and value people and situations beyond those people's perceptions, which are often locked into shadow prejudices.

When a leader has begun to achieve pattern recognition, reactions and decisions become less driven by shadow material. Being able to see the interconnection between things (the pattern) is an indication that more of the shadow material is being brought to consciousness and is being integrated into one's life.

Third, *practice is what one does when one is leading*. Practice is not about being perfect or arriving at some ultimate goal. Practice itself is the goal. Practice is the point of what a leader does every day. A meditator does not sit in meditation to achieve some transcendental state. The practice is to recognize the state that one is experiencing while meditating. In time, the meditator experiences some of the fruits of the practice: calmness, insight, compassion, etc. It is the same for a leader. Consider another example. For a leader to have a set of practices is like the gardener tending his garden every day. If it is not weeded, watered and pruned, no fruit will grow. If the leader does not work on pattern recognition, letting go or working with shadow material as a practice, development does not occur.

The word *practice* comes from the ancient Greek *prassein*, meaning "to do." Practice is not thinking about doing, it is acting—doing it habitually, regularly, day after day. The first section of this book described "The Practice of Leadership." It described some simple truths about leadership and what successful leaders *do* to be good leaders. If a leader is willing to be self-reflective, he will realize which areas he needs to practice at any given time. Each leader knows instinctively his limit for growth and learning. Moving forward requires taking a step *beyond* that limit. Practicing is doing something, taking action, taking the next step.

THE PERFECT LEADER?

There is an old Zen story that has been retold many times, but it fits the ending of this exploration of leadership. A Zen master was asked by a student how he would be different if he became enlightened. The master replied, "Before enlightenment, one will chop wood and carry water. After enlightenment, one will chop wood and carry water." One might ask what is different in a leader who cultivates the Four Powers. Leaders who have been cultivating the Four Powers may demonstrate no outward difference in their appearance or in their active leadership roles. But, as with any enlightened person who is chopping wood and carrying water, followers will sense in this leader a capacity—a breadth and width of approachability (Presence), a creativity and simplicity of problem solving and decision making (Wisdom), an inclination toward committed action (Intention), and a perspective about people that balances social and economic needs with spiritual ones (Compassion).

Leadership, in the end, is a state of being. We are human *beings*, after all, not human *doings*. One does things as a practice to *be*. One cultivates and develops to reveal one's natural state. Within the deep strata of a human being's psychological and spiritual core, one finds fertile ground for grappling with the challenge of becoming a leader. Leadership is a great mirror that teaches everyone—leaders and followers alike—about unifying and integrating the shadow and light of one's existence.

CHAPTER NOTES

Introduction

1. Peter Drucker describes that the leaders he knew or observed "knew four simple things." The four things were: a leader had followers; a leader is not someone who is loved or admired, but rather one who gets results; a leader is visible and sets examples; and a leader knows that leadership is not a privilege, but a responsibility. Drucker then goes on to list six issues leaders focus on: (1) What really needs to be done. (2) How to make a difference. (3) What constitutes performance and results. (4) How to be tolerant of diversity of followers, but intolerant of inconsistent performance, standards and results. (5) How not to react in fear to the strength of those around one. (6) "Confront the Mirror" test: Only do those things that one can be proud of. Don't do mean or petty things that one would not be proud to admit. *The Leader of the Future*, eds. Frances Hessellbein, Marshall Goldsmith and Richard Becknhard, Drucker Foundation Series (San Francisco: Jossey-Bass, 1996). See also Drucker's classic, *The Practice of Management* (San Francisco: Harper San Francisco, 1993).

2. The view of leadership as a state of being is described by Robert Fritz in his book *Corporate Tides: The Inescapable Laws of Organizational Structure* (San Francisco: Berrett-Koehler Publishers, 1996). Fritz is a friend and colleague of Peter Senge, and both posit some interesting ideas and theories about organizations. In this book on structure, Fritz cites seven elements of leadership that he has observed and that make for great leadership. (1) Leaders provide clarity to the organization through vision and values that are

translated into action. (2) Leaders take total responsibility for the organization. They willingly carry this burden. (3) Style is not the essence of leadership, substance is. Substance includes wise judgment, strength of character, purpose, and strong urges toward values and aspirations. (4) Organizational leadership doesn't need the charismatic personality. Leadership needs strategy, intelligence, ability to assess reality and a will to "get the job done"—to reach goals and achieve results. (5) Leaders encourage others to join them in creating results. (6) Leaders motivate others to focus on reality in order to get results. (7) Leaders know how to move followers to get from current reality to a vision of an agreed-upon outcome.

3. Are we born leaders? James Hillman argues in his acorn theory, "perhaps." With the metaphor of the acorn, he is using the notions of image, fate, destiny, soul and many other similar terms to indicate how both our character and the inner drive or calling grows, emerges and gets manifested within us. Hillman's argument would be, yes we are born leaders—but! And that "but" is determined by our response to many variables in the world around us. At the heart of his notion is awakening the seed of one's inner hearing so as to perceive what is most naturally who we are. Many of us should be leaders and don't listen. And those of us trying to be leaders aren't listening to what we really are called to be. James Hillman, *The Soul's Code: In Search of Character and Calling* (New York: Random House, 1996).

4. Neither extrovert nor introvert personality traits determine leadership. A review of the literature on leadership and personality types provides supporting evidence that personality type alone is not a leadership determiner. Christa L. Walck, "Using the MBTI in Management and Leadership: A Review of the Literature," in *Developing Leaders: Research and Applications in Psychological Type and Leadership Development*, ed. Catherine Fitzgerald and Linda Kirby (Palo Alto, Calif.: Davies-Black Publishing, 1997).

5. Leaders provide emotional and spiritual resources for the organization. Managers provide the physical resources for the organization. Warren Bennis and Burt Nanus, *Leaders: The Strategies for*

Taking Charge (San Francisco: Harper & Row, Perennial Library, 1985), 40–41, 92–93, 218. See also Warren Bennis, *On Becoming a Leader* (Menlo Park, Calif.: Addison Wesley, 1989), 44–47.

6. Those with technical, financial or organizational genius tend to receive acclaim as leaders. Note the current positive and negative views on Bill Gates, Andy Grove and Michael Milken.

7. Warren Bennis and Robert Townsend review differences between managing and leadership in their *Reinventing Leadership* (New York: William Morrow & Company, 1995). To cite some examples from their discussion: The manager administers; the leader innovates. The manager maintains; the leader develops. The manager focuses on systems and structure; the leader focuses on people. The manager relies on control; the leader inspires trust. The manager has a short-term view; the leader has a long-term view. The manager has an eye on the bottom line; the leader has an eye on the horizon.

8. James MacGregor Burns, *Leadership* (New York: HarperTorch Books, 1978). Burns is credited with coining the term *transformational leadership*. The book is acknowledged as the definitive classic on the macro view of leadership. It covers all forms of leadership: political, business, religious, etc.

9. Robert Fritz, *The Path of Least Resistance* (Salem, Mass.: Stillpoint Publishing, 1984).

10. Laurence J. Peter, *The Peter Principle: Why Things Always Go Wrong* (New York: Bantam Books, 1984).

11. Warren Blank, *The Nine Natural Laws of Leadership* (New York: American Management Association, 1995), 210–19.

12. Peter Senge, *The Fifth Discipline: The Art and Practice of the Learning Organization* (New York: Doubleday Currency, 1990).

13. John Kotter describes four key classical processes that make up the basics of good management. They are planning, budgeting, organizing and controlling. See his descriptions in *The Leadership Factor* (New York: Free Press, 1988), 21–24.

14. From a very different viewpoint of leadership characteristics Margaret Wheatley, in her book *Leadership and the New Science:*

Learning About Organization from an Orderly Universe (San Francisco: Berrett-Koehler Publishers, 1992), considers the principles of quantum physics and observes that effective leadership uses three "simple governing principles: guiding visions, strong values, organizational beliefs—the few rules individuals can use to shape their own behavior." Because of the impact of scientific knowledge on our culture, Wheatley argues that a different understanding of leadership is emerging. "Leadership is *always* dependent on the context, but the context is established by the relationships we value." She goes on to say that what relationship implies for leaders is to understand and use the complex network of people and systems that make up an organization. Not knowing how to do this limits and makes a leader ineffective. Pages 144–45.

15. Leading needs to be viewed in the context of different management approaches. Douglas McGregor, in his book *The Human Side of Enterprise* (New York: McGraw-Hill, 1960), puts forward the classic definition of two types of managers based on two sets of assumptions about human nature and what motivates employees and followers to complete their work. Some of McGregor's ideas are based on the motivational theory of Abraham Maslow. These two views of managing people McGregor calls Theory X and Theory Y. In simplest terms, Theory X represents the view that most managers believe that their employees are lazy, unambitious and need to be threatened, bribed, directed or punished in order to get them to work. Theory X is the carrot-or-stick approach to motivating people. Much of this viewpoint is based on Frederick Taylor's view that people have to be organized like machines in order to get the maximum amount of work from them. Theory Y views people as eager to participate, take responsibility, set goals and be self-directed. A Theory Y manager has to be more participatory and take more risks with employees. In essence the Y manager allows employees room for personal growth on the job, decision making and input into the job activity. Today this view seems self-evident, but it was McGregor's work at UCLA that stimulated the empowerment movement of today. See

also Abraham Maslow, *Motivation and Personality* (New York: Harper, 1954) and his classic book, *Toward a Psychology of Being* (New York: D. Van Nostrand Co., Inc., 1962). Here, Machiavellian principles of leadership are viewed as authoritarian, overcontrolling, Theory X–type attitudes toward followers. This form of leadership comes from Niccolo Machiavelli, *The Prince*, trans. Dominic Baker-Smith (New York: Knopf, Everyman's Library, 1992) and current books such as Wess Roberts, *Leadership Secrets of Attila the Hun* (New York: Warner Books, 1991).

16. Peter, *Peter Principle*.

17. Definitions and derivations of words come from *Webster's New Universal Unabridged Dictionary*, 2d ed. (New York: Simon & Schuster, 1979).

18. See chapter 3 for more on samurai and Irish warrior traditions.

19. Thomas A. Stewart, "Get with the *New* Power Game," *Fortune*, 13 January 1997, 58–62.

20. "Larry Bossidy Won't Stop Pushing," *Fortune*, 13 January 1997, 135–37.

21. Stephen Covey, *Seven Habits of Highly Effective People* (New York: Simon & Schuster, 1989).

22. See note 7 above.

23. Warren Bennis, *On Becoming a Leader* (Menlo Park, Calif.: Addison Wesley, 1989).

24. John Kotter, *The Leadership Factor* (New York: Free Press, 1988).

25. John Gardner, *On Leadership* (New York: Free Press, 1990).

26. Jay Conger, *The Charismatic Leader* (San Francisco: Jossey-Bass, 1989).

27. See note 1 above.

28. Peter Senge, *The Fifth Discipline: The Art and Practice of the Learning Organization* (New York: Doubleday Currency, 1990).

29. Robert Fritz, *The Path of Least Resistance* (Salem, Mass.: Stillpoint Publishing, 1984).

30. Wheatley, *Leadership and the New Science*. Wheatley's book

is the application of the *Tao of Physics* and other popular works on the "new science" to organizational understanding and problems. Wheatley applies these scientific concepts to the management of organizations and information, offering new insight on issues troubling people most: order and change, autonomy and control, structure and flexibility, planning and innovation.

31. Robert Moore and Douglas Gillette, *King, Warrior, Magician, Lover* (New York: William Morrow, 1991) and the individual books: *The King Within* (New York: William Morrow, 1992); *The Warrior Within* (New York: Avon, 1993); *The Magician Within* (New York: Avon, 1994); *The Lover Within* (New York: Avon, 1995).

32. Hillman, *Soul's Code.*

33. William Strauss and Neil Howe, *The Fourth Turning: An American Prophecy* (New York: Broadway Books, 1997). I have found this book both enlightening and deeply disturbing because of its obvious truth about the nature of cycles and the patterns we've been in as an Anglo-American culture for the past five hundred years. Strauss and Howe do an amazing and clear job of laying out the pattern we are in and the one that is to come. By their description we are in the third turning—the *Unraveling*—and soon to go into the *Crisis.* The following is from the card catalog description of the book presented online at *Amazon.com.*

> The authors look back five hundred years and uncover a distinct pattern: Modern history moves in cycles, each one lasting about the length of a human life, each composed of four eras—or "turnings"—that last about twenty years and that always arrive in the same order. First comes a High, a period of confident expansion as a new order takes root after the old has been swept away. Next comes an Awakening, a time of spiritual exploration and rebellion against the now-established order. Then comes an Unraveling, an increasingly troubled era in which individualism triumphs over crumbling institutions. Last comes a Crisis—the Fourth Turning—when society passes through a great and perilous gate in history. Together, the four turnings comprise history's seasonal rhythm of

growth, maturation, entropy, and rebirth.

By applying the lessons of history, *The Fourth Turning* makes some bold and hopeful predictions about America's next rendezvous with destiny. It also shows us how we can prepare for what's ahead, both individually and as a nation.

34. Moore's notion of our cultural failure to initiate people into the use of positive power is taken from a lecture in 1986 at the Mendocino Men's conference.

35. Moore and Gillette, *King, Warrior, Magician, Lover,* 3–8.

36. See also Riane Eisler, *The Chalice and the Blade: Our History, Our Future* (San Francisco: HarperCollins, 1987); Jean Bolen, *The Gods in Everyman: A New Psychology of Men's Lives and Loves* (San Francisco: Harper & Row, 1989); Robert Bly, *The Sibling Society* (Menlo Park, Calif.: Addison Wesley, 1996); Marija Gimbutas, *The Civilization of the Goddess: The World of Old Europe* (San Francisco: Harper & Row, 1991).

37. Joseph Campbell, *Myths to Live By* (New York: Arkana, 1993). The brilliant author of *The Masks of God* shares his ideas and speculations on our universal myths in a fascinating, very personal work that explores the enduring power of the myths that influence our lives, and examines the myth-making process from the primitive past to the immediate present.

38. Ibid.

39. Gorbachev was and is a commanding leader in the charismatic sense. Rather than sheer threat of power, Gorbachev used his personality and vision to change the course of history. At the core of his vision was *perestroika*, which according to his own press kit means "a moral cleansing of society and the opening up of creative possibilities for a free and all-round development of personality." As author Gail Sheehy writes, "The definition keeps broadening; *perestroika* started as a slogan for a new economic deal that would do away with the central-command system created under Stalin. Now Gorbachev uses it to mean a mass spiritual psychotherapy for his people. The definition keeps changing because he keeps changing."

And today after his political rejection in Russia, he still crusades, heading up his World Futures foundation and the prestigious annual world conference on global issues. Gorbachev has expanded *perestroika* to include a "cleansing" of the whole planet. Gail Sheehy, "Gorbachev: Red Star—The Shaping of the Man Who Shook the World," *Vanity Fair*, February 1990. See also Zhores Medvedev, *Gorbachev* (New York: W. W. Norton & Co., 1987); Mikhail Gorbachev, *Memories* (New York: Doubleday, 1996).

40. I began my consulting in the Soviet Union as one of ten consultants and presidents of companies in the United States who were invited by the Gorbachev government to work with the emerging cooperatives (the for-profit enterprises that he authorized as a step in moving away from the production economy that was devastating the economic health of the USSR). The result of our first trip in 1987 was to establish the Foundation for Soviet/American Economic Cooperation, headquarters in Seattle, Washington. After the collapse of the USSR, the name was changed to the Foundation for Russian/American Economic Cooperation. The foundation continues to foster economic development between midsize companies in the United States and Russia as well as to administer economic projects for AID. (Contact: Carol Vipperman, President, 1932 First Avenue, Suite 803, Seattle, WA 98101.) Citizen diplomacy during the 1980s had significant impact on Gorbachev and on the development of his plan to change the economy and politics of the USSR. When we talked with the people directly around Gorbachev, they told us that they had a plan to slowly change the economy and that it would take twenty-five years. Obviously events overtook Gorbachev, and he couldn't put the plan into effect. Gorbachev was concerned that to shift from a production economy to a market economy too quickly could devastate the country. He was both a realist and a pragmatist. Events are proving that his assessment was probably correct. Current information from Russia indicates that conditions for the common people are very bad. Most workers are not paid for months at a time and have to barter or steal to get food. "'You can go to any region of

Russia and find people who have not received their wages,' says Irene Stevenson, who works for the Free Trade Union Institute in Moscow, which supports independent trade-union growth in Russia. 'The state's debt is higher than it's ever been. It's broken all records,' she says, adding that as of March [1998] the government owed unpaid workers more than $8.5 billion." Genine Babakian, "Destitute Russians More Interested in Survival Than Politics," *USA Today*, 31 March 1998.

41. The United States is the largest exporter of military equipment on the planet. Excellent information on this topic comes from the Federation of American Scientists online Arms Sales monitoring project, and especially their *Arms Sales Table* at *www.fas.orgasmp/index.html* and their August 1997 (no. 35) edition. In the August 1997 edition they show that the U.S. market share for arms sales world-wide has grown to 70 percent. The same article outlines the huge push by the Pentagon into former Soviet-bloc countries where the current market is worth $30 billion and remains the only region of the world that has been denied Western military products. Also see online articles at *www.context.org* on "Is Militarism Fading?", and in particular "A Path to Global Disarmament" by Sarah van Gelder and "Military Spending and the American Economy" by Gary Chapman.

42. *Human Development Report* cited in *World Watch,* Sept./Oct. 1994. See also *State of the World Report* for years 1990 to 1998 and Donella Meadows, Dennis Meadows, and Jorgen Randers, *Beyond the Limits: Confronting Global Collapse, Envisioning a Sustainable Future* (Post Mills, Vt.: Chelsea Green Publishing, 1992). This book is the sequel to *Beyond the Limits of Growth* (published in 1972). Doing computer modeling, this team describes various scenarios for our future, focusing on five critical factors: natural resources, food production, population growth, industrial output and levels of pollution. At roughly 2040, all the curves come together. Resources experience a severe decline, population shoots up beyond food capacity, and industrial output and pollution peak. Not a pretty picture. The authors argue convincingly for focusing on a sustainable means of meeting these challenges.

43. Half a million Americans are users of heroin; 3 million, users of cocaine and crack; 15 million, alcoholics. These are the official statistics for 1995. Unofficial estimates run three times as high. Nicotine addicts are 53 million and spend $60 billion a year on tobacco. *State of the World Atlas*, 5th ed. (New York: Penguin, 1995).

44. In its lawsuit against the tobacco companies, the State of Minnesota forced them to hand over 33 million pages of documents related to health issues and young children, to determine what would get them to start smoking at the earliest age. These documents can be found online at *www.tobaccoresolution.com*. See also Shaifali Puri, "Bible Thumping: An Anti-tobacco Lawyer Takes on Philip Morris's Geoffrey Bible," *Fortune*, 30 March 1998, 30–31.

45. In my book *Human Robots and Holy Mechanics: Reclaiming Our Souls in a Machine World* (Portland, Oreg.: Swan-Raven & Co., 1993), I lay out many of the conflicting forces that are driving the worldwide economic culture and its negative impact on our lives. I argue that each of us must learn to shift from a victim view of the world to one that lets each of us become a resource to the situations we find ourselves in.

46. John Gardner, "The Antileadership Vaccine," in *Annual Report of the Carnegie Corporation* (New York: Carnegie Corporation, 1965), 12.

47. Strauss and Howe, *The Fourth Turning*.

48. Pierre Teilhard de Chardin, *The Phenomenon of Man* (New York: HarperCollins, 1980).

49. Michael Mead told this story about the crisis of the crossroads at a conference in San Francisco, January 1986.

1: The Structure of Power

1. Jung's premise is that "personal consciousness consists for the most part of complexes, the content of the collective unconscious is made up essentially of archetypes." Jung traces the history of archetypes back from the earliest Greek period to his contemporaries using

such terms as "categories of the imagination," "elementary" forms, and "primordial thoughts," and defining the word *archetype* as a "preexistent form." He then traces the psychological character of archetypes and concludes that they are "the unconscious images of the instincts themselves, in other words, that they are patterns of *instinctual behavior*." *Archetypes of the Collective Unconscious, Collected Works of C G Jung*, vol. 9, part 1, *The Archetypes and the Collective Unconscious*. (Princeton, N.J.: Princeton University Press, 1953), 3–44. In Jung's autobiography, *Memories, Dreams and Reflections* (New York: Random House, Vintage Books, 1961), he gives a brief description of the archetypes on page 347. The archetypes, he says, "are pre-existent to consciousness and condition it . . . as a priori structural forms of the stuff of consciousness. They do not in any sense represent things as they are in themselves, but rather the forms in which things can be perceived and conceived." He goes on to say that the archetype possesses "a specific energy which causes or compels definite modes of behavior or impulses. . . ." that can demonstrate a compulsive force in the personality. It is this compulsive force of the archetype that generates the power within a person. In my view the clearest description of Jung on archetypes comes from his essay "The Psychology of the Child Archetype" in *Collected Works* (vol. 9, part 1, p. 267). Jung says,

> Archetypes are, by definition, factors and motifs that arrange the psychic elements into certain images, characterized as archetypal, but in such a way that they can be recognized only from the effects they produce. They exist preconsciously, and presumably they form the structural dominants of the psyche in general. . . . As *a priori* conditioning factors they represent a special psychological instance of the biological "pattern of behavior," which gives all things their specific qualities. Just as the manifestations of this biological ground plan may change in the course of development, so also can those of the archetype. Empirically considered, however, the archetype did not ever come into existence as a phenomenon of organic life, but entered into the picture with life itself.

Jung's basic code word for archetype is "primordial image." By this notion of image, Jung meant all the historical, mythological stories and fairy tales, as well as dreams, visions and fantasies of the modern person.

For a clear and simple discussion of Jung's idea of archetypes, see the book by his longtime secretary, Jolande Jacobi, *Complex, Archetype, Symbol in the Psychology of C. G. Jung,* Bollingen Series no. 57 (Princeton, N.J.: Princeton University Press, 1959).

2. James Hillman, *Re-Visioning Psychology* (New York: Harper & Row, Perennial Library, 1975), xiii–xv.

3. Ibid., xiii–xv.

4. Ibid., xiii–xv.

5. Ibid., xiii–xv.

6. Ibid., xiii–xv.

7. Ibid., xiii–xv.

8. Ibid., xiii–xv.

9. John Sanford and George Lough, *What Men Are Like* (New York: Paulist Press, 1988).

10. Ibid., 14.

11. Ibid., 14.

12. Ibid., 14.

13. Ibid., 30.

14. Ibid., 30.

15. John Kotter, *The Leadership Factor* (New York: Free Press, 1988). Kotter defines leadership as "the process of moving a group (or groups) in some direction through mostly noncoercive means. Effective leadership is defined as leadership that produces movement in the long-term best interests of the group(s)" (page 5). John Kotter's *Power and Influence: Beyond Formal Authority* (New York: Free Press, 1985) has a significant discussion of power and influence by leaders. Kotter argues that the adage "power always corrupts" not only needs to be reexamined as a truism, but also needs to be confronted in our training and development of executives (pages 184–92).

2: Characteristics of the Four Powers

1. John Weir Perry, *Lord of the Four Quarters: The Mythology of Kingship* (New York: Paulist Press, 1991).

2. Robert Moore and Douglas Gillette describe the immature masculine as an expression of "boy" psychology, which is the "stunted masculine, fixated at immature levels." *King, Warrior, Magician, Lover* (New York: William Morrow, 1991), xvii.

3. Elder initiation was common in primitive cultures. This was considered the second initiation after the puberty initiation. Malidoma Somé describes this initiation taking place somewhere in the range of forty to sixty years old, depending on when the initiated elders deem the individual ready for this initiation. Malidoma says that in his African tribe the purpose of elder initiation is fundamentally to receive access to the magical language that is used in initiating the young, healing the sick, calling game and bringing changes in the weather. His description follows the anthropological descriptions of shaman initiation in many cultures. (Private discussions.) See also Mircea Eliade, *Rites and Symbols of Initiation* (New York: Harper & Row, 1958) on initiation rites. In *Ritual: Power, Healing and Community* (Portland, Oreg.: Swan-Raven & Co., 1993) Malidoma Somé shows the central role of elders in governing the archetypes of the community and the need to have elders initiated. See also my discussion of the need for modern elder initiation in *Human Robots and Holy Mechanics: Reclaiming Our Souls in a Machine World* (Portland, Oreg.: Swan-Raven & Co., 1993), 217–30. In the discussion, I indicate that myth, ritual and power are linked:

> In fact, all ancient cultures have known for thousands of years that power was an interaction between the seen and unseen. Power came from outside the material world, and myth (the cultural story that links the spirit world to this one) provided the understanding of the power. Myth gave the boundaries, conditions and approaches to the power. Ritual was a technique for using and determining how the power could be used. Ritual protected us from the power. Ritual

prescribed the conduit through which power could be channeled safely.

Rediscovering the relationship between myth, ritual and power may be one of the paths back to our ancient roots. The lessons of history and current anthropological research indicate that peoples worked with this power in communities. To revive our mythic roots, to restore vital and living ritual and become conscious and respectful so that we can interact with the power and force of Nature—of some Force beyond rational definition—this is the fundamental change we must make.

4. Moore and Gillette, *King, Warrior, Magician, Lover.*

5. In *The Fourth Turning: An American Prophecy* (New York: Broadway Books, 1997), William Strauss and Neil Howe give an excellent matrix and discussion of the four archetypes from several different authors and viewpoints, and examine how these archetypes influence generational attitudes and temperaments. As an example of many of the elements they compare, see the following:

Moore/Gillette	King	Lover	Magician	Warrior
Thompson	Headman	Clown	Shaman	Hunter
	(king)	(artist)	(priest)	(soldier)
Jung	Thinking	Intuition	Feeling	Sensation
Spranger	Theoretical	Aesthetic	Religious	Economic
Adickes	Traditional	Agnostic	Dogmatic	Innovative
Season	Spring	Summer	Fall	Winter
Deity	Prometheus	Dionysus	Apollo	Epimetheus
Kretschmer	Anesthetic	Hyperesthetic	Melancholic	Hypomanic
Howe/Strauss	Hero	Artist	Prophet	Nomad

6. William Irwin Thompson, *At the Edge of History* (New York: Irvington Publishers, 1971) describes the earliest pattern of the four archetypes to be headman, clown, shaman and hunter.

7. Moore's discussion of Jesus as a central psychic image for Western culture was given in a lecture at Mendocino Men's Conference in spring 1990.

8. See Jung's discussion of the central role of Christ as the symbol of the universal Self in history, dreams and other images in Western

culture in his "Introduction to the Religious and Psychological Problems of Alchemy," *Psychology and Alchemy (Collected Works,* vol. 12, revised second edition, [Princeton, N.J.: Princeton University Press, 1968], pages 8–19). Also, in *Symbols of Transformation* second edition (*Collected Works,* vol. 5, Bollingen series, no. 20 [Princeton, N.J.: Princeton University Press, 1967], 368) Jung says, "Christ, as a hero and god-man, signifies psychologically the self; that is, he represents the projection of this most important and most central of archetypes." In Jung's view the core of our Western archetype is the *imitatio Christi,* the imitation of Christ, which in his view forces us psychologically to be an outer, objective, extroverted, thinking culture. In this view we cannot evolve out of our problems because we need divine grace to get us out of our troubles. This is in contrast to the Eastern view of what Jung called the "self-liberating power of the introverted mind." See Jung's essay "Eastern and Western Thinking" in *The Portable Jung,* edited by Joseph Campbell (New York: Viking Press, 1971).

9. Jung describes the relationship between the unconscious and the shadow in the following way:

> The unconscious is commonly regarded as a sort of inscapsulated fragment of our most personal and intimate life—something like what the Bible calls the "heart" and considers the source of all evil thoughts. In the chambers of the heart dwell the wicked blood-spirits, swift anger and sensual weakness. This is how unconsciousness looks when seen from the conscious side. . . . Hence it is generally believed that anyone who descends into the unconscious gets into a suffocating atmosphere of egocentric subjectivity, and in this blind alley is exposed to the attack of all the ferocious beasts which the caverns of the psychic underworld are supposed to harbor.

Jung goes on to say that the confrontation with this unconscious world leads us to direct contact with our shadow. And "the shadow is a living part of the personality and therefore wants to live with it in some form. It cannot be argued out of existence or rationalized into harmlessness. This problem is exceedingly difficult, because it not only challenges the whole man, but reminds him at the same time of his helplessness and ineffectuality" ("Archetypes of the Collective Unconscious" in *Collected Works* of *C G Jung*, vol. 9, part 1, *The Archetypes and the Collective Unconscious* [Princeton, N.J.: Princeton University Press, 1953], 20–21).

10. Keith Crim, ed., *The Perennial Dictionary of World Religions* (San Francisco: Harper & Row, 1989).

11. Robert Graves, *The Greek Myths,* vol. 1 (Middlesex, England: Penguin Books, 1968).

12. Edward Whitmont, *The Symbolic Quest* (Princeton, N.J.: Princeton University Press, 1969) cited in Connie Zweig and Jeremiah Abrams, eds., *Meeting the Shadow: The Hidden Power of the Dark Side of Human Nature* (New York: Putnam, Tarcher/Perigree Books, 1991).

13. Adof Guggenbuhl-Craig, *Eros on Crutches: Reflections on Amorality and Psychopathy* (Dallas, Tex.: Spring Publications, 1980); cited in Zweig and Abrams, *Meeting the Shadow.*

14. William Eichman, "Meeting Darkness on the Path," *Gnosis,* winter 1990; cited in Zweig and Abrams, *Meeting the Shadow.*

15. Marsha Sinetar, *Do What You Love, the Money Will Follow* (New York: Dell Books, 1987); cited in Zweig and Abrams, *Meeting the Shadow.*

16. Karen Signell, *Wisdom of the Heart: Working with Women's Dreams* (New York: Bantam Books, 1990); cited in Zweig and Abrams, *Meeting the Shadow.*

17. Robert Bly, *A Little Book on the Human Shadow* (San Francisco: Harper & Row, 1988), 17.

18. Ibid., 19.

19. Robert Louis Stevenson, *Dr. Jekyll and Mr. Hyde* (New York: Everyman's Library, 1992).

20. Bly, *A Little Book on the Human Shadow.*

21. John Sanford, *Evil: The Shadow Side of Reality* (New York: Crossroads Publishing Co., 1984); cited in Zweig and Abrams, *Meeting the Shadow.*

22. Mary Henderson, *Star Wars: The Magic of Myth* (New York: Bantam, 1997).
23. Whitmont, *Symbolic Quest.*
24. Peter Nulty, "America's Toughest Bosses," *Fortune*, 27 February 1989.
25. Ibid.
26. Whitmont, *Symbolic Quest.*
27. Ibid.

3: The Warrior: The Power of Intention

1. Joseph Campbell, in *The Power of Myth* (Joseph Campbell with Bill Moyers; New York: Anchor, 1991), describes two types of deeds that the hero seeks to fulfill: "One is the physical deed, in which the hero performs a courageous act in battle or saves a life. The other is the spiritual deed, in which the hero learns to experience the supernatural range of human spiritual life and then comes back with the message" (page 152).

2. In the Japanese warrior tradition of the samurai, we have a blending of outer Warrior arts with inner spiritual development. The Zen Buddhist spiritual tradition was where the two were blended. At the heart of this blending was kendo—"the way of the sword." Besides the sword technique, Kendo incorporates the spiritual elements that control the art and discipline of fighting. The best example of how the two are blended is the classic kendo manual *A Book of Five Rings* by Miyamoto Musashi (trans. Victor Harris; Woodstock, N.Y.: Overlook Press, 1974). This is a book of strategy and can be applied to all types of "warrior" activity. Musashi is known to the Japanese as *kensei,* or "sword-saint." Musashi was born in 1584 and became Japan's most renowned samurai. *A Book of Five Rings* was written several weeks before his death in a cave he had been meditating in for two years. As with most samurai, Musashi meditated, did ink drawings, wrote poetry and practiced calligraphy.

In *A Book of Five Rings* he outlines a nine-step strategic "way" of living: (1) Do not think dishonestly. (2) The Way is in training. (3) Become acquainted with every art. (4) Know the Ways of all professions. (5) Distinguish between gain and loss in worldly matters. (6) Develop intuitive judgment and understanding for everything. (7) Perceive those things that cannot be seen. (8) Pay attention even to trifles. (9) Do nothing that is of no use. Other books that look at leadership from an Eastern Warrior perspective and apply these concepts to modern leadership challenges include: John Heider, *The Tao of Leadership* (Atlanta: Humanics, 1985), a modern leadership interpretation of the eighty-one verses of Lao-tzu's classic *Tao Te Ching;* Diane Dreher, *The Tao of Personal Leadership* (New York: HarperCollins, 1996), which applies the eighty-one sayings of the *Tao Te Ching* to modern leadership issues; Arnold Mindell, *The Leader as Marital Artist* (San Francisco: HarperSan Francisco, 1992), which uses the principles of martial art, such as *ki* energy, body movement, etc., to illustrate a Warrior leader's approach to leadership issues.

3. Anne W. Schaef and Diane Fassel, *The Addictive Organization* (San Francisco: Harper & Row, 1988), 57–58.

4. Bruce Shackleton, "Meeting the Shadow at Work," in Connie Zweig and Jeremaiah Abrams, eds., *Meeting the Shadow: The Hidden Power of the Dark Side of Human Nature* (New York: Putnam, Tarcher/Perigree Books, 1991).

5. Bryan Robinson, *Work Addiction* (Deerfield Beach, Fla.: Health Communications, 1989), vii–viii.

6. Dick Morris, *Behind the Oval Office* (New York: Random House, 1997).

7. The Warrior ethic has a long historical tradition. Murry Hope in *The Psychology of Ritual* (Dorset, England: Element Books, 1988) describes the five basic codes that historically have been the basis for cultural rituals and patterns of life. He calls these five codes: the Severity Code, the Emotional Code, the Contemplative Code, the Intellectual/Analytical Code and the Instinctive Code. Each code has its own style and period of history, but an individual code can also

show up within different cultural eras. The Severity Code epitomizes the Warrior tradition and showed itself strongly in the Hitler Youth movement, for example, as well as consistently in most modern military organizations. The Severity Code embodies "Teutonic Magic, the martial arts, Warrior and heroic rites, certain African and Amerindian rituals and the harsher Christian and Islamic practices. . . . [all of which] is of a disciplinary and sometimes punitive nature, and can involve physical mortification which may vary in intensity according to the traditions of the tribe or ethos concerned" (page 9).

8. Laurence J. Peter, *The Peter Principle: Why Things Always Go Wrong* (New York: Bantam, 1984).

9. Ibid., 19–27.

10. The "faker" is my term and it denotes a basic stress pattern that gets expressed through rationalization and procrastination. Mary Dempey and Rene Tihiata, in their book *Your Stress Personalities* (Novato, Calif.: Presidio Press, 1981) describe the faker stress pattern as the "Internal Con Artist." The Internal Con Artist is based on the principle of the double bind and giving oneself some kind of pleasure as an excuse to reduce tension and stress. When people are "faking it," they often procrastinate and put off until tomorrow what could be done today, because they really don't know what or how to do it. They are scared to ask people how to do something because they are "supposed" to know what to do. In this fear and tension of not knowing and not asking, they will insert something pleasurable to reduce this double bind. The easiest thing to try to relieve the stress is to work on something that's comfortable and "fun" to do, rationalizing that it is better to do something rather than nothing. In its extreme, the Internal Con Artist can overeat, drink, smoke, take drugs, etc., when the stress gets to be too much.

11. Shunryu Suzuki, *Zen Mind, Beginner's Mind: Informal Talks on Zen Meditation and Practice* (New York: Weatherhill, 1970). Suzuki, a Soto Zen priest, at fifty-three came to the United States for a short visit. Finding a great receptivity to Zen practice, he stayed and founded the San Francisco Zen Center as well as six other

locations. "In the beginner's mind there is no thought, 'I have attained something.' All self-centered thoughts limit our vast mind. When we have no thought of achievement, no thought of self, we are true beginners. Then we can really learn something. The beginner's mind is the mind of compassion. When our mind is compassionate, it is boundless. . . . This is the real secret of the arts: always be a beginner" (page 22).

12. Sun Tzu, *The Art of War* (Oxford, England: Oxford University Press, 1984). *The Art of War* is a classic Chinese book of strategy that has been popular reading with executives and managers.

13. Another useful book on Japanese warriors: *Zen and Japanese Culture* by D. T. Suzuki (Bollingen Series, no. 64, Princeton, N.J.: Princeton University Press, 1970). Suzuki was a Zen scholar. He came to the United States in the 1920s. He taught and wrote about Zen, and brought the first understanding of Zen practice and culture to the United States. His discussion of "Zen and the Samurai" provides an in-depth understanding of the spiritual focus of the samurai tradition. Another classic work is *Zen in the Art of Archery* by Eugen Herrigel (New York: Pantheon Books, 1964). Archery, like kendo or sword play, was used as a means to create an "artless art." This art demanded discipline, training, meditation and intense focus. Suzuki describes anyone who masters these "martial" arts as a "Zen artist of life." Aikido is a recently developed martial art that emphasizes the flow of energy within individuals and systems. Aikido was developed by a Japanese, Morihei Ueshiba. Two excellent books on aikido by John Stevens are: *Abundant Peace: Biography of Morihei Ueshiba, Founder of Aikido* (Boston: Shambhala, 1987) and *Aikido: The Way of Harmony* (Boston: Shambhala, 1984).

14. "Johari" comes from the first names of the two creators of the model (Joe and Harry). Joseph Luft, *Group Processes: An Introduction to Group Dynamics* (Mountain View, Calif.: Mayfield Publishing Company, 1970).

15. Two useful books on Alcoholics Anonymous are: *A Simple Program: A Contemporary Translation of the Book of Alcoholics Anonymous* (New York: Hyperion, 1996); and Deborah Thornton,

The Twelve Steps of Alcoholics Anonymous (Center City, Minn.: Hazelden, 1995). The first book is an interpretation by "J." of the original AA "Big Book," which was published in 1939. "J." is a long-time member of AA and, in keeping with its traditions, chooses to remain anonymous. The second book provdes a useful commentary on and discussion of the classic Twelve-Step program.

16. Warren Bennis and Burt Nanus, *Leaders: The Strategies for Taking Charge* (San Francisco: Harper & Row, Perennial Library, 1985), 187–89. Quotes are my description of the principles cited.

17. Robinson, *Work Addiction,* 159.

18. Ibid.

19. Donald Michael's five areas of leadership competency cited in Bennis and Nanus, *Leaders,* 82. An excellent example of this new competence that demonstrates all five points is a memo from a young CEO to his team. His company is a Silicon Valley start-up. In its first two years it confronted significant challenges. At the time of this memo to his direct reports (all functional VPs), the team had come through a couple months of implementing a new market strategy. I think the Warrior power of the memo speaks for itself about acknowledging, reexamining, encouraging, understanding his own limits, and continual learning within the context of the organization.

> To: execstaff
> Team,
>   There are a few important things I want to do as a team in the next ninety days. . . . Please be thinking of these and on the lookout for dates to talk about them.
>   (1) Have a great all hands and board meeting in April, digging into the whole demand generation program and starting to get some sense of our ability to impact the market . . . please start planning for the week of April 20th to be a "convergence point" where we check in on all the important things. . . . use the all hands, Sales Account reviews (4/22) and the board meeting to get a great checkpoint. (2) (Probably in May) Meet and review the metrics that each of you have for moving the ball down the field, and how we are

tracking to those goals. (3) Plan a two day session (tentatively June 30/July 1) with a facilitator to (a) review the first half, 199–, (b) set strategy and course and speed for 2H 199–, including changing direction wherever deemed appropriate, (c) answering the questions that we need to answer from the last couple board meetings, and (d) talk about the end of Concentration and the beginning of Momentum, and what we can/should do to complete concentration and kickstart momentum, including what a path to an IPO would look like starting in the July quarter. . . . I think we can know/assert our path substantially in this time frame.

So, I know you guys are kicking ass and taking names, and THE most important thing you can be doing (with your teams) is holding the vision, maintaining focus, and driving for measurable progress every single day on the major campaigns. . . . push as hard as you think you can live with to forward the action. Expect a lot, and be public that you expect a lot, just tell people why it matters that we really execute in these next few crucial months.

My job is to notice what structures and processes (and what timing) would be useful to install that allow us to reflect, learn, change, and then get back to the mission.

It is a pleasure to have an execstaff that can execute brilliantly with little supervision. . . . it is the power of what we can do as a TEAM that will make the difference in keeping us together in a high growth mode.

Food for thought, a few things to plan for. Thanks in advance for your participation.

John

20. Bennis and Nanus, *Leaders,* 187–217. These five points are my summary of key leadership characteristics from throughout the book. Particularly note chapter 6, "The Development of Self."

4: The Magician: The Power of Wisdom

1. *Fantasia*, Walt Disney Productions, 1940.

2. Joseph Campbell, *The Historical Atlas of World Mythology,* vol. 1, *The Way of the Animal Powers: Mythologies of the Primitive Hunters and Gatherers* (New York: Harper & Row, 1988); Mircea Eliade, *Shamanism: Archaic Techniques of Ecstasy* (New York: Pantheon, 1964); Joan Halifax, *Shaman: The Wounded Healer* (New York: Crossroads, 1982); Robert Lawlor, *Voices of the First Day: Awakening in the Aboriginal Dreamtime* (Rochester, Vt.: Inner Traditions, 1991).

3. John Granrose, "The Archetype of the Magician," diploma thesis, C. G. Jung Institute, Zurich, 1996.

4. The first step toward becoming a shaman usually entailed some sort of initiation into the way of the magician. Often for shamans, this initiation takes the form of a near-death experience by means of physical illness or accident, or the occurrence of some strange mental and emotional break with conscious reality. If the elders in the community observe certain conditions, the individual may be considered to have the potential to become a shaman. Such an individual would act as apprentice to a practicing shaman in order to acquire the skill and knowledge necessary to travel in the spirit world, work with herbs and other healing remedies, master incantations and healing songs, etc.

On the initiation rites of shamans, see Victor Turner, *The Ritual Process: Structure and Anti-structure* (Ithaca, N.Y.: Cornell University Press, Cornell Paperbacks, 1969). Turner, an anthropologist, gained from his research an in-depth knowledge of how initiation proceeds through stages of what he called liminal space, or thresholds, that changed both perception and experience of the person being initiated. Liminal space is a ritual process of unstructuring and then restructuring, or reconstellating, a new view of the world and the initiate's place in it.

5. Aleister Crowley, *Confessions of Aleister Crowley* (New York: Arkana, 1989).

6. Robert Moore, in a lecture at a conference in Mendocino, California, in 1990, outlined the thresholds of initiation and development in each of the four power archetypes that we are discussing. These stages proceed from unconscious to supraconscious awareness. From my notes they are as follows:

> *Awareness that there is power to access.* Before any initiation can start, there has to be a recognition that there is a power. Without beginning awareness that some kind of power is in my world of possibility, no initiation can begin for me.
>
> *Connection to the power through someone else.* Either projection of the power on others or admiration of the power qualities in them. I can perceive power at work in others, but may not recognize that the power is possible in me.
>
> *Connection to the power in ourselves in some way.* It could be recognition that we can display force and energy in a situation, that we know something, have passion for someone or something, or influence an outcome in some situation (without knowing the source of this power in us to do it).
>
> *Unconscious incompetence.* I am unaware of the quality and dynamics of the power itself. I feel or think I am wonderful because I can demonstrate the power. An example is: "new leaders give many orders" when they gain a new position of influence. They haven't integrated the power of the position into the personal power of their lives.
>
> *Conscious incompetence.* **Student stage.** I know I don't know very much. I begin to develop skills that are needed to use the power.
>
> *Unconscious competence.* **Apprenticeship stage.** I am constantly practicing the skills and capabilities in many settings with the power. I am not conscious of my own capability. I am learning from a mentor.
>
> *Conscious competence.* **Journeyman stage.** I know how to transfer skills to different situations when using the power. I can

coach others about developing the power. I continue to refine my capability and capacity to use the power.

Integration and stewardship of power. **Master stage.** I have a clear purpose, mission and direction for the power. I am in service to the power. I am a vessel by which the power works through me clearly and fully.

7. S. L. Mathers, *Book of the Sacred Magic of Abramelin the Magi* (London: Dover Publishers, 1975); C. G. Jung, *Collected Works*, vol. 12, *Psychology and Alchemy* (Princeton, N.J.: Princeton University Press, 1953); Terence McKenna, *Food of the Gods* (New York: Bantam Books, 1992). McKenna provides a concise description of alchemy both in China and Europe:

Alchemy was a slowly evolving, loosely knit, and not mutually exclusive group of Gnostic and Hermetic theories concerning human origins and the dichotomy of spirit and matter. Its roots reached back deep into time, to at least Dynastic Egypt and the slow accumulation of jealously guarded secrets of processes for dyeing fabric, gilding metals, and mummifying bodies. Upon those ancient foundations had risen an edifice of pre-Socratic, Pythagorean, and Hermetic philosophical ideas, which ultimately came to revolve around the notion of the alchemical work as the task of somehow gathering into a unity and thereby rescuing the Divine light that had been scattered through an alien and unfriendly universe. (pages 145–46)

8. Martin Pawley, *Buckminster Fuller* (Jersey City, N.J.: Parkwest Publishers, 1991).

9. J. Baldwin, *Bucky Works: Buckminster Fuller's Ideas for Today* (San Francisco: Wiley & Sons, 1997).

10. R. Buckminster Fuller, *Critical Path* (New York: St. Martin's Press, 1987). This is Fuller's seminal work.

11. Donald Tyson, *The New Magus* (St. Paul, Minn.: Llewellyn Publications, 1987).

12. Ibid., 4.

13. Malidoma Somé, *Ritual: Power, Healing and Community*

(Portland, Oreg.: Swan-Raven & Co., 1993), 9.

14. Robert Moore and Douglas Gillette, *King, Warrior, Magician, Lover* (New York: William Morrow, 1991), 97–118.

15. James Hillman, *The Soul's Code: In Search of Character and Calling* (New York: Random House, 1996), 234.

16. Robert Moore and Douglas Gillette, *The Magician Within* (New York: Avon, 1994), 163–74.

Mary Shelley's *Frankenstein* provides a literary example of the morality issues resulting from the modern scientific Magician's deteriorating into his shadow. Through his practice of black magic, Dr. Frankenstein creates a being that wreaks havoc on the world around him. Robert Moore observes that "His experiment goes haywire because of his complete insensitivity to the feelings of the unfortunate being he created. The outcome of the story is a dire reminder of the effects of a technology prematurely unleashed upon the world by the morally immature."

17. C. G. Jung, "On the Psychology of the Trickster-Figure" in *Collected Works*, vol. 9, part 1, *The Archetypes and the Collective Unconscious* (Bollingen Series, no. 20, Princeton, N.J.: Princeton University Press, 1959). For our discussion Jung notes that:

> The trickster motif does not crop up only in its mythical form but appears just as naively and authentically in the unsuspecting modern man—whenever, in fact, he feels himself at the mercy of annoying 'accidents' which thwart his will and his actions with apparently malicious intent. He then speaks of 'hoodoos' and 'jinxes' or of the 'mischievousness of the object.' Here the trickster is represented by counter-tendencies in the unconscious, and in certain cases by a sort of second personality, of a puerile and inferior character. . . . I have, I think, found a suitable designation for this character-component when I called it the *shadow*. (page 262)

It was Hermes, the archetypal magus who traversed back and forth into the darkness of Hades, that created so many problems among the Greek gods. It was Hermes who was known as the god of criminals and is called the Trickster.

18. Moore and Gillette, *The Magician Within*.

19. Jeanie Russel Kasindorf, "What to Make of Mike," *Fortune*, 14 September 1996, 86–96.

20. An example of shadow business magic is the insight that a client has gained as he has negotiated three major deals with Microsoft Corporation. This client was influential in helping to stimulate the Justice Department to initiate legal action against Microsoft. My client's view is that Microsoft's strategy of dominance follows the manipulation pattern of the shadow Magician. What follows is a page summary of his view.

MICROSOFT MAGIC IN DOMINATING THE BUSINESS WORLD

Overview

Microsoft has developed an almost magical formula to create domination in the high-technology software sector. Initially the capabilities for dominating markets were almost accidental in how they were created. Since Microsoft figured out the formula, they have become adept at replicating the formula in each business they enter. Part of what they do has a strong benefit in providing products that consumers want at good prices. The shadow side is that eventually Microsoft will control all the means of delivering electronic information to consumers, which will result in Microsoft being able to control the information you see and how much you have to pay to access it.

The accident that revealed the secret formula was when IBM contracted with Microsoft to create PC/DOS and subsequently allowed Microsoft to create their own version, MS/DOS. Microsoft leveraged their newfound expertise and fortune to dominate the DOS operating system market for all PCs.

While this dominance was beneficial, Microsoft's decision to build applications for the Macintosh platform gave them the skills and experience to both build a windowing environment on top of

DOS as well as a significant lead in the knowledge of how to build applications for this environment.

While the rest of the applications vendors were distracted building applications for OS/2, being built in partnership by IBM and Microsoft, Microsoft was changing course by building its own windowing environment (MS Windows) and leveraging their applications from the Macintosh platform to create a strongly linked operating systems and applications environment.

The Formula: Link and Leverage

From this experience they hit upon the magic formula:

1. Partner with industry-dominant players (IBM) to create new technologies that leverage the position of the dominant player.

2. Create disagreement with dominant player. Get divorce that results in ownership and rights to the technology that is key to a market sector (PC operating systems). This is Microsoft's CORE market. Divorce is predicated on a "may the best man win" equal rights divorce settlement. Microsoft goes in with nothing and gets full rights to any benefits of the partnership.

3. Link that technology with another marketplace (applications) and leverage it by creating unique and proprietary ties between the two markets (operating systems and applications). This is the TARGET market.

4. Create a partnership with other vendors (PARTNERS) who are dependent on the CORE product. Force these partners to promote the CORE product or face being cut off from CORE product either technically or from a marketing and promotion standpoint.

5. Compete against PARTNERS in TARGET market by utilizing proprietary linkages to CORE technology and by doing bundled or linked pricing which provides a single package that combines the CORE and TARGET products in a way that competitors cannot match.

6. Competitors in TARGET market lose massive market share (Lotus, Borland, WordPerfect, Corel, Aldus . . .). TARGET product becomes part of CORE.

7. Pick new TARGET market to dominate. Repeat steps 1 through 7.

21. Jung lays out the process in the classical alchemical tradition. *Psychology and Alchemy,* 228–41.

22. Stephen Batchelor, *Buddhism Without Beliefs* (New York: Riverhead Books, 1997), 10.

23. Ibid., 10.

24. Lama Surya Das, *Awakening the Buddha Within* (New York: Broadway Books, 1997).

25. Joseph Goldstein, *Insight Meditation: The Practice of Freedom* (Boston: Shambhala Publications, 1993).

26. Mark Epstein, *Thoughts Without a Thinker: Psychotherapy from a Buddhist Perspective* (New York: Basic Books, 1995).

27. My paraphrase of John 14:2–3, New English Bible.

28. Thomas Byrom, trans., *The Dhammapada: The Sayings of the Buddha* (New York: Random House, Vintage Books, 1976), 146.

5: The Artist: The Power of Compassion

1. Tenzin Gyatso, *Freedom in Exile: The Autobiography of the Dalai Lama* (New York: HarperCollins, 1990). Translated, the terms *dalai* and *lama* mean "ocean of wisdom." Because he is also considered the earthly manifestation of Avalokiteshvara, Bodhisattva of Compassion, he also holds the title Ocean of Compassion. A Bodhisattva in Buddhism is:

> Someone on the path to Buddhahood who dedicates themselves entirely to helping all other sentient beings towards release from suffering. The word Bodhisattva can best be understood by translating the *Bodhi* and *Sattva* separately: *Bodhi* means the

understanding or wisdom of the ultimate nature of reality, and a *Sattva* is someone who is motivated by universal compassion. The Bodhisattva ideal is thus the aspiration to practice infinite compassion with infinite wisdom. (pages 204–5)

The Dalai Lama says about himself, "To me 'Dalai Lama' is a title that signifies the office I hold. I myself am just a human being, and incidentally a Tibetan, who chooses to be a Buddhist monk" (page xiii).

2. Sharon Salzberg, *A Heart as Wide as the World: Living with Mindfulness, Wisdom and Compassion* (Boston: Shambhala, 1997).

3. Following Strauss and Howe's discussion of the four archetypal powers I choose the "Artist" to more fully express the archetype of Compassion. Some of the terms they give the Artist more fully reflect our interest in a leadership quality: interdependent, experimental, pluralistic, sensitive, liked, protective, caring, open minded, humanist, progressive, seeking enlightenment. *Fourth Turning: An American Prophecy* (New York: Broadway Books, 1997), 98.

4. Robert Moore and Douglas Gillette, *The Lover Within* (New York: Avon, 1995).

5. Robert Moore and Douglas Gillette, *King, Warrior, Magician, Lover* (New York: William Morrow, 1991), 119–41.

6. Robert E. Staub, *The Heart of Leadership* (Provo, Utah: Executive Excellence Publishing, 1996); Jack Canfield and Jacqueline Miller, *Heart at Work* (New York: McGraw-Hill, 1996).

7. Coleman Barks, trans., with John Moyne, *The Essential Rumi* (San Francisco: Harper San Francisco, 1995), 104. (This is the first few lines of the poem.)

8. Thomas Stewart, "Why Leadership Matters," *Fortune,* 2 March 1998, 80.

9. Ibid.

10. Ibid.

11. Pierre Teilhard de Chardin, *The Phenomenon of Man* (New York: Harper & Row, 1959).

12. Ted Harrison, *Stigmata: A Medieval Mystery in a Modern Age* (New York: Penguin, 1996).

13. Charles Carty, *Padre Pio the Stigmatist* (Rockford, Ill.: Tan Books, 1989).

14. Arthur Koestler, *Act of Creation* (New York: Arkana, 1990). Originally published in 1964 this is a cult classic about the spontaneity of creativity. Koestler argues that we are the most creative when rational thought is limited.

15. Mihaly Csikszentmihalyi, *Flow: The Psychology of Optimal Experience* (New York: HarperCollins, 1991), philosophy and religion editors' recommended book for *Amazon.com*:

> You have heard about how a musician loses herself in her music, how a painter becomes one with the process of painting. In work, sport, conversation or hobby, you have experienced, yourself, the suspension of time, the freedom of complete absorption in activity. This is "flow," an experience that is at once demanding and rewarding—an experience that Mihaly Csikszentmihalyi demonstrates is one of the most enjoyable and valuable experiences a person can have. The exhaustive case studies, controlled experiments and innumerable references to historical figures, philosophers and scientists through the ages prove Csikszentmihalyi's point that flow is a singularly productive and desirable state. But the implications for its application to society are what make the book revolutionary. Synopsis: People enter a flow state when they are fully absorbed in activity during which they lose their sense of time and have feelings of great satisfaction. The author, a pioneer in this astonishing field of study, clearly explains the principles of "flow" and shows how it can be introduced into every level of life.

16. D. T. Suzuki, in *Zen Mind, Beginner's Mind: Informal Talks on Zen Meditation and Practice* (New York: Weatherhill, 1970), describes the notion of flow as "naturalness."

> Naturalness is, I think, some feeling of being independent from everything, or some activity which is based on nothingness. Something which comes out of nothingness is naturalness, like a seed or plant coming out of the ground. The seed has no idea of

being some particular plant, but it has its own form and is in perfect harmony with the ground, with its surroundings. As it grows, in the course of time it expresses its nature. . . . This is what we mean by naturalness. (page 108)

17. Brewster Ghiselin, ed., *The Creative Process: Reflections on the Invention of Art* (Berkeley, Calif.: University of California Press, 1996). An excellent anthology examining all types of artistic creation.

18. Abraham Maslow, *Eupsychian Management* (Homewood, Ill.: Richard Irwin, Inc.; Dorsey Press, 1965). This is a classic work by Maslow giving his observations on business organizations. His chapter "Notes on Creativeness" gives a clear, concise, practical definition of creativity in our daily leadership.

Here-now creativeness is dependent on . . . the ability to forget about the future, to improvise in the present, to give full attention to the present, e.g. to be able fully to listen or to observe. This general ability to give up future, structure, to give up control and predictability, is also characteristic of loafing, or to the ability to enjoy—to say it in another way—which itself is also essentially unmotivated, purposeless, without goal, and therefore without future. (page 188)

19. Michael Ray and Rochelle Meyers, *Creativity in Business* (New York: Doubleday, 1989). Ray and Meyers teach how creativity and innovation can be available to every person with a little work. The book describes a group of successful innovative and creative thinkers. Much emphasis is put on intuition and instinct, the value of being naive, and forging onward without a definitive game plan. Passion and an instinctual trust in one's own ability to succeed are recurrent character traits of most of those interviewed. The book was based on much of what they learned teaching the course on creativity in the Business School at Stanford University in the 1980s.

20. Peter Senge, *The Fifth Discipline: The Art and Practice of the Learning Organization* (New York: Doubleday Currency, 1990), 341.

21. Ibid., 341.

22. Jeffrey Moore, *Crossing the Chasm* (New York: Harper Business, 1995).

23. Robert Fritz, *The Path of Least Resistance: Principles for Creating What You Want to Create* (Salem, Mass.: Stillpoint Publishing, 1984).

24. Ibid., 54–58.

25. James Carse, *Finite and Infinite Games: A Vision of Life as Play and Possibility* (New York: Free Press, 1986), 31–32.

26. One of the most innovative consulting organizations I know is the Generative Leadership Group, headquartered in New Jersey. Mel Toomy and Ed Gurowitz are the founding partners. They introduced me to Carse and to their deeply creative strategy to systematically design organizations operating from a field of possibility rather than certainty. Possibility, in their model, creates genuine breakthroughs in organizational results rather than just being locked into the model of continuous improvement. Their view is that leaders can consciously design a continuously expanding field of possibilities that moves toward the future. This process they call "generative leadership."

27. Cited in Canfield and Miller, *Heart at Work,* 200.

28. Cited in Canfield and Miller, *Heart at Work,* 205.

29. Drucker, Bennis, Nanus, Senge, Fritz and many other leadership thinkers posit values as one of the key personal and organizational conditions that make successful leaders. In his study of leaders over the years since his first book *Leaders* came out, Bennis insists that personal integrity is the core of leadership values. "Integrity is the basis of trust." Empathy for others, he says, is the complement to trust.

30. Terry Cole-Whittaker, "Spirituality—The Heart and Soul of Every Successful Business" cited in Canfield and Miller, *Heart at Work,* 256.

31. Lao Tzu, *Tao Te Ching,* trans. Stephen Mitchell (New York: HarperPerennial Library, 1992).

32. Private newsletter, *The Performance Edge,* Chris Thorson, ed.

33. Quote from the adaptation of the *Tao Te Ching,* John Heider, *The Tao of Leadership* (Atlanta: Humanics, 1985), 143.

34. Cited in Connie Zweig and Jeremaiah Abrams, eds., *Meeting the Shadow: The Hidden Power of the Dark Side of Human Nature* (New York: Putnam, Tarcher/Perigree Books, 1991), 233.

35. Moore and Gillette, *King, Warrior, Magician, Lover,* 131.

36. Ibid., 133–41.

37. James Hillman, *The Soul's Code: In Search of Character and Calling* (New York: Random House, 1996), 214–48.

38. An excellent little book that touches deeply the heart of compassionate relationships between spouses is Sobonfu E. Somé's, *The Spirit of Intimacy: Ancient Teachings in the Way of Relationships* (Berkeley, Calif.: Berkeley Hills Books, 1997). Sobonfu says about conflict in relationships: "Conflict usually comes when things start to stagnate, when our ego and controlling self start to take over our relationship. Conflict comes as a notice that spiritual energy is being stopped and needs to move" (page 116).

39. Salzberg, *A Heart as Wide as the World.*

40. My practice of the Four Sacred Homes of loving and the *metta,* or loving kindness, meditation has been guided by Michelle McDonald-Smith and Steven Smith, teachers with the Insight Meditation Society center in Barre, Massachusetts, and at their own center, Vipassana, Hawaii in Honolulu.

41. Sharon Salzberg, *Lovingkindness: The Revolutionary Art of Happiness* (Boston: Shambhala, 1995).

42. Thomas Thompson and John Nieder, *Forgive and Love Again: Healing Wounded Relationships* (Eugene, Oreg.: Harvest House Publishers, 1991).

43. Lewis Smedes, *The Art of Forgiveness: When You Need to Forgive and Don't Know How* (New York: Ballantine Books, 1997).

44. Maslow, *Eupsychian Management.* His chapter "Notes on Leadership" outlines the power of Compassion by focusing on how a leader needs to respond and be with followers. Using his principles of hierarchy of needs, he describes a strong leader as "one who has all his basic needs gratified, that is, the need for safety, for belongingness, for loving and for being loved, for prestige and respect, and

finally for self-confidence and self-esteem. This is the same as saying that the closer a person approaches toward self-actualization, the better leader or boss he is apt to be in the general sense of the largest number of situations." Maslow makes another observation specifically related to the Artist archetype with regard to caring and concern for others: "the good leader in most situations must have as a psychological prerequisite the ability to take pleasure in the growth and self-actualization of other people" (pages 130–31).

6: The Sovereign: The Power of Presence

1. John Weir Perry, *Lord of the Four Quarters: The Mythology of Kingship* New York: Paulist Press, 1991).

2. Sacred kingship was presented in a penetrating analysis by Mircea Eliade in *The Myth of the Eternal Return* (Bollingen Series, no. 46, (New York: Pantheon, 1954).

3. Perry, *Four Quarters*, 21.

4. Donald Peterson's vision and leadership at Ford were dramatic when he took over in 1985. See John W. Gardner, *On Leadership* (New York: Free Press, 1990).

5. Tom Peters and Robert Waterman, *In Search of Excellence* (New York: Harper & Row, 1982).

6. Matthew Fox, *Original Blessing* (Santa Fe, N. Mex.: Bear & Co., 1984).

7. Vision in leadership has been discussed in many ways. Two useful sources: Staub, *Heart of Leadership* (see the chapter on "Providing Guidance Through Shared Vision"); Warren Blank, *The Nine Natural Laws of Leadership* (New York: American Management Association, 1995). See section on "Quantum Leader Vision."

8. Warren Bennis and Burt Nanus, *Leaders: The Strategies for Taking Charge* (New York: Harper & Row, 1985), 92.

9. Burt Nanus, *Visionary Leadership* (San Francisco: Jossey-Bass,

1992). The main message of his book is, "There is no more powerful engine driving an organization toward excellence and long-range success than an attractive, worthwhile, and achievable vision of the future, widely shared."

10. The research done by my former project management, training and consulting company, Ontara Corporation, in eleven major corporations in the San Francisco Bay area demonstrated that the number-one characteristic of a successful project leader was knowing how to create a shared vision with the project team.

11. Quoted in Viktor Frankl, *Man's Search for Meaning* (New York: Washington Square Press, 1963), 164.

12. Gardner, *On Leadership*, 132.

13. Al Chungliang Huang and Jerry Lynch, *Mentoring: The Tao of Giving and Receiving Wisdom* (San Francisco: Harper San Francisco, 1995). Their view of mentoring is not technique-based, but rather, encourages the deeper nurturing that influences the mentor as well as the mentee. For more technique-based books see: William Hendricks, *Coaching, Mentoring and Managing* (Franklin Lakes, N.J.: Career Press, 1996) and Floyd Wishman and Terrie Sjodin, *Mentoring* (Irwin Professional Publishing, 1996).

14. Huang and Lynch, *Mentoring*, 17.

15. Peter Nulty, "America's Toughest Bosses," *Fortune*, 27 February 1989.

16. Albert Dunlap, *Mean Business: How I Save Bad Companies and Make Good Companies Great* (New York: Times Books, 1996); Joseph Nocera, "Confessions of a Corporate Killer," *Fortune*, 30 September 1996.

17. Dunlap, *Mean Business*.

18. Jolande Jacobi, *Individuation* (New York: Meridian/Penguin, 1965), 38. See Jung's essays: "Conscious, Unconscious and Individuation" and "A Study in the Process of Individuation," both in *The Archetypes and the Collective Unconscious, Collected Works* vol. 9. 1 op. cit. He defines individuation as "the process by which a person becomes a psychological 'in-dividual,' that is, a separate,

indivisible unity or 'whole.' It is generally assumed that consciousness is the whole of the psychological individual" (page 275). And he
expands later in this same essay:

> Conscious and unconscious do not make a whole when one of them
> is suppressed and injured by the other. . . . Consciousness should
> defend its reason and protect itself, and the chaotic life of the
> unconscious should be given the chance of having its way too—as
> much of it as we can stand. This means open conflict and
> open collaboration at once. . . . This, roughly, is what I mean by the
> individuation process. As the name shows, it is a process or course
> of development arising out of the conflict between the two
> fundamental psychic facts. (page 288)

19. Frankl, *Man's Search for Meaning*, 164.

20. Ibid., 157.

21. Mitchell L. Marks and Philip H. Mirvis, "The Merger
Syndrome," *Psychology Today*, 1986: 42. See also Paul Shrivastava,
"Post Merger Integration," *Business Strategy*, Fall 1987: 65–76.

22. Gardner, *On Leadership*, 24.

23. Jacobi, *Individuation*, 13.

24. Ibid., 13.

25. William Miller, *Your Golden Shadow: Discovering and
Fulfilling Your Underdeveloped Self* (New York: HarperCollins,
1989) cited in Connie Zweig and Jeremaiah Abrams, eds., *Meeting
the Shadow: The Hidden Power of the Dark Side of Human Nature*
(New York: Putnam, Tarcher/Perigree Books, 1991).

26. Ibid.

27. Jung, *Two Essays on Analytical Psychology, Collected Works*,
vol. 7, 266. See also Jacobi, *Individuation*, 83.

REFERENCES

Babakian, Genine. "Destitute Russians More Interested in Survival Than Politics." *USA Today*, 31 March 1998.

Baldwin, J. *Bucky Works: Buckminster Fuller's Ideas for Today.* San Francisco: Wiley & Sons, 1997.

Barks, Coleman, with John Moyne, trans. *The Essential Rumi.* San Francisco: Harper San Francisco, 1995.

Batchelor, Stephen. *Buddhism Without Beliefs.* New York: Riverhead Books, 1997.

Bennis, Warren. "The Four Competencies of Leadership." *Training and Development Journal* (August 1984): 15–19.

———. *On Becoming a Leader.* Menlo Park, Calif.: Addison Wesley, 1989.

Bennis, Warren, and Burt Nanus. *Leaders: The Strategies for Taking Charge.* New York: Harper & Row, 1985.

Bennis, Warren, and Robert Townsend. *Reinventing Leadership.* New York: William Morrow & Company, 1995.

Blank, Warren. *The Nine Natural Laws of Leadership.* New York: American Management Association, 1995.

Bly, Robert. *A Little Book on the Human Shadow.* San Francisco: Harper & Row, 1988.

———. *The Sibling Society.* Menlo Park, Calif.: Addison Wesley, 1996.

Bolen, Jean. *The Gods in Everyman: A New Psychology of Men's Lives and Loves.* San Francisco: Harper & Row, 1989.

Bradford, David L., and Allan R. Cohen. "The Postheroic Leader." *Training and Development Journal* (January 1984): 41–49.

Brown, Lester, ed. *State of the World, 1992.* New York: W. W. Norton & Co., 1992.

Burns, James MacGregor. *Leadership.* New York: HarperTorch Books, 1978.

Byrom, Thomas, trans. *The Dhammapada: The Sayings of the Buddha.* New York: Random House, Vintage Books, 1976.

Campbell, Joseph. *The Historical Atlas of World Mythology.* vol. 1, *The Way of the Animal Powers: Mythologies of the Primitive Hunters and Gatherers.* New York: Harper & Row, 1988.

————. *Myths to Live By.* New York: Arkana, 1993.

Campbell, Joseph, ed. *The Portable Jung.* New York: Viking Press, 1971.

Campbell, Joseph, with Bill Moyers. *The Power of Myth.* New York: Anchor, 1991.

Canfield, Jack, and Jacqueline Miller. *Heart at Work.* New York: McGraw-Hill, 1996.

Carse, James. *Finite and Infinite Games: A Vision of Life as Play and Possibility.* New York: Free Press, 1986.

Carty, Charles. *Padre Pio the Stigmatist.* Rockford, Ill.: Tan Books, 1989.

Chapman, Gary. "Military Spending and the American Economy." *In Context* 20 (Winter 1989): 16. Also on the Web at *www.context.org.*

Conger, Jay. *The Charismatic Leader.* San Francisco: Jossey-Bass, 1989.

Covey, Stephen. *Seven Habits of Highly Effective People.* New York: Simon & Schuster, 1989.

Crim, Keith, ed. *The Perennial Dictionary of World Religions.* San Francisco: Harper & Row, 1989.

Crowley, Aleister. *Confessions of Aleister Crowley.* New York: Arkana, 1989.

Csikszentmihalyi, Mihaly. *Flow: The Psychology of Optimal Experience.* New York: HarperCollins, 1991.

Dempey, Mary, and Rene Tihiata. *Your Stress Personalities.* Navato, Calif.: Presidio Press, 1981.

Dreher, Diane. *The Tao of Personal Leadership.* New York: HarperCollins, 1996.

Dunlap, Albert. *Mean Business.* New York: Times Books, 1996.

Dunnigan, James, and Daniel Masterson. *The Way of the Warrior.* New York: St. Martin's Press, 1997.

Eichman, William. "Meeting Darkness on the Path." *Gnosis,* winter 1990.

Eisler, Riane. *The Chalice and the Blade: Our History, Our Future.* San Francisco: HarperCollins, 1987.

Eliade, Mircea. *Rites and Symbols of Initiation.* New York: Harper & Row, 1958.

————. *Shamanism: Archaic Techniques of Ecstasy.* New York: Pantheon, 1964.

Epstein, Mark. *Thoughts Without a Thinker: Psychotherapy from a Buddhist Perspective.* New York: Basic Books, 1995.

Fitzgerald, Catherine, and Linda Kirby, eds., *Developing Leaders: Research and Applications in Psychological Type and Leadership Development.* Palo Alto, Calif.: Davies-Black Publishing, 1997.

Frankl, Viktor. *Man's Search for Meaning.* New York: Washington Square Press, 1963.

Fritz, Robert. *Corporate Tides: The Inescapable Laws of Organizational Structure.* San Francisco: Berrett-Koehler Publishers, 1996.

————. *The Path of Least Resistance: Principles for Creating What You Want to Create.* Salem, Mass.: Still Point Publishing, 1984.

Fox, Matthew. *Original Blessing.* Santa Fe, N. Mex.: Bear & Co., 1984.

Fuller, R. Buckminster. *Critical Path.* New York: St. Martin's Press, 1987.

Gardner, John. "The Antileadership Vaccine." In *Annual Report of the Carnegie Corporation.* New York: Carnegie Corporation, 1965.

————. *On Leadership.* New York: Free Press, 1990.

Ghiselin, Brewster, ed. *The Creative Process: Reflections on the Invention of Art.* Berkeley, Calif.: University of California Press, 1996.

Gimbutas, Marija. *The Civilization of the Goddess: The World of Old Europe.* San Francisco: Harper & Row, 1991.

Goldstein, Joseph. *Insight Meditation: The Practice of Freedom.* Boston: Shambhala Publications, 1993.

Gorbachev, Mikhail. *Memories.* New York: Doubleday, 1996.

Granrose, John. "The Archetype of the Magician." Diploma thesis, C. G. Jung Institute, Zurich, 1996.

Graves, Robert. *The Greek Myths,* vol. 1. Middlesex, England: Penguin Books, 1968.

Guggenbuhl-Craig, Adolf. *Eros on Crutches: Reflections on Amorality and Psychopathy.* Dallas, Tex.: Spring Publications, 1980.

Gyatso, Tenzin. *Freedom in Exile: The Autobiography of the Dalai Lama.* New York: HarperCollins, 1990.

Halifax, Joan. *Shaman: The Wounded Healer.* New York: Crossroads, 1982.

Harrison, Ted. *Stigmata: A Medieval Mystery in a Modern Age.* New York: Penguin, 1996.

Heider, John. *The Tao of Leadership.* Atlanta: Humanics, 1985.

Hendricks, William. *Coaching, Mentoring and Managing.* Franklin Lakes, N.J.: Career Press, 1996.

Herrigel, Eugen. *Zen in the Art of Archery.* New York: Pantheon Books, 1964.

Hessellbein, Frances, Marshall Goldsmith and Richard Becknhard, eds. *The Leader of the Future: New Visions, Strategies and Practices for the Next Era.* The Drucker Foundation Future Series. San Francisco: Jossey-Bass, 1996.

Hillman, James. *Re-Visioning Psychology.* New York: Harper & Row, Perennial Library, 1975.

―――. *The Soul's Code: In Search of Character and Calling* New York: Random House, 1996.

Hope, Murry. *The Psychology of Ritual.* Dorset, England: Element Books, 1988.

Huang, Al Chungliang, and Jerry Lynch. *Mentoring: The Tao of Giving*

and Receiving Wisdom. San Francisco: Harper San Francisco, 1995.
["J."]. *A Simple Program: A Contemporary Translation of the Book of Alcoholics Anonymous.* New York: Hyperion, 1996.
Jacobi, Jolande. *Complex, Archetype, Symbol in the Psychology of C. G. Jung.* Bollingen Series. Princeton, N.J.: Princeton University Press, 1959.
———. *Individuation.* New York: Meridian/Penguin, 1965.
Jung, C. G. *Archetypes of the Collective Unconscious, Collected Works of C. G. Jung.* vol. 9, part 1: "The Archetypes and the Collective Unconscious." Princeton, N.J.: Princeton University Press, 1953.
———. *Memories, Dreams and Reflections.* New York: Random House, Vintage Books, 1961.
———. *Psychology and Alchemy. Collected Works.* Vol. 12. Princeton, N.J.: Princeton University Press, 1953.
———. *Symbols of Transformation, Collected Works.* Vol. 5. Bollingen Series, no. 20. Princeton, N.J.: Princeton University Press, 1967.
Kasindorf, Jeanie Russel. "What to Make of Mike." *Fortune,* 14 September 1996, 86–96.
Kidron, Michael, and Ronald Segal. *State of the World Atlas,* 5th ed. New York: Penguin, 1995.
———. *State of the World Reports 1990 to 1998.* New York: W. W. Norton & Co., 1998.
Koestler, Arthur. *Act of Creation.* New York: Arkana, 1990.
Kotter, John. *The Leadership Factor.* New York: Free Press, 1988.
———. *Power and Influence: Beyond Formal Authority.* New York: Free Press, 1985.
Kyle, David. *Human Robots and Holy Mechanics: Reclaiming Our Souls in a Machine World.* Portland, Oreg.: Swan-Raven & Co., 1993.
Lao Tzu. *Tao Te Ching.* Trans. Stephen Mitchell. New York: Harper Perennial Library, 1992.
"Larry Bossidy Won't Stop Pushing." *Fortune,* 13 January 1997, 135–37.

Lawlor, Robert. *Voices of the First Day: Awakening in the Aboriginal Dreamtime.* Rochester, Vt.: Inner Traditions, 1991.

Luft, Joseph. *Group Processes: An Introduction to Group Dynamics.* Mountain View, Calif.: Mayfield Publishing Company, 1970.

Machiavelli, Niccolo. *The Prince.* Trans. Dominic Baker-Smith. New York: Knopf, Everyman's Library, 1992.

Maslow, Abraham. *Eupsychian Management.* Homewood, Ill.: Richard Irwin, Inc.; Dorsey Press, 1965.

———. *Motivation and Personality.* New York: Harper, 1954.

———. *Toward a Psychology of Being.* New York: D. Van Nostrand Co., Inc., 1962.

Mathers, S. L. *Book of the Sacred Magic of Abramelin the Magi.* London: Dover Publishers, 1975.

McGregor, Douglas. *The Human Side of Enterprise.* New York: McGraw-Hill, 1960.

McKenna, Terence. *Food of the Gods.* New York: Bantam Books, 1992.

Meadows, Donella, Dennis Meadows, and Jorgen Randers. *Beyond the Limits: Confronting Global Collapse, Envisioning a Sustainable Future.* Post Mills, Vt.: Chelsea Green Publishing, 1992.

———. *The Limits of Growth.* New York: Universe Books, 1972.

Medvedev, Zhores. *Gorbachev.* New York: W. W. Norton & Co., 1987.

Miller, William. *Your Golden Shadow: Discovering and Fulfilling Your Underdeveloped Self.* New York: HarperCollins, 1989.

Mindell, Arnold. *The Leader as Martial Artist.* San Francisco: Harper San Francisco, 1992.

Moore, Jeffrey. *Crossing the Chasm.* New York: Harper Business, 1995.

Moore, Robert, and Douglas Gillette. *King, Warrior, Magician, Lover.* New York: William Morrow, 1991.

———. *The King Within.* New York: William Morrow, 1992.

———. *The Lover Within.* New York: Avon, 1995.

———. *The Magician Within.* New York: Avon, 1994.

————. *The Warrior Within.* New York: Avon, 1993.

Morris, Dick. *Behind the Oval Office.* New York: Random House, 1997.

Musashi, Miyamoto, and Victor Harris, trans. *A Book of Five Rings.* Woodstock, N.Y.: Overlook Press, 1974.

Nanus, Burt. *Visionary Leadership.* San Francisco: Jossey-Bass, 1992.

New English Bible: New Testament. Oxford, England, and Cambridge, England: Oxford and Cambridge University Presses, 1961.

Nocera, Joseph. "Confessions of a Corporate Killer." *Fortune,* 30 September 1996.

Nulty, Peter. "America's Toughest Bosses." *Fortune,* 27 February 1989.

Pawley, Martin. *Buckminster Fuller.* Jersey City, N.J.: Parkwest Publishers, 1991.

Perry, John Weir. *Lord of the Four Quarters: The Mythology of Kingship.* New York: Paulist Press, 1991.

Peter, Laurence J. *The Peter Principle: Why Things Always Go Wrong.* New York: Bantam Books, 1984.

Peters, Tom, and Robert Waterman. *In Search of Excellence.* New York: Harper & Row, 1982.

Puri, Shaifali. "Bible Thumping: An Anti-Tobacco Lawyer Takes on Philip Morris' Geoffrey Bible." *Fortune,* 30 March 1998, 30–31.

Quesada, Alvaro Unama. "Taking the Reigns of Leadership." *Stanford Magazine,* December 1989.

Ray, Michael, and Rochelle Meyers. *Creativity in Business.* New York: Doubleday, 1989.

Reps, Paul, and Nyogen Senzaki. *Zen Flesh, Zen Bones.* Boston: Shambhala, 1994.

Roberts, Wess. *Leadership Secrets of Attila the Hun.* New York: Warner Books, 1991.

Robinson, Bryan. *Work Addiction.* Deerfield Beach, Fla.: Health Communications, 1989.

Rubin, Irwin M., and David E. Berlew. "The Power Failure in Organizations." *Training and Development Journal* (January 1984): 35–38.

Salzberg, Sharon. *A Heart as Wide as the World: Living with Mindfulness, Wisdom and Compassion.* Boston: Shambhala, 1997.

————. *Lovingkindness: The Revolutionary Art of Happiness.* Boston: Shambhala, 1995.

Sanford, John. *Evil: The Shadow Side of Reality.* New York: Crossroads Publishing Co., 1984.

Sanford, John, and George Lough. *What Men Are Like.* New York: Paulist Press, 1988.

Schaef, Anne W., and Diane Fassel. *The Addictive Organization.* San Francisco: Harper & Row, 1988.

Senge, Peter. *The Fifth Discipline: The Art and Practice of the Learning Organization.* New York: Doubleday Currency, 1990.

Sheehy, Gail. "Gorbachev: Red Star—The Shaping of the Man Who Shook the World." *Vanity Fair,* February 1990.

Signell, Karen. *Wisdom of the Heart: Working with Women's Dreams.* New York: Bantam Books, 1990.

Sinetar, Marsha. *Do What You Love, the Money Will Follow.* New York: Dell Books, 1987.

Smedes, Lewis. *The Art of Forgiveness: When You Need to Forgive and Don't Know How.* New York: Ballantine Books, 1997.

Somé, Malidoma. *Ritual: Power, Healing and Community.* Portland, Oreg.: Swan-Raven & Co., 1993.

Somé, Sobonfu E. *The Spirit of Intimacy: Ancient Teachings in the Way of Relationships.* Berkeley, Calif.: Berkeley Hills Books, 1997.

Staub, Robert E. *The Heart of Leadership.* Provo, Utah: Executive Excellence Publishing, 1996.

Stevens, John. *Abundant Peace: Biography of Morihei Ueshiba, Founder of Aikido.* Boston: Shambhala, 1987.

————. *Aikido: The Way of Harmony.* Boston: Shambhala, 1984.

Stevenson, Robert Louis. *Dr. Jekyll and Mr. Hyde.* New York: Everyman's Library, 1992.

Stewart, Thomas A. "Get with the *New* Power Game." *Fortune,* 13 January 1997, 58–62.

———. "Why Leadership Matters." *Fortune,* 2 March 1998, 80.

Strauss, William, and Neil Howe. *The Fourth Turning: An American Prophecy.* New York: Broadway Books, 1997.

Sun Tzu. *The Art of War.* Oxford, England: Oxford University Press, 1984.

Surya Das, Lama. *Awakening the Buddha Within.* New York: Broadway Books, 1997.

Suzuki, D. T. *Zen and Japanese Culture.* Bollingen Series, no. 64. Princeton, N.J.: Princeton University Press, 1970.

Suzuki, Shunryu. *Zen Mind, Beginner's Mind: Informal Talks on Zen Meditation and Practice.* New York: Weatherhill, 1970.

Teilhard de Chardin, Pierre. *The Phenomenon of Man.* New York: HarperCollins, 1959.

Thompson, Thomas, and John Nieder. *Forgiveness: Forgive and Love Again: Healing Wounded Relationships.* Eugene, Oreg.: Harvest House Publishers, 1991.

Thompson, William Irwin. *At the Edge of History.* New York: Irvington Publishers, 1971.

Thornton, Deborah. *The Twelve Steps of Alcoholics Anonymous.* Center City, Minn.: Hazelden, 1995.

Tichy, Noel M., and Mary Anne Devanna. "The Transformational Leader." *Training and Development Journal* (July 1986): 27–32.

Turner, Victor. *The Ritual Process: Structure and Anti-structure.* Ithaca, N.Y.: Cornell University Press, Cornell Paperbacks, 1969.

van Gelder, Sarah. "A Path to Global Disarmament." *www.context.org.*

Webster's New Universal Unabridged Dictionary, 2d ed. New York: Simon & Schuster, 1979.

Wheatley, Margaret. *Leadership and the New Science: Learning About Organization from an Orderly Universe.* San Francisco: Berrett-Koehler Publishers, 1992.

Whitmont, Edward. *The Symbolic Quest.* Princeton, N.J.: Princeton University Press, 1969.

Wishman, Floyd, and Terrie Sjodin. *Mentoring.* New York: Irwin Professional Publishing, 1996.

Zweig, Connie, and Jeremiah Abrams, eds. *Meeting the Shadow: The Hidden Power of the Dark Side of Human Nature.* New York: Putnam, Tarcher/Perigee Books, 1991.

INDEX

About the Author

David T. Kyle, Ph.D., is an organizational consultant in the management and executive development arenas, with thirty years' experience in teaching, managing and consulting. Currently, he is a partner in Lind & Kyle Consultants, an executive development company based in Portland, Oregon. Besides his academic responsibilities, he has worked in a variety of organizational settings and positions as a manager, director and executive. Mr. Kyle's consulting focuses primarily on executive development and coaching, but also includes strategic planning, organizational redesign, change strategies and senior-team development. Mr. Kyle works with both start-up and mature organizations. His client base comprises companies from both the public and private sectors, including for-profit and nonprofit organizations. His international consulting includes work in Asia, Africa, the Middle East and the former Soviet Union.

As a professor, Mr. Kyle taught for ten years at San José State University, the University of Phoenix, Foothill College and the Findhorn Foundation in Scotland.

Mr. Kyle is former chairman of the board of the Foundation for Russian/American Economic Cooperation, a nonprofit foundation in Seattle, Washington, that fosters economic development between medium and small businesses in the two countries. He also has served on the boards of other for-profit and nonprofit organizations.

In 1993, Mr. Kyle authored *Human Robots and Holy Mechanics: Reclaiming Our Souls in a Machine World,* a critique of postindustrial machine consciousness that advocates rediscovering a conception of ourselves as "holy mechanics" who can alter the effects the machine "imagination" has on us and on our society.

Mr. Kyle can be contacted at *www.lindandkyle.com.*

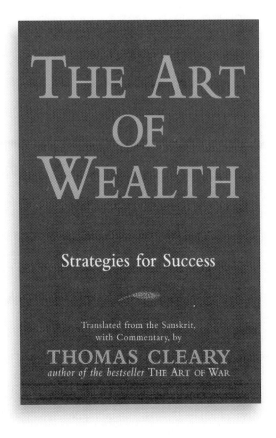

THE ART
OF
WEALTH

Strategies for Success

Translated from the Sanskrit,
with Commentary, by

THOMAS CLEARY
author of the bestseller THE ART OF WAR

The Art of Wealth
Strategies for Success
Translated from the Sanskrit with commentary by Thomas Cleary, Ph.D.

This book is based on the celebrated works of Kauthilya, an ancient philosopher popularly called the Aristotle and Machiavelli of India. Dr. Cleary's commentary is characteristically rich, with insightful parallels from Eastern and Western philosophical traditions no other living Western author/translator could draw with such authentic clarity. His vivid translation and accompanying interpretation of each aphorism offer modern readers the opportunity to benefit from the lucidity and wisdom of ancient thought and tradition by inviting them to integrate these gifts into their everyday, contemporary lives. **Code 5416, $11.95**

Little Souls Will Inspire the Spirit

The Goodness Gorillas

The friends of the Goodness Gorilla Club have lots of great plans! But what will they do about Todd, the meanest kid in the class? *Code 505X, hardcover, $14.95*

The Best Night Out with Dad

Danny has a new friend, and an important decision to make. Will he get to see the circus after all? *Code 5084, hardcover, $14.95*

The Never-Forgotten Doll

Ellie wants to give a special gift to Miss Maggie, the best babysitter in the world. But everything is going wrong! How will she show Miss Maggie how much she loves her? *Code 5076, hardcover, $14.95*

A Dog of My Own

Ben's wish comes true when his mom finally says he can have a puppy. But, on the way to pick up the puppy, Ben and his friend Kelly stumble upon a discovery that could change everything! *Code 5556, hardcover, $14.95*

The Braids Girl

When Izzy helps Grandpa Mike with his volunteer work at the Family Togetherness Home, the girl in the corner with the two long braids makes a lasting impression on her. But, Izzy just can't seem to make the braids girl happy! *Code 5548, hardcover, $14.95*

More from the *Chicken Soup for the Soul®* Series

Selected books are also available in hardcover, large print, audiocassette and compact disc.

Available in bookstores everywhere or call **1-800-441-5569** for Visa or MasterCard orders. Prices do not include shipping and handling. Your response code is **BKS**.

New for Kids

Chicken Soup for the Kid's Soul

Jack Canfield, Mark Victor Hansen, Patty Hansen and Irene Dunlap

Young readers will find empowerment and encouragement to love and accept themselves, believe in their dreams, find answers to their questions and discover hope for a promising future.

Code 6099, $12.95

Chicken Soup for the Teenage Soul II

Jack Canfield, Mark Victor Hansen and Kimberly Kirberger

The stories in this collection will show teens the importance of friendship, family, self-respect, dreams, and life itself.

October 1998 Release • Code 6161, $12.95

Chicken Soup for the Teenage Soul Journal

Jack Canfield, Mark Victor Hansen and Kimberly Kirberger

This personal journal offers teens the space to write their own life stories, as well as space for their friends and parents to offer them words of love and inspiration.

October 1998 Release • Code 6374, $12.95

The New Kid and the Cookie Thief

Story adaptation by Lisa McCourt
Illustrated by Mary O'Keefe Young

For a shy girl like Julie, there couldn't be anything worse than the very first day at a brand new school. What if the kids don't like her? What if no one ever talks to her at all? Julie's big sister has some advice—and a plan—that just might help. But will Julie be too scared to even give it a try?

October 1998 Release • Code 5882, hardcover, $14.95

New from *Chicken Soup for the Soul*®

Code 5629—$14.95

Code 6226—$12.95